Rick Searle has been a full-time freelance writer and film maker for over 40 years. He has worked in radio, television and film, and lectured in television writing at the Queensland University of Technology. Rick has had a lifelong interest in aviation. He is the author of five books, including *The Man Who Saved Smithy*, about the life of Australian flyer and navigator Sir Gordon Taylor.

Charles Ulm overseeing the refuelling and mechanical checks of the *Southern Cross*, Italy, 1929. National Library of Australia

CHARLES ULM

The untold story of one of Australia's
greatest aviation pioneers

RICK SEARLE

ALLEN&UNWIN
SYDNEY•MELBOURNE•AUCKLAND•LONDON

Allen & Unwin
83 Alexander Street
Crows Nest NSW 2065
Australia
Phone: (61 2) 8425 0100
Email: info@allenandunwin.com
Web: www.allenandunwin.com

 A catalogue record for this book is available from the National Library of Australia

ISBN 978 1 76029 427 4

Maps by Map Graphics, Brisbane, unless otherwise attributed
Index by Puddingburn
Set in 12/19 pt Minion Pro by Bookhouse, Sydney
Printed and bound in Australia by Griffin Press

10 9 8 7 6 5 4 3 2 1

MIX
Paper from
responsible sources
FSC® C009448

The paper in this book is FSC® certified. FSC® promotes environmentally responsible, socially beneficial and economically viable management of the world's forests.

In memory of Don Gough
1948–2017

CONTENTS

List of maps

Foreword

When my father's name is mentioned, it is usually in the context of his 1928 trans-Pacific flight in the *Southern Cross*. But Charles Ulm accomplished a great deal more than that, and for both family and historical reasons I am delighted that there is at last a book that examines his extraordinary life in detail.

Meticulously researched, thoughtfully crafted, crisply written, Rick Searle's *Charles Ulm: The untold story of one of Australia's greatest aviation pioneers* should rest easily in the pantheon of our Great—a poignant record of Australian endeavour.

As a very little boy (I'm told) my father took me up in his flimsy biplane—speed maybe 100 kilometres per hour. At that time it took some Intrepids a month and more to fly England–Australia. Ten years later in his specially built very long-range trimotor *Faith in Australia* he shrank the space to just under one week.

Our world quartered.

Flying to England after the Second World War, I enjoyed some five days of comfort. Jets reduced this to a day or so. Now we're doing it non-stop. We jump on and off planes like buses.

Charles Ulm foresaw all this, and it was his mission to create an airline network that would shrink our island continent and span our oceans, linking Australians with each other, and the world.

But boy, were there headwinds!

John Ulm
May 2018

Prologue

One morning towards the end of 1934, the postman delivered a large envelope to the offices of C.T.P. Ulm, Aircraft Operator, at 16 Barrack Street, in the heart of Sydney's business district. Ellen Rogers was expecting it. It was the manuscript of her boss's latest flight, and it was her job to type it up, ready for the printers.

After almost six years as Charles Ulm's secretary, Miss Rogers could read his handwriting easily, but this manuscript was untidy. Almost every page had words overwritten or crossed out, with second thoughts squeezed between lines and in the margins. Ellen's brow furrowed . . . this was going to be a challenging job. Inserting a sheet of paper, a carbon and a flimsy into her machine with practised ease, she began to type.

Chapter One—Thank you!!!

Thank you; that is my first feeling as I set off to write this book which will be an attempt to record the 'Stella Australis' all-British transpacific flight of 1934 and answer some of the seemingly endless, but often logical questions that are often asked about such flights.

Yes—thank you—those hundreds of people who made the flight a success—from the designers, mathematicians, engineers, to the junior engineering apprentices who brought into being the aircraft, the engines, instruments, the wireless and other equipment used; to the firms and individuals who to a small or great extent supported the undertaking; to the meteorologists, to the wireless operators of ship and shore stations; to my colleagues George McCorquord Littlejohn and John Joseph Leonard Skilling who saw the job through to conclusion with me.

After this triumphant, if somewhat overblown opening, Ulm's writing descended to a more prosaic level, and 'Rog', as he affectionately called her, found herself transcribing pages dealing with the reasons for making a second trans-Pacific flight, the problems faced, the choice of aircraft, the navigation, and the selection of the crew. It was all straightforward stuff, expressed in Ulm's direct and positive style. But when she came to the section about the route that the *Stella Australis* had traversed, from San Francisco to Honolulu to Fanning Atoll, thence to Canton Island, Suva, Auckland, Sydney and on to Melbourne, there was a problem. Ulm had sketched out rough, hand-drawn tables containing the distances between the various ports along the route, but had left the adjacent column, intended for the times taken to fly each sector, blank.

Ellen's fingers stopped their dance across the keyboard. She couldn't enter the figures because they were not yet known. The trans-Pacific flight had yet to take place; *Stella Australis* was still sitting firmly on the ground at San Francisco. The manuscript that she was so faithfully transcribing was pure conjecture.

She allowed herself a wry smile; this kind of thing was typical of Charles Ulm. A consummate publicist, he knew that timing was everything, and had written a rough draft in advance, so as to have the book in the shops as soon as the trans-Pacific flight was a fait accompli.

Ellen Rogers never filled in the blanks: before she had finished transcribing the manuscript, word came through that Ulm and his companions had come down in the Pacific, somewhere between San Francisco and Honolulu. Despite an exhaustive search, no trace of *Stella Australis* or her crew was ever found.

Had Charles Ulm lived, there is little doubt that the story of civil aviation in Australia would have taken a different course, and he would have been a major player.

His unpublished manuscript, and Ellen Rogers' incomplete transcription, are now in the Charles Ulm Collection in the National Library of Australia; poignant metaphors for a life in aviation that, tragically, was unfulfilled.

AKA Charles Jackson

Charles Thomas Phillippe Ulm was born on 18 October 1898 at his family's home at 5 Mills Street, Albert Park, Melbourne, not far from where the Formula One motor racing circuit now stands. The baroque spelling of his third Christian name was perhaps a nod to his ancestors; his father, Emile Gustavus Ulm, a Parisian artist, had emigrated during the previous decade.

Emile did not become a household name, and so far as we know, his works did not reach the walls of a major gallery. But he did well enough to decide to stay in Australia and establish a family, and on 4 May 1888 he married Ada Emma Greenland. He was 25; she was 26, born in Australia to English parents. Ulm was the third of five children, four sons and one daughter. He described himself as 'a very ordinary child, quick of temper, inclined to obstinacy, truthful, but outrageously inquisitive': 'Any toy which was handed to me was quickly taken apart, thoroughly examined, and probably wrecked beyond all hope of usefulness.'[1]

A similar fate awaited his first bicycle. After he had taken it to pieces and reassembled it, he set off on a headlong dash down a steep hill with his brother balancing precariously on the parcel tray at the rear. At the bottom of the hill a jetty offered ample space to slow down, but the brakes failed and they ended up in the sea. 'I vaguely recall rescuing my palpitating brother and then salvaging the precious bicycle. This, I suppose, was my first crash.'[2]

Ulm realised quite early that he had not inherited his urge for adventure from his parents: 'To discover the origin of that spirit, it seems that I must look back as far as my great grand-father, a seven-foot [2.1-metre] giant of a man who served in the Royal Bodyguard of King Louis of France. He was a soldier born and bred, devoid of humour, who lived and died without ever experiencing that sensation which men label "fear".'[3]

The family moved around, and Ulm went to the local state schools in Melbourne, and later, after the family moved yet again, in Sydney, in the harbourside suburb of Mosman. As was common in those days, Charles left school at 14, in 1913, and began work as a clerk at a firm of stockbrokers. At his age, and with his restless spirit, he was no doubt bored by the tedium of office routine, but he probably picked up the art of writing a business letter and reading a balance sheet. He would have also seen his first prospectus. He may even have realised that the smartly presented document that he held in his hands was much more than dry text and columns of figures. It was a nexus between men who had ideas and men who had money.

Charles Ulm would have plenty of ideas.

A year later, Great Britain declared war on Germany, and Australia followed her lead. Thousands of young Australian men, motivated by a mix of patriotism and a desire for adventure, lost no time in joining up.

One of the earliest recruits was a young man described on his enlistment form as Charles Jackson, 19 years and 11 months old, 5 feet 7 inches (170 centimetres) tall, of fair complexion, with brown eyes and hair. His next of kin was listed as John Charles Jackson, his address as 27 Keaton Avenue, Mosman, Sydney. Apart from an appendix scar, there were no distinguishing marks on his body, and the medical officer signed the form that certified him fit for service overseas.[4] Two days later, Charles Jackson took the oath pledging allegiance to his sovereign lord, the King.

The only problem, of course, was that Charles Jackson did not exist. The newly minted soldier was in fact Charles Thomas Phillippe Ulm, not yet 16. Under age, but looking much older, he had bluffed his way in.

Ulm's subterfuge would not have held up to scrutiny. He had forged the signature of a parent, because even a 19 year old needed written permission to enlist, but he had supplied his real address, probably because he wanted the army to have an eventual point of contact with his parents. He was hoping that officialdom would not intervene until he was on a troopship on the high seas.

His ruse worked. The 1st Battalion of the AIF arrived in Egypt on 2 December 1914 and after a brief period of training, Charles Jackson AKA Ulm was among the first contingent of ANZACs to land at Gallipoli in April 1915. He received a minor shrapnel wound in the foot and was evacuated to a military hospital at Alexandria. Upon being discharged, he was ordered to report to a nearby camp, where other Australians were awaiting orders to rejoin their units. The fleshpots of Alexandria acted like a magnet for the lusty young Diggers, who began to seek out the camp medical officer in increasing numbers with embarrassing symptoms, Charles among them.

In those days, there was a stigma attached to venereal disease. Penicillin had yet to be invented, and the available treatment regimens were invasive, painful and the subject of much salacious gossip. Fortunately, Charles was not seriously affected, but even so was not considered fit for return to active service. On 5 June 1915, he boarded His Majesty's Hospital Ship *Ballarat* to return to Australia.

Many young men put their ages up in order to enlist, so his mother Ada was probably not altogether surprised when she found out that her 15-year-old son had done so too. About when Charles was preparing to land at Gallipoli she wrote to the army, to let them know he had used a fake name, and asked that it be corrected in their records. She also requested that 'some portion of his pay . . . be sent to [her], to put aside for him in the event of casualty or death whilst on active service abroad'. She never revealed how young he truly was, only that he was not yet 21.

Presumably she received no response, because Ada continued to write to the army seeking the whereabouts of her son. Finally, six months after her first letter, she received a tactful reply, letting her know her son had arrived in Australia by hospital ship. 'Owing to the nature of his illness he will remain in Melbourne for at least a month before proceeding to Sydney', she was told, but that 'it should, however, be understood he is not seriously ill'.[5]

Once recovered, and with his true age and identity now known, Charles Jackson AKA Ulm received an honourable discharge on 13 April 1916. But despite his experiences at Gallipoli, and the prospect of placing himself in harm's way once again, he wanted desperately to return to the army. Being under 21, he still needed the approval of a parent before he could re-enlist, and his father Gustave agreed. On 21 January 1917, Charles Ulm signed up again, joining the 4th Battalion under his own name. There were no repercussions.

Interestingly, at his second medical he measured 5 feet 10 inches (177 centimetres) tall, 7 centimetres taller than his alter ego!

The 4th Battalion sailed to England for training, and then deployed to France, where Ulm was once again wounded. According to a second-hand account written many years later, he was buried by earth thrown up by an exploding shell during a skirmish at the Corbie Canal on the Somme.[6] When his mates found him, only a hand was sticking out. He had wounds to his left thigh, stomach and right knee and foot. He was also temporarily shell-shocked. The knee wound was quite serious, requiring surgery. He regained full movement, but suffered pain for the rest of his life.

Even while recuperating in England, he did not let the grass grow under his feet: 50 quid invested in a dodgy deal quickly returned £3000, in those days enough to buy a couple of houses back home in Sydney.

It is believed that Ulm was selected for officer training at Netheravon, on Salisbury Plain, but the war ended before he could complete the course. No mention of this appears in his official service record, but in a handwritten caption to a photograph taken in Australia shortly after the war he is identified as Lieutenant Ulm. He would soon gain a reputation for stretching the truth in the interests of publicity, so perhaps this is an early example.[7]

At Netheravon, Ulm was introduced to a fellow Australian, Captain Gordon Campbell 'Billy' Wilson, who was a flying instructor responsible for training aircrew before they went to France. Although not classified as an ace, Wilson had shot down a number of enemy aircraft, earning both the Military Cross and the Air Force Cross. At this stage of his war, Charles Ulm would have been quite accustomed to the sight and sound of aeroplanes. At Gallipoli and in France, he would have heard the rattle of machine guns and the screaming of over-revving engines. He would have looked up to see sunlight flashing off wings as the combatants twisted and turned high in the air. He perhaps witnessed the final dive of a doomed fighter, spiralling down, bearing its unfortunate occupant to a violent and often fiery death.

Until 1918, such encounters would always have been at a distance. But now, probably due to his association with Wilson, he saw an aeroplane at close quarters, and flew for the first time. After several flights as a passenger, 'innumerable questions' and short periods of dual control training, Ulm, without authority, made his first solo flight: 'By the grace of God it was more or less satisfactory. I got the aircraft off the ground, circled once or twice, and managed to bump back to the ground without injuring myself or the plane. Had the outcome been unlucky, I probably would have been faced with a court-martial.'[8]

There is no official record of this episode, for if Charles Ulm kept a pilot's logbook its whereabouts are unknown. This says a lot about the man, and the way he viewed aeroplanes and flying. For most pilots, their first solo flight is a significant event, something they remember for the rest of their lives. For Ulm, it appears to have had no emotional impact whatsoever. There is no doubt that the course of his life was changed after he first flew, but it was not the romance of flying aeroplanes that captured his imagination.

He was more interested in what aeroplanes could *do*.

The science of powered flight had developed in leaps and bounds since 1914, driven by the exigencies of war. At the beginning of hostilities, few took the aeroplane seriously, but by 1919, aircraft designers had a deeper understanding of aerodynamics, structures were lighter and stronger, and engines were more powerful and more reliable. Aeroplanes could now fly higher, faster and further than their predecessors, and the advent of the bomber in the later years of the war meant that they could also carry heavier loads. Now, with peace in sight, enterprising people could see that aeroplanes could perhaps be used to carry passengers and parcels instead of bombs and bullets. Aeroplanes could be used to make money.

It was already happening in Britain. Aircraft Transport and Travel was carrying passengers four at a time between London and Paris in de Havilland DH.16 aircraft, adapted from the military DH.9.[9] Handley Page Transport soon followed, with O/400 bombers converted to carry as many as 16 passengers.[10] On the other side of the Channel, several French airlines were planning to operate fourteen-passenger Farman F.60 Goliaths, also converted bombers, on the same route.[11]

Ulm could not have failed to notice.

He returned to Australia after the war, and was honourably discharged as a sergeant on 20 March 1919, entitled to wear the British War Medal, the Victory Medal and the 1914–15 Star.[12] While his damaged knee was a constant reminder of the horrors of the trenches, he was determined to put the past behind him. He had done his duty and the future beckoned. Unlike many of his comrades-in-arms, who were struggling to come to terms with the return to civilian life, he had money in his pocket, and he had plans.

Although he was intense by nature, and committed to starting a career for himself in civil aviation, life wasn't all work for Charles. Shortly after his return to Australia, he met Isabel Winter at a club in Market Street that catered for returned Diggers. Isabel worked behind the linen counter at Farmers department store during the day, and at night was one of a group of young women who acted as hostesses at the club. The adventurer in Ulm no doubt appreciated that her father had been a member of the Shackleton expedition to Antarctica. They were married at St John's Anglican Church, Darlinghurst, on 20 November 1919, and their only son, John, was born in 1921.

It was not a happy marriage. They both possessed strong, organising personalities, and their problems were no doubt compounded by a shortage of money, Ulm's obsession with aviation, and his consequent frequent and prolonged absences from home. He soon left Isabel and they eventually divorced in 1926.[13] Young John seldom saw his father.

The month before Ulm's marriage, the Overseas Institute of Aircraft Engineering (OIAE) was registered in Sydney on 8 October 1919, with offices in the Lyceum Building at 241 Pitt Street. A press release announced that the company was backed by a number of 'exceedingly wealthy men' who were 'keen on the development of commercial aviation'. Charles Ulm was the company secretary, among the first shareholders and had also written the press release. The company was founded just ten days before his 21st birthday.[14]

Initially, the OIAE offered a correspondence course in aviation science, open to students anywhere in Australia. This was a subterfuge, because Ulm's aim was the development of air services, not education. He was on the lookout for pilots and mechanics. The course would attract recently discharged servicemen hoping to improve their chances of finding work in aviation, and he could have his pick of the best. The problem, of course, was that Australia did not yet have an aviation industry. Ulm intended to do something about that.

Rather than establishing an air link between Sydney and Melbourne, OIAE intended to focus on the development of regional air services, linking major centres with each other and with the capital cities. Bathurst, about 200 kilometres north-west of Sydney in the central highlands of New South Wales, would be the hub of their operations. The oldest inland settlement in Australia, Bathurst had come into prominence during the gold rush of the 1860s, attracting fortune seekers from all over the world. By 1919, the gold was gone, but it was still a prosperous town with many fine buildings, large railway workshops and a cannery, and surrounded by a thriving agricultural community.

Early the next year, the *Bathurst Times* reported on a visit by a Lieutenant James Ovens, an OIAE representative looking for a suitable site for a landing ground. Lieutenant Ovens said the company was planning to establish an air service that would enable a busy Sydney man to leave his office and visit Mount Victoria, Bathurst and Orange and return the same day. Fifty thousand pounds would be spent on workshops and hangars; Bathurst would be made the overhauling centre of the west. The report went on to say that the company owned 25 machines and had options on others.[15]

In fact, the OIAE did not own a single aeroplane. The press release that formed the basis of the article had been written by Charles Ulm. In reality, Ulm had secured only the options on 25 Sopwith Dove biplanes that had been imported from England by the Larkin-Sopwith Aviation Company.

Ten days later, Lieutenant Ovens was in Bathurst again, this time to interview applicants for the correspondence course. He could not have chosen a better moment, because that morning there was a stir of excitement: the Vickers Vimy G-EAOU carrying Ross and Keith Smith, Wally Shiers, Jim Bennett and the photographer Frank Hurley was due to pass over the town following its momentous first–ever flight from England to Australia.

In due course the Vimy appeared, and Ross Smith rocked the wings gracefully in salute before setting a stately course towards the Blue Mountains and Sydney. Never one to miss an opportunity, Charles Ulm had already written to Smith. The letter no longer exists, but Ulm almost certainly sought Smith's services, not only as a pilot, but also as a 'name' that would improve the OIAE's prospects. Smith's reply was courteous, and non-committal. While he was 'grateful' for the offer in connection with the OIAE, he wrote, 'I would like to talk over matters with you as at present I know nothing of your aims or plans of your scheme'.[16] Ulm did not take the matter any further. It is not known how many students enrolled in the correspondence course, but it is certain that not one graduated, because the Overseas Institute of Aviation Engineering failed to attract sufficient investors, and within three months ceased to exist, with one of its principals absconding overseas.

For Charles, this was a just a minor setback, and the following year he registered the Aviation Service Company, appointing himself secretary and manager. At a well-attended public meeting in the Bathurst Town Hall, he made his intentions known. The nominal capital of the company was to be £25,000, to be distributed as 25,000 shares at £1 each. He proposed to buy six Sopwith Dove biplanes, which had been imported from England by the Larkin-Sopwith Aviation Company, and were then located in Melbourne. Bathurst would be the centre of regional operations, with a weekly link to Sydney. The Aviation Service Company would also establish a base at an aerodrome soon to be built at Manly, on Sydney's northern beaches. From here Sopwith Gnus, which had more powerful engines, would fly on interstate routes.

In the audience were Mayor Havenhand and a prominent local pharmacist, P.J. 'Perce' Moodie, who had recently flown for the first time, in a DH.6 biplane. Exhilarated by the experience, Moodie had become an instant convert. Ulm was a persuasive speaker, and Moodie quickly saw the benefits that air travel could bring to regional areas. Moreover, in Charles Ulm he recognised a man who, he believed, could make things happen. Moodie became a director of the company and one of Charles Ulm's staunchest supporters. It was the beginning of a lasting friendship.

In the prospectus for the new company, Ulm's enthusiasm for the future of aviation in Australia knew no bounds: 'There is no country in the world so ideally suited to aerial development; its geographical and weather conditions being extraordinarily favourable. It consists of huge areas of flat country, an immediate result of which may be seen by its cloudless skies, absence of fogs, and general atmospheric uniformity.'

Ulm noted that the average motorcar and a Sopwith Dove biplane consumed the same fuel per miles per hour, with the advantage that in flying you could travel straight to your destination. 'There is not the slightest question,' he concluded, 'but that aviation will introduce to Australia a new era of prosperity.'[17] What he conveniently omitted to say that was that the Dove was not much faster than a car, could carry only a light load, and was uncomfortable and dangerous.

The prospectus was a handsome typeset document, with maps showing an impressive route network. Passenger services would begin immediately, and aircraft would be available for delivery flights and aerial advertising. Joy-riding would be an important source of revenue. Based on two machines, flying for a minimum of three hours each per day, Ulm anticipated a net profit of £15,955 per year—a return on capital of no less than 63.82 per cent.

The figures added up, but to experienced eyes it all looked too good to be true. Despite Perce Moodie's enthusiasm, an endorsement from the mayor and Ulm's formidable promotional skills, the general public was not yet ready to accept the aeroplane as a regular means of public transport, and the stock issue was undersubscribed.

Short on working capital, Ulm decided to purchase just two Doves instead of the original six, and recklessly announced that, on their delivery flight, both aircraft would fly from Melbourne to Bathurst nonstop, in formation. To impart a degree of gravitas to the venture, Perce Moodie and Mayor Havenhand would fly as passengers. However, there were last-minute delays with the installation of long-range tanks, and Ulm was forced to issue a statement saying that only one aircraft would make the flight.

On the appointed day, flight commander Johnson, the Aviation Service Company's chief pilot, with the plucky mayor as passenger, attempted to take off from a rain-soaked aerodrome at Glen Huntly. The first two runs were aborted due to the heavy going, and on the third attempt the machine rose briefly then dropped, tearing off the undercarriage and damaging the propeller. Nobody was injured, but Mayor Havenhand was badly shaken, together with his faith in the aeroplane as a reliable form of transport. In Bathurst, Ulm was dismayed when he heard the news. Hastily reassuring his shareholders that the Sopwith was fully insured, he evaded the waiting press and caught the next train to Melbourne.

It took him almost three weeks to sort things out, and it was mid-July before the Dove taxied out once more at Glen Huntly.

This time the pilot was P.H. 'Skip' Moody, with the redoubtable Perce Moodie (no relation) as passenger. They took off without further mishap, but had to return five times because of bad weather. Finally, on 15 July they arrived in Bathurst after a refuelling stop at Albury. Ulm was waiting to congratulate pilot and passenger, but no amount of spin could hide the fact that the whole exercise, intended to promote flying as a safe and reliable form of transport, had been an unmitigated disaster.

Nevertheless, the company did get off the ground commercially, with passenger and parcel-delivery flights between Sydney and Melbourne, but without capital it could not carry on, and at a shareholders' meeting at Bathurst on 12 April 1921, the Aviation Service Company was quietly wound up.

Just one week earlier, another aerial enterprise, the Diggers' Co-Operative Aviation Company, had arrived in Bathurst. They were a freewheeling, boozy lot, whose main business was barnstorming from town to town offering joy-rides in war-surplus Avro 504s. Their chief pilot and star attraction was a charismatic, decorated ex-fighter pilot, stunt flyer and all-round knockabout bloke. His name was Charles Kingsford Smith.[18]

Ulm had already met Smithy briefly some months earlier, but didn't bother to renew their acquaintance.

The stars were not yet in alignment.

CHAPTER 2

Late nights at Lavender Bay

Following the demise of the Aviation Service Company, Charles again tried to pick up the pieces and establish a regular air service, but without success: 'In those days I received about as much encouragement as a coal dealer in Hades. Those people who did not regard me as a mild sort of lunatic always buttoned up their pockets or produced writs whenever I came within 100 yards of them.'[1]

Short of money, Ulm teamed up with wartime pal Billy Wilson for what he considered the airman's last resort: travelling from town to town selling joyrides, a practice known as barnstorming. To attract the customers, they recognised the need for publicity— free publicity, if possible. Anything to alert the public that they were open for business.

A member of an organisation named Smith's Suicide Club had recently driven a car up virtually non-existent roads to Careys Peak in Barrington Tops, the highest inhabited point in Australia. Charles and Billy decided to emulate the feat by aeroplane. It was madness, and a reflection of Ulm's inexperience, because any publicity they gleaned from the adventure would likely be of the worst possible kind. And so it turned out to be.

Ulm and Wilson took off from Mascot and headed north, carrying an apprehensive reporter from the *Wingham Chronicle and Manning River Observer,* who in the next edition shared the experience with his readers.

> Aboard the machine was a six-valve wireless set with which the results of the races and other news were received in the air and which would have come in handy had our little band of history makers become snowed in on the Tops and be forced to winter there for a week. Looking back on Mascot aerodrome shrinking into a tiny garden plot, Wilson, who was used to more daring adventures, settled down at ease in the pilot's seat. C.P. Ulm, his brother pilot, looked as contented as though he had just passed an order over for a whiskey and soda. As for myself, I began fumbling my pockets for my insurance policy. Newcastle, our first stop, was reached three quarters of an hour after leaving Sydney.

They landed at Newcastle to refuel and have a quick cigarette, then took off again into a strong headwind, which stirred up huge clouds of red dust, obscuring the ground. They were soon lost, but pressed on, hoping that the dust would clear sufficiently to enable them to identify a landmark. Suddenly they glimpsed a small town through the murk, and by circling low over the railway station, they were able to identify it as Scone. Back on track once again, and climbing hard to clear the mountain tops that lay ahead, they passed over the village of Gundy, then Belltrees Station, skimming the mountain peaks with metres to spare. At Moonan Flat, fuel was once again running low, so Wilson searched for a landing place.

Moonan Flat is locked in by hills, and practically all the flat is sparsely timbered. At the back of the hotel there happens to be a small cultivation paddock but a bad landing ground owing to the fact that it was an oblong tract with a crosswind over it making it impossible to land the orthodox way, head on to the wind. Only one thing remained—to do a side slip, and we did it as gracefully and as cleverly as though it were an everyday occurrence to land in a garden plot not much bigger than a pocket handkerchief. Nose into the crosswind, the machine was swerved quickly a few feet from the ground, and rising momentarily, slid back again sideways and landed in its own length. A closer inspection of the paddock disclosed the fact that to get off again was going to be a harder job than the landing, owing to the rough nature of the ground and the fact that it was riddled with rabbits' burrows. Taxiing up to the fence a few minutes after landing the tailskid sank into a rabbit burrow and snapped off. This meant a delay while the village blacksmith built up new stays for the damaged portion. The delay was annoying, but when a howling gale blew up, followed by showers of hail that almost pierced the fabric of the machine, we realised that all had happened for the best. Had we attempted to land on the Tops in such a terrific gale and a mist that blanketed out the open spaces, the odds are that we would have crashed.

While they were waiting for the blacksmith to repair the tailskid, word came through that a motorcyclist had become lost while attempting to ride across the Tops from Dungog to Moonan Flat, and Billy Wilson was asked to search for him.

The repairs completed, they took off, but bad weather drove them back. It was too late for another attempt, so they were forced to stay the night. That evening they were invited to a bush dance, which lasted until 4 a.m.

At first light they took off again, circling to gain height. As the needle of the altimeter registered 10,000 feet, the Barrington Range came into view, with Careys Peak, the highest point, protruding above the ragged clouds that draped the escarpment. They flew back and forth along the range, but in such rugged, heavily timbered country they could not see the ground through the dense canopy, which was itself, more often than not, obscured by the fast-moving clouds. In such conditions they knew that they would never see the missing man. All they could hope for was a wisp of smoke, swirling up through the trees, to reveal his location.

There was nothing.

It was impossible for us to cruise around any longer and have enough petrol left to get back to Moonan. To go back and wait for a clear day meant perhaps a delay of the week or more, so Wilson decided to wait for an opening in the mist and dive for it and land in a side slip on the first patch of clear ground that he could see. An opening came and closed just as quickly, but the pilot's practised eye saw that it had laid bare a clear patch and a few seconds later the bumping of the undercarriage indicated that we had come down to earth. The landing, perilous as it was, had forged another link in the chain of aviation achievements, for it was the highest point in Australia that a plane had ever landed upon—4500 feet [1370 metres] above sea level. Stopping only long enough to take a photograph and make an adjustment to the carburettor owing to the high altitude and the need for a different petrol mixture, the pilot got ready to take advantage of another break in the clouds to take off. It came sooner than expected, and helped by a sharp head-wind, the 'plane rose and just scraped over the edge of the trees that fringed the plain. Leaves of the topmost branches of one tree actually touched the starboard wing. It was the thrill of a lifetime.[2]

It all made exciting copy for the *Chronicle*, but unfortunately for Ulm and Wilson, it was also effective in keeping all but the most avid thrillseekers away. The barnstorming tour was a complete disaster. Ulm retreated to Sydney, broke, separated and soon to be divorced from his wife. In desperation, he turned to his considerable skills as a snooker player, hanging around saloons in the hope of partnering other players for a fee. He found lodgings at a flat in Lavender Bay, with Mary Josephine Callaghan, a schoolteacher, and her sister Amy, a nurse, who was able to help him improve the mobility of his knee and give him a degree of pain relief.

According to aviation historian Ian Mackersey, Jo Callaghan was a 'plain, bespectacled, academic-looking woman, regarded with universal affection', unfailingly 'gracious, cheerful, and generous'.[3] She and Ulm soon became soulmates, and would remain so for the rest of his life. It was here, at Lavender Bay, during long late-night conversations with Jo, that his plans for the future began to crystallise.

> Looking back, I can see now that it was at this period that my main ambition was born—the urge to establish and control major air services over long distances for the carriage of passengers and mails. My idea was to establish a fleet of aeroplanes to operate between Melbourne and Perth, and finally, right round Australia.[4]

At the back of his mind he harboured an even loftier ambition so outlandish that he hardly dared think about it. Now was not the time to share it, not even with Jo. But one day he was going to fly the Pacific.

His feet back firmly on the ground, Ulm spent many hours preparing detailed proposals for a Melbourne–Perth service, which government officials acknowledged, then ignored. Undeterred, he sought private backing, once again without success.

But his fortunes were about to change. On 27 November 1923, an armada of British warships sailed from Devonport on an extended cruise around the world. Known as the Special Service Squadron, it comprised two battlecruisers, five light cruisers and an assortment of destroyers. The flagship, HMS *Hood*, was the largest and most heavily armed warship afloat. The Royal Navy intended to show the flag wherever possible in countries that had supported Britain during the First World War.

Australians followed the progress of the Special Service Squadron with great interest via frequent updates that were published almost daily in the major newspapers. The culmination of the whole exercise, so far as they were concerned, would be on the morning of Wednesday 9 April 1924, when the fleet was scheduled to sail majestically into Sydney Harbour. As the ships worked their way around the coast from Fremantle, interest rose to fever pitch.

Charles Ulm sensed an opportunity. He wrote to Herbert Campbell Jones, the managing editor of Sydney's *The Sun* newspaper, offering to supply aerial photographs of the ships at sea as they approached the Heads in the early morning light. The timing would suit *The Sun* perfectly, because as an afternoon paper it would scoop the morning editions by at least 18 hours. Campbell Jones agreed immediately and a deal was struck: *The Sun* would provide the photographer and Ulm would supply the aircraft, to be flown by Billy Wilson.

As these words are written, anybody with a smartphone can take a photograph and make it available to the world almost immediately via the internet, but such a thing was unheard of in 1924. Although pictures had been transmitted experimentally along telephone lines, the technology was not in general use, and newspaper editors needed physical photographs in order to reproduce them in print.

Even though both sides had used aerial photographs extensively for mapping and reconnaissance during the First World War, news photography from aeroplanes was definitely not routine. The standard press camera, used by most photographers, including those at *The Sun*, was the American Graflex, which captured negative images on plates of silver halide film measuring 5 inches by 4 inches (12 centimetres by 10 centimetres) that had to be loaded shot by shot. Aiming a heavy, bulky Graflex from an open cockpit at 150 kilometres per hour would be a difficult process.

Taking the pictures was the photographer's business, and Wilson would look after the flying. But overall responsibility for the enterprise weighed heavily on Ulm's shoulders. He was asking his colleagues to fly out to sea in an elderly Sopwith Dove; three men squeezed into two tiny cockpits behind a cantankerous rotary engine that constantly sprayed them (and the camera) with castor oil. His presence aboard was not necessary, but there was no way he was going to miss out on the action. He knew that strong winds could prevent them even from leaving the ground; low cloud, fog or heavy rain could conceal the ships. Publishable pictures were not a foregone conclusion and, if he didn't deliver, he would not be paid. Ulm knew he was taking a gamble, and he relished the challenge.

On the day the armada arrived in Sydney, the front page of *The Sun* was dominated by a large aerial photograph, four columns wide, of HMS *Hood* steaming towards the Heads, framed by the bracing wires and interplane struts of the Sopwith's wing. It was accompanied by purple prose extolling the glories of the British Empire, the strong ties between Australia and England, and the might of the Royal Navy: 'And as the lord of the Seven Seas, the majestic "Hood" revealed herself to the strained, silent, awed assemblage that waited like a settled flock of dark birds on the long bastion of rocks, the might of our race became manifest. Here was a sign that could not be mistaken, the lordship of the oceans, the pledge of our protection, the security of a peaceful virile race, intent only on the development of their great heritage . . .'[5]

Charles Ulm was more interested in another item, also on the front page. Headed 'THE SUN' ALOFT. SPECIAL PICTURE PLANE A SPECK IN THE WEST, it was the story behind the story—a dramatic account of the way the pictures of *Hood* had been obtained.

> At 8 a.m. the plane was winging its way eastward over the Heads, rushing out to meet the fleet at sea. At 20 minutes to 9 'The Sun' photographer and Mr Ulm arrived breathlessly on the top floor of 'The Sun' office with the first set of plates. They had just driven in from Mascot in a fast car, which waited to take them back to the aerodrome where the pilot was waiting to carry them out again on a second flight in order to secure further pictures for today's later editions.[6]

Ulm was delighted. This was the kind of publicity you simply couldn't buy. He had earned a modest fee for his efforts, but more importantly, he had established a relationship with Herbert Campbell Jones that he knew could be of immense value in the years ahead. Another flight for *The Sun* soon followed, this time to take aerial photographs of Newcastle.

Despite the success of the photographic sorties, he had his eyes firmly fixed on the goal that he had discussed with Jo. He wanted to make interstate, intercity flights, carrying passengers and mail. And now there was an opportunity to turn his dream into reality: tenders were invited for a government contract to operate a service between Adelaide and Perth. Norman Brearley's

Western Australian Airways, which already had experience on the route, were the favourites, but Ulm, ever the optimist, was determined to make a bid for it.

By now, experience had taught him that to stand even the remotest chance of winning the contract he needed to find an established outfit with bigger, faster machines, pilots to fly them and mechanics to maintain them. He needed to win their trust, and work his way in.

He had a prospect in mind. It was called Interstate Flying Services, a new company set up by two pilots, Keith Anderson and Charles Kingsford Smith. They had recently been in the news after flying two Bristol Tourers from Perth to Sydney in an attempt to break the west-to-east record of three days, established in 1920. Their attempt had failed, but they had made headlines anyway because one of their passengers, the wife of a newspaperman, had thereby become the first woman to cross Australia by air.

Ulm knew Smithy mainly by repute: by all accounts the man was an excellent pilot, but he had a habit of breaking aeroplanes. He had not met Anderson, but this didn't particularly bother him. The main attraction was their two aircraft.

The Bristol Type 28 Tourer was an adaptation of the famous Bristol Fighter, one of the most successful military aircraft of the First World War. For civil use, the airframe had been stripped of all military equipment and the rear cockpit modified to carry two passengers in a semi-enclosed cabin. The 230 horsepower

Siddeley Puma water-cooled engine gave the aircraft a cruising speed of about 90 knots (170 kilometres per hour) and a range of 400 miles (644 kilometres).

Interstate Flying Services' Tourers were not new. Since December 1921, Norman Brearley's Western Australian Airways had used them to operate a scheduled service from Perth to Derby, so they had a lot of hours in their logbooks. But they were sturdy and reliable, and definitely a step up from the Sopwith Dove.

Kingsford Smith and Anderson had been partners in a trucking company, Gascoyne Transport, based in Carnarvon, Western Australia. It had been a sizable operation with a fleet of six heavy trucks and trailers servicing the wool industry. They had recently sold the company to finance the purchase of the Bristol Tourers, which they planned to fly to New Guinea where they could earn big money flying equipment, supplies and personnel to the goldfields. This would then provide the funds for their ultimate dream: Kingsford Smith and Keith Anderson intended to be the first men to fly across the Pacific.

Charles Ulm, of course, knew nothing of their lofty ambitions, nor of their financial position. Interstate Flying Services had an office in Pitt Street, and a leaflet that advertised 'Aeroplane flights to any part of the world', but, as a publicist of some experience, Ulm no doubt read it with a wry grin for he knew the limitations of the aircraft of the day. He was also aware that their tiny serviced office, in the centre of Sydney's business district, was probably just for show. But on the other hand, maybe Interstate Flying Services offered him the chance that he had been waiting for.

He resisted the urge to pick up the telephone himself. It was important to make a good impression right from the start, so he called his solicitor and asked him to set up a meeting.

Even though he was almost stony broke, the impression that Charles Ulm projected the next day was of a tall, dark, successful businessman, smartly dressed in a well-cut suit, complete with hat and shiny briefcase. He exuded self-confidence.

Kingsford Smith made the introductions, which were formal, as was the custom in those days: Mr Keith Anderson, pilot; Mr Bert Pike, Kingsford Smith's brother-in-law; and Mr Leofric Kingsford Smith, his brother and financial advisor. They all addressed their visitor as Mr Ulm. Smithy explained that the other member of the team, Mr Bob Hitchcock, was at Mascot, where he maintained the Tourers.

Ulm quickly got down to business, speaking with an intensity that captured their attention: Australia's vast distances were calling out for air services, and he could see them eventually linking all the major capitals. There was money to be made, he was certain. He had read in the papers about their Perth to Sydney flight, and had been impressed. He was about to make a bid for a government contract to operate an Adelaide–Perth air service. Would they be interested in joining forces with him to submit a tender?

He produced a document and put it on the table for their perusal. As usual, he had done his homework. Neatly bound and professionally typed, it contained, among other items, a complete cost–revenue estimate for the proposed service. Kingsford Smith was impressed. Nobody else in the room was capable of producing such a document. Here was a man to be taken seriously.

While they sat in a haze of cigarette smoke, scanning the submission in turn, trying to make quick sense of the columns of figures, Ulm made his pitch. While he was not an aviator, he understood the aviation business. He had management skills and a natural flair for publicity and fundraising. Interstate Flying Services had pilots, aircraft and the means to maintain them. Working together as a team, they could make a formidable combination. They could win the contract.

To Smithy, Ulm's presentation made perfect sense: he and Ulm were striving for the same objective from different directions. But reactions in the room were mixed. Although he didn't show it, Keith Anderson was uneasy. He noticed that Ulm never smiled, and wondered what impact this intense, humourless man might have on the easygoing friendship that he had developed with Smithy. Bert Pike felt downright threatened. As well as Smithy's brother-in-law, he was his business manager of long standing, first with the trucks, now with the aeroplanes. Would there still be a place for him if Ulm joined Interstate Flying Services?

Pike's fears were not unfounded. It didn't take long for Interstate Flying Services to invite Ulm to join them, and in April

1927 they drew up a partnership agreement, valid for the period of the tender, and found him a desk at the office in Pitt Street.

Ulm quickly discovered that the company was in a deplorable state. There were substantial debts and there was very little money in the bank. The phone seldom rang because charter work had dried up and Pike seemed devoid of ideas for drumming up new business. Kingsford Smith and Anderson were seldom to be seen.

Ulm immediately applied himself to turning the company around. He had plenty of contacts in the aviation world, and the phone soon began ringing again. Totally eclipsed by Ulm's intellect and overwhelmed by his forceful personality, Bert Pike offered his resignation, which was reluctantly, but immediately, accepted. Ulm replaced him as business manager on a retainer of 30 shillings per week, a reasonable sum, and a figure quickly boosted by a commission on the extra charter business that he attracted.

He was aware of the disquiet that Bert's demise caused within the Kingsford Smith family, but shrugged it off. In his eyes, all was fair in love and war—and business. Bert had been an unfortunate, but necessary, casualty; a 'good-natured, unimaginative plodder'.[7]

Ulm had formed impressions of the other partners, too. Keith Anderson was 'a gentle giant; a simple soul with a broad grin and an intensely parochial outlook', and Kingsford Smith, 'wizard pilot though he was, had little more idea of organising big-scale finance than he had of conducting a Sunday school'.[8]

Ulm's reservations notwithstanding, he and Charles Kingsford Smith were beginning to develop a firm friendship. It was the genesis of one of the most potent partnerships that the aviation world would ever see.

Keith Anderson watched, and worried, and kept his opinions to himself.

In May 1927, thousands of people converged on Canberra for the official opening of the new Parliament House, which was presided over by the Duke and Duchess of York. The Royal Australian Air Force was represented by a flight of Avro 504 training aircraft, which flew in formation over the assembled throng.

Ulm made sure that Interstate Flying Services was there too, offering joyrides. While many roads were still tracks and the Molonglo River had yet to be dammed to create Lake Burley Griffin, the general layout of Australia's capital was apparent from the air, so a quick circuit in a Bristol Tourer provided a unique perspective. Business was brisk. The Tourer was quite well suited to joy-riding. It had two cockpits: the pilot sat in the front, with two passengers in a larger cockpit behind him. Smithy and Anderson did the flying while Ulm took care of the business, touting for customers and collecting the money. Hitchcock kept the aircraft serviceable. They camped on the makeshift airfield and, with the familiarity brought on by the close quarters of the tents, finally began to call each other by their first names.

Back in Sydney, with Interstate Flying Services now heading in the right direction, Ulm turned his attention to the tender.

Borrowing money at a high rate of interest to cover their expenses, he created a syndicate to support their application, with war hero Major General Sir Charles Rosenthal as chairman to add prestige to the venture.

It was not enough. The contract for the Adelaide–Perth service was awarded to Norman Brearley's West Australian Airways. Ulm was disappointed, but not surprised; against the brand-new 14-passenger, three-engine de Havilland DH.66 Hercules airliners that Brearley proposed to use on the route, three obsolescent two-passenger Bristol Tourers simply did not stack up.

Moreover, he knew that Interstate Flying Services was regarded as a cowboy operation within government circles, and that his personal reputation was not entirely squeaky clean.

With the tender process done and dusted, it could have been time for Ulm to move on, but Smithy and Anderson pressed him to stay. The friendship between Ulm and Kingsford Smith continued to develop, and Smithy often drove Charles home to Jo's flat at Lavender Bay, on Sydney's lower North Shore, where they would sit over a beer, smoking and chatting late into the night. The topic was usually some aspect of aviation, their hopes, their dreams.

But in May 1927, the dreaming came to an abrupt end. An event on the other side of the world galvanised them into action.

Charles Ulm, photographed with his parents during the First World War. National Library of Australia (NLA)

Ulm's first aircraft, a Sopwith Dove, 1920. Ulm is standing on the right, partially obscuring the registration letters. Pilot 'Skip' Moody is in the cockpit, 'Perce' Moodie at the trailing edge of the wing. Charles T.P. Ulm Collection of Aviation Photographs, Mitchell Library, State Library of NSW (ML SLNSW)

Bob Hitchcock, Charles Kingsford Smith (on wing), Keith Anderson and Ulm pose for a publicity shot on 20 June 1927 after the abortive start on an attempt to break the around-Australia record. They are all smiles for the camera, but Ulm's divisive tactics had alienated Anderson and Hitchcock. NLA

Harry Lyon, Ulm, Smithy and Jim Warner, the crew of *Southern Cross*, at Los Angeles, 23 May 1928, shortly before their attempt to cross the Pacific by air. NLA

A posed shot of Warner at the controls of his radio. The name of the aircraft is visible in reverse through the thin fabric covering of the fuselage. NLA

The rear cabin of *Southern Cross* as fitted out for the trans-Pacific flight, looking towards the cockpit. The massive tank blocked all access; the only means of communication between the pilots and their navigator and radio operator was by means of written messages, passed to and fro on a long stick. NLA

Southern Cross lands at Albert Park, Suva, Fiji, at the end of the long hop from Honolulu, Hawaii. It was a difficult short-field landing, and despite his exhaustion, Smithy managed to bring her safely to a stop. NLA

Southern Cross taxies in after landing at Eagle Farm, Brisbane, on 9 June 1928 upon completion of the Pacific flight. The two distant figures beneath the left wing are Warner and Lyon, who had been disembarked at the end of the landing run. NLA

Southern Cross surrounded by the crowds who flocked to Eagle Farm airfield to witness the triumphant arrival. Queensland State Archives

Ulm and Smithy basking in the glow of public adulation in Sydney, following their historic flight. Fairfax Images

Crowds in New Zealand at an official function to celebrate the first trans-Tasman flight, September 1928. NLA

A photograph taken from Les Holden's aircraft on 12 April 1929, shortly after he discovered *Southern Cross* on the mudflat in north-western Australia that came to be known as Coffee Royal. NLA

Southern Cross, showing the makeshift tents erected by the crew. NLA

Bertie Heath was the first pilot to reach Coffee Royal, landing beside the stranded *Southern Cross* on 13 April 1929. He was borne shoulder-high by the emaciated Tom McWilliams, Smithy, Ulm and Harold Litchfield, but their elation would be short-lived. ML SLNSW

Joining the search for the *Southern Cross*: Hitchcock and Anderson in front of the *Kookaburra*. State Library of Western Australia

The *Kookaburra* is finally spotted from the air. In front of the plane can be seen attempts at clearing made by Hitchcock and Anderson. NLA

An aerial view of the newly completed Australian National Airways (ANA) hangar at Mascot, Sydney, 1929. ML SLNSW

Not a good start: the ANA airliner *Southern Sky* and passengers after a forced landing at Old Bonalbo, New South Wales, on the first day of the airline's operations, 1 January 1930. Kingsford Smith later flew the aircraft out. NLA

Southern Moon in flight: the state of the art in airline equipment in 1930. Charles Ulm later bought this aircraft and renamed it *Faith in Australia*. NLA

Although the passenger cabin of an ANA Avro Ten represented the ultimate in passenger comfort in 1929, there were no seatbelts. In heavy turbulence, passengers were sometimes thrown about the cabin. ML SLNSW

The pilot's cockpit, *Faith in Australia,* 1933. Using these rudimentary instruments and manual controls Ulm and his colleagues flew *Faith in Australia* halfway around the world and back again. ML SLNSW

Ulm casts a critical eye over the two massive long-range tanks in *Faith in Australia*'s tubular steel fuselage in Mascot, 1933. There is just enough room for a crew member to access the cockpit from the rear cabin. NLA

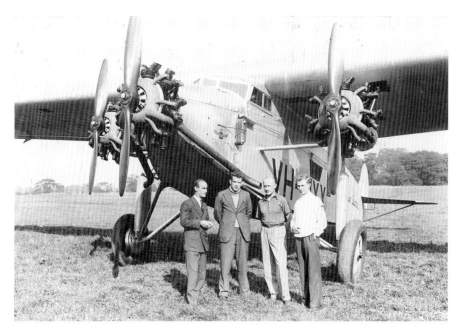

Faith in Australia at Heston, England, with the crew for the trans-Atlantic flight.
G.A. Allan, co-pilot; Ulm, commander–pilot; P.G. Taylor, navigator–relief pilot;
J.A. Edwards, wireless operator. ML SLNSW

Charles Ulm and Scotty Allan assess the damage after *Faith in Australia*'s undercarriage collapsed on Portmarnock Beach, Ireland, 28 July 1933. ML SLNSW

Her engines wrapped in tarpaulins to give a measure of protection from the rising sea, a crippled *Faith in Australia* awaits her fate. ML SLNSW

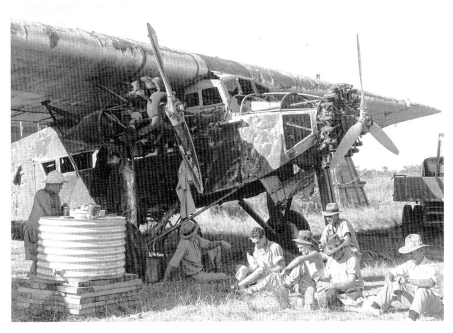

An ignominious end for a grand old lady. Workmen pause for smoko beside the derelict hulk of *Faith in Australia*, Garbutt Airfield, Townsville, 1943. The aircraft was later bulldozed into a dump. Courtesy of the Airways Museum, Essendon

On 4 December 1933, Ulm's wife, Jo (left), and his secretary, Ellen Rogers (right), became the first women passengers to cross the Tasman Sea by air. Ellen is shown alighting from *Faith in Australia* at New Plymouth, New Zealand. NLA / ML SLNSW

Faith in Australia on the beach at Murawai, ready for take-off with the first official air mail from New Zealand to Australia, 17 February 1934. The photograph was signed by Charles Ulm. ML SLNSW

Charles and Jo Ulm photographed at Richmond Aerodrome shortly before *Faith in Australia*'s departure on the first official airmail flight to New Zealand, 12 April 1934. NLA

Ulm spent many hours at the controls of both *Faith in Australia* and *Southern Cross*. This rare photograph was taken on one of the few occasions when both aircraft could be seen in the air together. Museum of Applied Arts and Sciences, Sydney

Charles Ulm speaking with the American aviator Amelia Earhart minutes before *Stella Australis* departed Oakland Airport, California. Within three years she, too, would vanish into the vastness of the Pacific. ML SLNSW

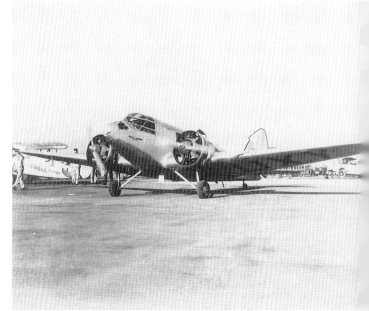

Stella Australis shortly before taking off on the ill-fated crossing to Honolulu, 3 December 1934. ML SLNSW

CHAPTER 3

The other man in
the picture

At 7.54 a.m. on 20 May 1927, a young unknown American aviator named Charles Lindbergh coaxed his heavily laden Ryan NYP monoplane from the rain-sodden runway at Roosevelt Field, Long Island, banked gently to avoid some trees, and headed off into the misty morning.[1] Thirty-three hours later he was circling Le Bourget Airport, a hero overnight, and the recipient of the Orteig Prize of US$25,000 for the first flight from New York to Paris.[2]

It was an amazing achievement whichever way you looked at it, but, in Australia, Kingsford Smith read the newspaper reports of the flight with a growing sense of disquiet. 'Lucky Lindy' undoubtedly had skill and courage, he had the right aircraft, and now, with runs on the board, he had money and influence.

Would he soon have the Pacific in his sights?[3] Smithy and Ulm met at Jo's flat to discuss the record flight.

Smithy's long-held ambition to be the first to fly the Pacific had been no secret, but at this meeting Ulm revealed that he, too, had the same dream. Surprised and delighted, Smithy felt a surge of renewed interest. Until this evening, his vision had seemed out of reach, untouchable. But now . . . ?

Ulm already had a plan. A Ryan monoplane similar to Lindbergh's seemed a suitable aircraft for a Pacific crossing, possessing both the range and a reliable Wright Whirlwind engine, but for the moment it was beyond their means. Therefore, to attract the necessary funding, he proposed a two-stage strategy. Firstly, they would use one of the Bristol Tourers to break the record for flying around Australia—some 12,000 kilometres in 23 days—which had been established in 1924. Secondly, with the record in the bag and the resultant publicity, their names would be mentioned in high places, and they could persuade somebody important to fund the Pacific flight.

Sensing that he had captured Smithy's attention, Ulm lost no time in pointing out that he and Kingsford Smith had complementary skills; Smithy's business was flying, while his expertise lay in the flying business. If they joined forces, they could make this Pacific flight together.

It didn't take much effort to sell the idea. Smithy's face cracked into the grin that would soon become his trademark, and he held out his hand in agreement. They shook on it.

As he waved Kingsford Smith off into the dawn, Ulm knew in the back of his mind that there would be trouble when Keith Anderson found out. But he would cross that bridge when he came to it.

Initially, Anderson accepted the idea of the around-Australia flight with enthusiasm. As Smithy's mate, fellow pilot, business partner and co-owner of the aeroplanes, he naturally assumed that he would be the second member of the crew.

But not so. Ulm announced that he and Kingsford Smith would be making the flight.

Anderson's jaw dropped. How could this be? Charles Ulm could not even fly an aeroplane! Ulm airily dismissed his protest by announcing that he had already entered into a financial arrangement with Herbert Campbell Jones to cable exclusive reports that would be published in the Sydney *Sun*, as well as the Melbourne *Herald* and the Brisbane *Daily Mail*.[4] To accomplish this he would have to go on the flight to experience events firsthand. In addition, he had arranged for the Vacuum Oil Company to make petrol and oil available along their proposed route. At each stop, he would supervise the refuelling while Smithy took a break.

Anderson persisted: the rear cockpit of the Tourer could accommodate two passengers; if they took two pilots to share the flying, the off-duty man could travel with Ulm in the rear seat. Ulm countered that if they were to break the record, they would have to limit refuelling stops to minimise time on the ground. To accomplish this, they would need to carry extra petrol in cans, stowed in the rear cockpit, to top up the tanks in flight. There would be no room for an extra passenger.

Anderson said no more, for there was nothing more he could say. He could taste defeat. With his easygoing nature and straight-forward approach to life he simply could not compete with the fast-talking Charles Ulm.

Despite his confident manner, Ulm felt vulnerable. He was acutely aware that he was not a qualified pilot. But his strength was *ideas*: he could organise, he could persuade, he could sell. He hoped with all his heart that this would be enough.

There was a pause. It was time for a decision, and both men turned to Kingsford Smith. Legally, Smithy had no more right to decide than Anderson, who was his equal partner in Interstate Flying Services. But such was the power of his personality that both men deferred to him. Like it or not, the ball was in his court.

Smithy looked at Keith Anderson and saw a mate. He saw trucks and trailers and bleating sheep. Dusty roads, flooded rivers, hard work, cold beers. Adventures shared, on the ground and in the air. History.[5]

He looked at Charles Ulm. He recalled no history, for there was none. But in his mind's eye he clearly saw a glittering prize, far away across the trackless wastes of a great ocean. The future.

Ambition trumped loyalty. The decision was made: just he and Ulm would be making the trip.

Keith Anderson had had enough. He exploded in an outburst of emotion that had been building for weeks. He had never trusted Ulm, right from their very first meeting. So what if he was good with figures? So what if he could scribble fluffed-up nonsense for a newspaper? So what if he could cobble together a few lousy cans of petrol? Because of Charles Ulm, Bert Pike had lost his job. The man could not fly. He was not an aviator. He was a carpetbagger. He did not belong.

The outburst was so uncharacteristic that Smithy and Ulm sat for several moments in stunned silence. With so much resentment in the air, Ulm could see that the situation at Interstate Flying Services was highly unstable. The partnership could collapse, taking his plan to fly the Pacific with it. Something had to be done to pacify Anderson, and quickly.

Within a few days, he had found a second sponsor. Both Tourers would now fly around Australia. Smithy and Ulm would fly one aircraft, as originally proposed, and the second aircraft would be crewed by Anderson and Bob Hitchcock.

Keith Anderson knew that Ulm was offering him a consolation prize, but it was better than nothing, so he agreed. Out at Mascot, Bob Hitchcock, who had been feeling rather left out of things, was overjoyed at the news that he had been included in the flying team.

But they soon discovered that there was a catch. To raise extra finance for the second Tourer, Ulm had entered into a commercial agreement with George Bond and Company, a well-known clothing manufacturer, to carry their advertising manager, Charles

Vivian, around Australia.[6] With three people on board, there was no room for extra petrol, so Anderson and Hitchcock would have to land more frequently to refuel; consequently there was little chance that they would break the record. Furthermore, the contracts with both sponsors stipulated that they could not leave until Ulm and Smithy had completed their flight, or abandoned it.[7]

Ulm had extended an olive branch to Anderson with one hand and emasculated him with the other. It was treachery of the first order.

Ulm and Kingsford Smith left Sydney on Saturday, 19 June 1927, on the first leg of their record attempt. Ulm's detailed account of the first day's flying was published the next day in *The Sun*, as contracted, and preceded by the byline, 'C.T.P. Ulm, Copyright'.[8]

They had encountered engine trouble immediately and returned to Mascot to swap to the other aeroplane, which then also started to fail as they approached Lake Macquarie.

> Our first indication of any trouble was when our instruments recorded general engine inefficiency, which gradually became worse but still not serious. About 2 miles from Boolaroo Kingsford Smith told me via ear phone that a forced landing was inevitable—but where? The race course was the only possible ground, and, whilst it was quite large enough in total area, it became apparent when we were within 300 feet of it that the surface was very bad and covered with large, hard tufts of grass and scattered with logs and burnt-off timber.

Ulm had been in 30 forced landings by then but this one was shaping up to be the worst.

> Large pot-holes, more than big enough to wreck a machine, were all over the ground, and to make matters worse, adjoining the field over which we had to approach were fairly high trees and some houses . . . Kingsford Smith cleverly side-slipped the 'bus over a house and between two of the taller trees, and then over the race-track fence, and, when just about to sit her down, noticed a large hole which was grown-over with ferns, making it appear a level surface. He then performed one of the prettiest pieces of flying work I have seen for years. By keeping on full rudder he put the machine on the ground on a turn. It was then that the real skill and judgement of an experienced aviator came to play. As the machine, which lands at over 60 miles per hour, was finishing her run on the ground of about 150 yards, the pilot had to make her turn in and out, zigzagging potholes, stumps, logs, and tufts of grass, each big enough to cause a smash. To his credit it can be recorded that when the machine came to a standstill there was not even a wire strained or a scratch or a mark anywhere on the 'bus.

A mere 150 kilometres into their 12,000-kilometre journey, they were downed. All they could see from an inspection of the Tourer was that 'the gauges had ceased to function due to some internal trouble'. They judged it would be grounded in Boolaroo for some two or three days. Their first attempt at the record was over almost as soon as it had begun.

Irrepressible Ulm arranged for the racecourse caretaker to drive them to town, from where he called Mascot with the new plan: Smithy and Ulm would immediately return to Sydney by train while Anderson and Hitchcock readied the other Tourer for a renewed attempt at the record the next morning, and then retrieved and repaired the downed machine.

Ulm clearly realised this wasn't painting a picture of safe or reliable flight and he hastened to assure his readers that the aviators had 'experienced the "million to one against" chance' (which does not quite gel with the constant engine trouble and 30 previous forced landings). Ulm wrote that their 'bad luck and difficulties . . . [were] only spurring [them] on to greater efforts':

> We are going to break these records. It means working hard all night tonight, no time for sleep—flying all day tomorrow and thereafter; flying all day and working through the best part of all night but we will do it and we will get there. Interstate Flying Services' motto is 'Do your job,' and we are going to do it.

In the event, Anderson and Hitchcock did not catch the train to Newcastle as ordered, because they had to work through the night to get the second machine ready. The next morning, Ulm made sure that a photographer from *The Sun* captured the four men at Mascot, all smiles, just before he and Smithy took off for the second attempt. The image was that of a happy, cohesive team, but nothing was further from the truth.

Ulm and Smithy finally got away on the Sunday. This time the flight was uneventful, but when they reached Brisbane they were exhausted, having been awake for the best part of 24 hours. After a night's rest, they took off for Longreach in fine, clear weather, but with a strong headwind that eased during the course of the day.

Early in the afternoon, the slipstream snatched their map from Ulm's hand as he was attempting to pass it to Kingsford Smith in the front cockpit, and they were forced by a malfunctioning compass to keep their course by the sun and landmarks on the ground.

> We struck for the railway line linking Jericho and Blackall, but in view of the fact that we had no map we did not know how far east or west along the railway line we were, so after nosing around for about 10 minutes we decided to land on a station nearby to discover our exact whereabouts. This place proved to be Malvern Hills Station. A perfect landing was made, but while waiting for people to walk out to the machine, one of our tyres blew out.[9]
>
> We went into town, had a quick dinner, and this story was written in the Q.A.N.T.A.S. hangar with petrol tins as a table. The 'bus was filled up for today's flight, and the engine gone over and tuned up. Before we went to bed we installed and fixed a special lead to our oil tank which

41

will allow us to fill up oil in the air. This is necessary for the long non-stop flights, which we will be making after leaving Camooweal.

Upon arrival in Darwin, Ulm wrote:

We believe we have a new motto—'A record a day keeps our troubles away.' We believe that yesterday we broke the Australian non-stop record for commercial aircraft, in our flight from Camooweal to Darwin. The total distance flown was 820 miles in 9½ hours.

The country from Camooweal to Darwin was practically featureless. We came by the longer route so that we might be over fairly decent country and near communication if forced to land. After leaving Brunette Downs we had to fly on a compass course, and eventually struck the telegraph line about two miles north of Newcastle Waters. Messages to *The Sun* were dropped at Katherine. They landed right in between two houses.

From Camooweal to Newcastle Waters there is a good open country, but from Newcastle waters right to Darwin the country is very bad. Except for the prepared landing ground at Katherine there are practically no points at which a safe landing could be made. From Katherine to Darwin there is no place at all to land safely. Where there are no rugged hills the country is heavily timbered. We delivered last Sunday's 'Sun' and Monday's Brisbane

'Daily Mail' in Darwin yesterday. Both were much appreciated by general public.

Ulm could not resist the urge to avail himself of some free publicity.

> Interstate Flying Services is the first organisation to fly
> from Sydney to Darwin via Brisbane in four days, and the
> residents here are asking us to use our best endeavours
> to interest the authorities in subsidising air mail services.

They left Darwin early on the Friday morning, but about 20 minutes after take-off an exhaust valve cracked, causing the engine to misfire. To return to Darwin was out of the question, because they knew that they would have to wait for at least three weeks for spare parts, and this would mean the end of the record attempt. They decided instead to press on for Broome, where they knew that the engine could be repaired. They kept the coast in sight all the way and dropped messages for *The Sun* at Wyndham. Ulm claimed another record:

> Interstate Flying Services is the first to fly from Darwin
> to Broome, non-stop. Yesterday's flight was not by any
> means in a direct line, as we kept over the best of the bad
> country, because a forced landing was likely at any time
> owing to the valve trouble becoming worse.
>
> On arrival here at 4:40 pm Darwin time we checked
> our map course, and worked out the mileage flown as

860, flying time being 10 hours 20 minutes. The engine was taken down last night. I worked on it all night and Kingsford Smith until midnight. I can perhaps get some sleep in the air today. We had no aero mechanic to assist us. We hope to have the engine tested by 8 o'clock this morning, and leave here by 8.30. We intend to reach Carnarvon this afternoon without stopping. Since leaving Brisbane the weather has been perfect for flying but we have been uncomfortably hot wearing our Sidcott suits.[10]

They had no spare clothes to wear under their flying suits, and by the time they had reached Darwin their shirts had become so filthy that they discarded them, travelling in just trousers, coats and singlets. Before Carnarvon they ran into heavy rain, the first bad weather of the trip, forcing them to fly very low to keep within sight of the ground.

They were getting by on four hours' sleep per night and one meal per day. During the initial stages of the flight they carried no food and little water to save weight, but, by the time they had left Longreach, wisdom had prevailed and they took sandwiches, ginger ale and a spare half gallon of drinking water to sustain them along the way. Even so, it was a Spartan existence. When they reached Perth they were very tired, dozing off while talking to the people who came to meet them.

From Perth they turned east and continued on their weary way across the southern half of the continent, via Kalgoorlie, Nareetha, Cook, Wirraminna, Adelaide and Melbourne, and thence to Sydney, where they arrived on Wednesday, 29 June, to an enthusiastic welcome from New South Wales Premier Jack Lang, dignitaries and clamouring press. Suddenly, they were famous. Flashbulbs popped, and they appeared for the first time on the front pages of the nation's newspapers.

Even in those early photographs, whatever the angle, Kingsford Smith tends to dominate the frame. Ulm is there, for they were pictured as dual celebrities, but as the pilot of the aircraft, Smithy tended to be the focus of attention. It helped that he was also photogenic, with a natural charm that would soon make him a favourite with the press, and the darling of the newsreel cameras.

Charles Ulm would always be the other man in the picture.

The following day they were guests at a lavish luncheon given by the directors of Sun Newspapers. Speaking to reporters afterwards, Ulm praised everyone who had helped with their flight, especially the Vacuum Oil Company. 'Their co-operation extended a great deal further than the laying down of supplies at given points, difficult enough job as it was,' he said. 'Their agents everywhere did everything in their power to help us. They found us our hotels and hot baths and food. In outback places they met us by car, took off their coats, and helped us with our work.' He modestly omitted to say that he had been the driving force behind the whole operation.

On their flight around Australia, both Ulm and Kingsford Smith had been impressed by the sheer size of the Outback. For hour upon hour, vast tracts of desolate country had passed beneath their wings, with not a sign of human habitation. Even on the coast, settlements were few and far between.

To Charles Ulm, the region's remoteness and sparse population constituted a risk to national security and, exploiting his new-found celebrity status, he made his concern public in a dramatic article in the Newcastle *Sun* headlined 'SECRET BASES POSSIBLE'. 'Give Charlie and me a few million pounds and we could guarantee to bomb every capital city of Australia, and you would not know where we came from,' he told a reporter. 'Perhaps the chief lesson taught them by their record-breaking flight around Australia [was] ... that an enemy could easily establish an air force base in the north. Both Captain Kingsford Smith and Mr. Ulm are satisfied that the aeroplane is Australia's only possible means of defence.'[11]

The article failed to make a stir.

Prior to leaving Sydney, Ulm had promised Jo that they would be married as soon as he returned. He was as good as his word, and immediately after the official welcome they were married at the North Sydney Congregational Church.[12]

It had been a busy time and things were about to get a lot busier.

CHAPTER 4

Quest for an aircraft

It was time to move on to the second part of their plan. Ulm quickly approached the Vacuum Oil Company and asked them to fund the purchase of a Ryan monoplane, and to provide fuel and oil for a Pacific crossing. Basking in the reflected glow of favourable publicity emanating from the around-Australia flight, Vacuum Oil readily agreed, on the condition that the cost of the aircraft was underwritten by the New South Wales state government. Ulm sought a meeting with Premier Lang, and the Cabinet subsequently undertook to provide a guarantee capped at £3500 to fund the venture, provided the flight was made within six months. Ulm also secured a £500 deal with Sun Newspapers for the news rights, and, following an appeal through the pages of the same newspaper, donations from the public began coming in. Ulm booked passages to San Francisco for himself and Smithy on the *Tahiti*.[1]

There was good reason for all this activity: both Ulm and Smithy were uncomfortably aware that aviators were beginning to focus on the Pacific, in particular the long stretch between the United States and Hawaii. The US Navy had already made one unsuccessful attempt to fly to Honolulu in 1925, with two Naval Aircraft Factory PN-9 flying boats. Soon after leaving San Pablo, California, one came down in the sea with engine trouble. The other machine pressed on, but ran out of fuel several hundred miles short of the islands. Undaunted, the crew sailed their fragile craft under a jury rig across open ocean for nine days until, with the island of Oahu tantalisingly close, they were rescued by a submarine.

That had been two years prior, but on 29 June 1927, as he and Smithy landed in Sydney at the end of their around-Australia flight, Ulm was disturbed to hear that *Bird of Paradise*, a US Army Air Corps Fokker trimotor, crewed by lieutenants Lester Maitland and Albert Hegenberger, had touched down at Wheeler Field, on the island of Oahu, 25 hours and 50 minutes after taking off from Oakland, California.[2]

Then came the announcement that James Dole, a millionaire who had made his fortune growing pineapples on the Hawaiian island of Lanai, had offered a prize of US$25,000 for the first fixed-wing aircraft to fly from Oakland to Honolulu, and US$10,000 for the aircraft that came in second.[3] Army fliers were ineligible, which ruled out Maitland and Hegenberger as they had already completed their journey. Fifteen aircraft entered the race, which soon became known as the Dole Derby, and American interest in aviation intensified.

For Ulm and Smithy, on the far side of the ocean they so fervently hoped to cross, the situation was becoming desperate. They feared that after the Dole Race it would be only a matter of time before somebody ventured beyond Hawaii and flew across the Pacific. They had to get to America, get an aircraft and get cracking, or be left stranded at the starting line.

While Ulm and Smithy were wrestling with this prospect, Keith Anderson, Bob Hitchcock and Charles Vivian landed in Melbourne, the penultimate stop on their flight around Australia. Carrying a gigantic chip on his shoulder after the shabby way he had been treated, Anderson had decided to ignore Ulm's order to wait, and had started off as soon as they had repaired the engine of the first Tourer.

Even though he made a navigation error over outback Queensland that put them 150 miles (241 kilometres) off course, they had made good progress, arriving in Melbourne just four days after Smithy and Ulm completed their record flight.

There, flicking through the newspaper, Anderson received another body blow. His so-called partners had announced that they intended to participate in the Dole race. They were about to board a ship for America.

Anderson, Hitchcock and Vivian arrived back at Mascot on 8 July after being held up by bad weather over the Australian Alps. As newly minted celebrities, Smithy and Ulm were prominent among the press, family and friends who gathered at the aerodrome to welcome them home. But behind the smiles and the handshakes the atmosphere was tense. Anderson wasn't much interested in celebration or listening to speeches. He wanted to confront Smithy alone; just the two of them, face to face.

The next 48 hours were action packed and emotionally charged, with decisions made and things said that would have legal repercussions for them all.

That evening, as Kingsford Smith and Anderson met at the house of Bon Hilliard, Anderson's fiancée, Charles Ulm waited, chain-smoking, at Lavender Bay. He was worried. The experience of the around-Australia flight had strengthened his conviction that he and Smithy, with their complementary skills, made a great team. But it was a team of two. There was no place for Keith Anderson. He had made this clear to Smithy, and hoped fervently that Smithy would have the fortitude to pass it on to Anderson. But he knew what Smithy was like. He drew deeply on a cigarette. It was out of his hands now. All he could do was wait.

The three men met the next day in a private bar at the Carlton Hotel in Castlereagh Street. There, to Ulm's consternation, Smithy announced that he wanted Anderson in the team.

Ulm refused point-blank to accept the decision, but Anderson wouldn't back down. Still smarting over his treatment during the around-Australia flight, and deeply hurt that they had not told him about the Dole Race, he once again accused Ulm of treachery. The Pacific flight had been just a pipe dream, but now, with government funding, it was a distinct possibility, and once again Ulm was trying to cut him out. It was Ulm who should be left behind.

The same old argument raged back and forth, but this time Smithy was not prepared to arbitrate between Ulm and Anderson, each of whom he now regarded as a friend.

The room fell quiet. They had reached a stalemate.

In the silence, Ulm felt desperately insecure. As a non-pilot, and stony broke, he really needed Smithy, and Smithy was quite obviously not prepared to discard Anderson. Ulm realised that unless he conceded something, this could be the end of his Pacific dream.

He looked at Smithy. 'I don't mind including Anderson and making the party three. We will sink or swim together,' he said.[4]

They shook hands on it. Charles Ulm had cleared the impasse, but he was not happy.

The following Monday, after paying for their sea passages to San Francisco (and lending Ulm £60 to pay his), the three men went to Parliament House and signed the agreement for the government's £3500 guarantee. Upon their arrival in America, the money would be made available as needed by the Vacuum Oil Company, acting as the government's agent.[5]

When they returned to their office, Anderson dropped another bombshell: Bob Hitchcock had telephoned, asking to be included in the team going to America. Ulm reacted angrily: 'Damn Hitchcock! We have had enough worry about making arrangements for *three* to go on the flight!'[6] Smithy's reaction was more measured. He felt sorry for Hitchcock, but there would be no room for four people in a Ryan. Furthermore, Hitchcock had no experience working on American aircraft.

Anderson, having recently flown around Australia with Hitchcock, felt a degree of loyalty towards him and refused to pass on the bad news; if Ulm and Smithy wanted to dump Hitchcock, they would have to do it themselves.

Hitchcock was summoned to a meeting at the office of Interstate Flying Services the next day. He pointed out that he had left his job in Western Australia especially to make the Pacific flight. As far as he was concerned, he was part of the team.

Kingsford Smith did not see it that way. He told Hitchcock that their funds were limited. There was only enough money to pay for three passages and, consequently, it had been decided that he would not be going to America. By way of consolation, Smithy promised Hitchcock a handsome cash reward when they returned.

Crestfallen, and now well aware that his status was not that of a partner, but of a mere employee, Bob Hitchcock retired to Mascot to lick his wounds.

In the days leading up to their departure, Hitchcock tried to meet with Ulm, Smithy and Anderson again, but they were caught up in a round of celebratory parties and too busy to see him. Finally, he tracked them down at the Carlton. Realising that a noisy, smoke-filled bar room was not the best place to make a final appeal, he went back to the office and waited.

When they finally appeared, it was obvious that they had been partying hard. Ulm was not pleased to see Hitchcock, but Smithy appeared sympathetic. 'We're very sorry to leave you behind, but it can't be helped, old man. On our arrival back here, Bob, there'll be a thousand hard for you,' he said.

Ulm joined in. 'Yes, you'll hear a knock on the door, and I'll say "Sir Charles, Robert awaits outside about his thousand."'

'And I'll say, "Show the boy in,"' continued Smithy.[7]

They were mocking him, and Bob Hitchcock didn't like it. He would not forget.

⸻ ⸻ ⸻ ⸻ ⸻ ⸻ ⸻ ⸻

Charles Ulm, Charles Kingsford Smith and Keith Anderson left Sydney aboard the *Tahiti* on 14 July 1927. They travelled in style, first class. During the long, leisurely days at sea they at last had plenty of time to consider the practical details of the challenge that lay before them, and they soon realised that they knew very little about long-distance transoceanic flying.

Firstly, the aircraft. The Ryan monoplane that had carried Lindbergh across the Atlantic from New York to Paris had been eminently suited to the task. It had, in effect, been a flying fuel tank, with a range of almost 6500 kilometres, certainly capable of reaching Hawaii. But with the weight of three men, a Ryan would not be able to uplift as much fuel as Lindbergh's NYP; its range would therefore be significantly reduced.

The single engine was also a matter for concern. The Wright Whirlwind had proven itself to be extremely reliable, but, if it failed, they would come down in the sea. Perhaps an aircraft with two engines, maybe even three, would be a better choice, although multiple power plants increased the statistical chance of failure.

While Wheeler Field, near Honolulu, was a well-established air base, they did not know if the islands further out in the Pacific where they hoped to refuel, such as Fanning Atoll (Tabuaeran) and the Phoenix Islands (Rawaki) in Kiribati, even had landing grounds. Rather than risk it, they planned to fit the Ryan with floats at Hawaii and land in island lagoons thereafter. But floats imposed additional weight and drag, further reducing the range.

Transoceanic navigation was another concern. They knew that Lindbergh had plotted his course across the Atlantic in detail before he left Roosevelt Field. During the flight, he navigated by dead reckoning, using a compass and watch to make pre-determined course changes at regular intervals, following a great circle route, which offered the shortest distance across the ocean. Charles Ulm knew that this method had succeeded for Lindbergh, firstly because he was a navigator of long experience after years of flying the US Air Mail in all weather, day or night, and secondly, because Lindbergh had been aiming for France, a target several hundred kilometres wide. He could hardly miss it and, once he made landfall, he could rectify any drift errors by turning north or south.

Drift, that was another problem. Crosswinds caused an aircraft to deviate left or right from its intended track. A small drift error would have been of little consequence to Lindbergh, with the entire coastline of western France stretching across his path, but in the Pacific it was a different story entirely. Ulm knew that their destinations would be small islands, mere pinpricks on the map. A drift error of just a few degrees and they could miss an island entirely and fly on, vainly searching, to vanish into the vast Pacific. It was a sobering prospect.

The only way to establish a position reliably over a feature-less ocean was to use a sextant to take sightings on the stars. Celestial navigation had been used by mariners for hundreds of years, and it was now finding an application aboard aircraft. Once an accurate position was found, corrections could be made for drift. It was essential that they became competent in the art as soon as possible. Their lives would depend on it.

As first-class passengers, Ulm, Smithy and Anderson social-ised with the *Tahiti*'s officers and befriended a fellow Australian, Second Officer William Todd, who tried to impart the rudiments of using a sextant. Ulm, keen to acquire a skill that would be of use in the air, applied himself diligently, but it quickly became apparent that he would not master the complex art of celestial navigation any time soon; certainly not before they set out to cross the Pacific.

The *Tahiti* docked in San Francisco on 5 August, and Ulm, Smithy and Anderson were met by Harold, Kingsford Smith's brother. Also on the wharf was Herbert Dickie from the Vacuum Oil Company, who announced that he had taken out an option on an aircraft that could possibly be suitable for the Dole Race. Entering that race might grant them experience that could help them when the time came to tackle the Pacific. The aeroplane was aptly named *Miss Hollywood*. Excited to have something tangible happening on their very first day in the United States, they lost no time in driving to the airfield to inspect it.

As soon as they saw *Miss Hollywood* all notions of stardom evaporated. It was an open-cockpit, fabric-covered, single-engine biplane, for their purposes vastly inferior to the Ryan, and not at all suitable for long-distance ocean flying. There was no way that the aircraft could accommodate the heavy load of fuel required to take them to Hawaii. In fact, the undercarriage would collapse under load during pre-race testing.

With Dickie as their guide, they examined several machines that had been entered in the race and decided they could not possibly prepare a machine in time. Reluctantly, they withdrew.

It was just as well; the Dole Race was a disaster. Fifteen aircraft were entered, but three crashed during preparations for the race, killing their pilots. By race day, 16 August, the field had narrowed to eight aircraft. Grossly overloaded with fuel, two crashed on take-off, and three more subsequently went missing. A fourth had to return for repairs before taking off to search for the lost aircraft, and was itself never seen again. Only two competitors, *Woolaroc* and *Aloha*, eventually reached Honolulu. Ulm and Smithy noted with interest that *Woolaroc*'s navigator, William V. Davis Jnr, had flown a great-circle course, using a sextant and smoke bombs to calculate his course and drift.[8]

Overall, ten people lost their lives during the Dole Race, and six aircraft were totally destroyed, but despite the tragic circumstances, or perhaps because of them, Ulm, Kingsford Smith and Anderson came to two important conclusions. Firstly, they realised that it would be folly to attempt a long Pacific crossing in a single-engine aircraft. And secondly, that an experienced professional navigator was absolutely essential.

Shortly after arriving in San Francisco, they met Locke Harper, the west-coast manager of the Vacuum Oil Company, who made them welcome and placed his office at their disposal. They would use it as their headquarters, through thick and thin, for the next eight months.

Their first priority was to find an aircraft. After the Dole fiasco, a single-engine aircraft was absolutely ruled out, and the big three-engine, record-breaking Fokker F.VIIb/3m quickly emerged as the main contender. The Fokker trimotor had been used by Maitland and Hegenberger for their Oakland–Honolulu flight, and also by Admiral Richard Byrd in his 1926 flight over the North Pole. The Fokker's Wright Whirlwind engines were renowned for their reliability and its massive wooden wing could lift a prodigious load of fuel. As well as two pilots, its capacious fuselage could house a navigator and a radio operator. It appeared to be ideal, but, unfortunately, no F.VIIb/3m was currently available.

Immediately upon arrival, Charles Ulm had, almost instinctively, begun to cultivate the local press and his assiduous efforts were starting to bear fruit. Visiting fellow Australian and Arctic explorer Hubert Wilkins read a newspaper article about their proposed Pacific flight, and their quest for a suitable aircraft, and sent them a telegram. He happened to have a Fokker F.VIIb/3m for sale. The price was US$15,000, without instruments or engines.

They were soon facing each other across a table in Locke Harper's office, and quickly established a rapport for, like Ulm and Smithy, Wilkins was an adventurer. He had two Fokkers for sale: a single-engine F.VII named *Alaskan*, and *Detroiter*, a three-engine F.VIIb/3m. He had been using both aircraft on exploratory work in the Arctic, but now needed to dispose of them urgently to fund the purchase of a Lockheed Vega, in which he hoped to make a trans-Arctic flight in the spring.

Ulm and Kingsford told him their plans and Wilkins agreed that *Detroiter* would suit their purposes very well. He would sell them the aircraft, but on the condition that he appoint a pilot to carry out all performance tests and instruct Kingsford Smith in handling a large multi-engine aircraft.[9]

Money remained a problem. The funds guaranteed by the New South Wales government were sufficient to buy the airframe, but not to fit it out with engines and instruments, and the fuel tanks required to extend *Detroiter*'s range. Ulm cabled Premier Lang, asking for additional money, and Wilkins, desperate to make a sale, offered to accept payment in installments.

Ulm's efforts to increase their public profile continued to pay dividends, as the three men began to receive invitations from wealthy and influential people keen to meet the putative Pacific fliers. They were seldom disappointed, for at social occasions Kingsford Smith was at his charming best: totally at ease in almost any company and a great hit with women. Ulm could also turn on the charm, but he lacked Smithy's charisma and was quite intense beneath the veneer.

At one event they met the Australian businessman Sidney Myer, who was in the United States for the northern summer, and were invited to stay at his house at Burlingame, outside San Francisco. With the Dole Race a recent and disturbing memory, Myer viewed the prospect of the Pacific flight with dismay, and tried to talk Ulm, Smithy and Anderson out of it. But when he saw that they were committed, he contributed £1500 (over $100,000 in today's money), stressing that it was not a loan, but a gift. More good news followed, in the form of a cable from the New South Wales government advising that their request for a further £1000 had been approved. The flyers were jubilant; they could seal the deal.

They had an airframe. Now they needed three Wright Whirlwinds, but there was a strong demand for the world's most popular radial engine, and the Wright Company was approximately ninety units behind with its orders, some of which were earmarked for military aircraft.

Never afraid to go to the top, Ulm sought help from the naval and military authorities in San Francisco, and on their advice asked the British ambassador in Washington to put their case to the US Secretary of War. His bold strategy paid off: three engines were subsequently diverted from the government order and installed in the aircraft, which was at Seattle. Ulm finalised the purchase with Wilkins and in the late autumn *Detroiter* took to the air again, in the hands of Commander George Pond, Wilkins' nominated test pilot, with Smithy in the right-hand seat. After acceptance trials, they were all on board when she was flown down to San Francisco.

Kingsford Smith was happy; at long last he had his hands on an aeroplane. Ulm was cautiously optimistic; it appeared that the finances were all in place. And Keith Anderson proposed a change of name for the aircraft that they hoped would carry them across the Pacific.

He suggested *Southern Cross*.[10]

CHAPTER 5

Captain Hancock

They now had an aeroplane with engines, but much remained to be done: long-range tanks to be fitted, wheels and undercarriage to be strengthened, blind-flying instruments and radio equipment to be installed. It all cost money and Ulm, the only member of the partnership who kept an eye on their bank balance, realised with alarm that their funds were rapidly running out.

They had continued to socialise with the officers of the *Tahiti* whenever the ship was in port and, when it appeared that the Pacific flight was imminent, Smithy asked Second Officer William Todd to take unpaid leave and join them as navigator and wireless officer. Ulm, always sensitive when new personalities came on the scene, objected on the grounds that Todd was too heavy. Kingsford Smith disagreed; in his opinion, while Todd was indeed a big man, his navigational skills made him 'worth his weight'. Todd left the ship and took up residence at the Roosevelt Hotel, at their expense.[1]

Charles Ulm and William Todd soon fell out. It appears that the ill feeling was mutual. Todd grew tired of waiting for Ulm and Smithy to complete their arrangements for the Pacific flight, and began to drink heavily. Ulm resented Smithy's support of someone whom he perceived as a drunk, unproductive and an unnecessary drain on their finances. Finally, when Todd borrowed their car and rolled it, Ulm seized the opportunity and sacked him. It was a pattern that would be repeated throughout Ulm's life. He did not tolerate people who did not measure up to his standards, and his brusque manner often rubbed people the wrong way.

In late October, there was a state election in New South Wales, and the Lang Labor government was replaced by a coalition led by Thomas Bavin. The new premier regarded the proposed Pacific flight as dangerous, irresponsible and a waste of taxpayers' money, and immediately revoked the government guarantee.

The bedrock underpinning the entire Pacific enterprise, £4500, or over $350,000 today, in government-backed funding crumbled to dust overnight.

Charles Ulm was devastated when he heard the news. They had yet to pay Wilkins the final installment on the aircraft, but without a government guarantee the Vacuum Oil Company could make no further funds available. And there were creditors coming out of the woodwork, both in America and Australia, clamouring for their money. Even Keith Anderson's mother, who had lent him £400, was asking him to pay her back.

In Australia, there were newspaper headlines urging them to abandon their plans and come home. But Ulm knew that they had come too far, achieved too much, owed too much, to contemplate giving up now. If nothing else, honour demanded that they stick it out.

The Vacuum Oil Company may not have been able to advance them any more money, but their west coast manager could, and did. Locke Harper lent them US$7500 out of his own pocket, enabling them to pay Wilkins the final installment on the aeroplane. It was a wonderful gesture of affection and trust, but in practical terms it was akin to moving the deckchairs around on a sinking ship. Sooner or later, the money would have to be paid back.

One thing they could do was to settle their debts in Australia, so they cabled Leofric Kingsford Smith to sell one of the Bristol Tourers and pay their creditors with the proceeds.

Sorting things out in America was a much more difficult proposition. Kingsford Smith and Anderson were hopeless when it came to financial matters, so the heavy burden of responsibility fell onto Charles Ulm's shoulders. Despite his best efforts, he could not find a sponsor, and finally, in desperation, he mortgaged the *Southern Cross* to the *San Francisco Chronicle* for US$10,000. He was moving deckchairs again, but at least it kept their creditors at bay.

There was a glimmer of hope when he talked the Associated Oil Company of California into supplying fuel and oil for an attempt on the world flight endurance record, which then stood at 52 hours and 22 minutes. If *Southern Cross* succeeded in breaking this record, Associated Oil would clear all their debts. It was a long shot and probably their last chance to redeem themselves.

The aircraft was still not fully equipped to spend a long time in the air; it needed extra tankage, and a strengthened under-carriage to carry the weight of the extra fuel. These measures would be necessary in any case should the Pacific flight ever go ahead. But they all cost money.

Keith Anderson had already asked his uncle several times for money to support the Pacific venture, and Harry Vincent, a successful Melbourne builder, had refused. But Ulm persuaded Anderson to approach his uncle one more time and, to their surprise, Vincent agreed. He would lend Keith £600, provided that Smithy and Ulm allowed his nephew to share the flying.

Now that they had some money, the aircraft was fitted out for the record attempt at the Douglas factory in Santa Monica. As well as extra tankage and a stronger undercarriage, the fuselage was re-covered and repainted, and the name *Southern Cross* was revealed to the world for the first time, in bold white lettering against a blue background.

Perhaps in recognition of Vincent's contribution, but more likely with a shrewd eye on future developments, Ulm drew up an agreement between himself, Kingsford Smith and Anderson, in which all three were declared equal owners of *Southern Cross*. However, the document also stipulated that if any one of them withdrew from the Pacific flight, he would cease to be a partner, and the other two would acquire all the assets and liabilities. The partners would also divide equally any profits from any flight made by 'any of them' in the aircraft.[2]

Everything was now set for *Southern Cross* to make the record attempt, but Ulm and Smithy had not bothered to notify the *San Francisco Chronicle*. When they found out, the newspaper's management served them with a writ; the flight could not go ahead until the mortgage was paid out.

Ulm and Smithy were devastated. This seemed like the end. But once again, their friend Locke Harper came to the rescue.

> On the spur of the moment I told them I would lift this $10,000 mortgage, they in turn to mortgage the plane to me, and this they did. Two or three days before they were due to take to the air, it suddenly occurred to me that if they cracked up, my mortgage would not be worth a great deal. Consequently I went round to a newly formed insurance Company in San Francisco who wrote airplane insurance and for a premium $1480 I secured protection for 55 hours. This protection consisting of a policy of three pages typed on both sides in very small print which probably contained every 'out' in the world so far as they were concerned if a crack up took place. And you can believe it or not, it was numbered 13.[3]

Kingsford Smith and George Pond made three attempts on the world endurance record, flying in wide circles for hour upon hour over San Francisco and the bay. During the first flight they stayed aloft for approximately 49 hours, but encountered technical difficulties that obliged them to dump their remaining fuel and make an emergency landing in fog. It was Monday morning—washing day—and in several suburbs aviation gasoline rained down on clothes hanging out to dry. Somehow word got around that Locke Harper was connected with the flyers, and in the following months he paid off a number of claims for fuel-damaged garments made by irate San Francisco housewives.

Despite the conditions attached to his uncle's loan, Smithy refused to allow Keith Anderson to fly with him or Pond this time, or on the other unsuccessful attempts on the record that followed. The reason for this is not known. Anderson was a competent and experienced pilot, of that there was no doubt, but he had had virtually no time at the controls of a large multi-engine aircraft and, with so much at stake, perhaps Kingsford Smith was not prepared to take a risk. Whether Ulm had any say in this decision is also not known, but it was an unwritten and inviolable law among them all that in any matters related to flying, Smithy had the last word.

If Keith Anderson was gutted by what he no doubt perceived as a broken promise, Harry Vincent was incensed. In the months to come, when he could perhaps have helped them further, he turned his nephew's entreaties down flat.

After the fifth failed record attempt, even Kingsford Smith, who was by nature an optimist, was forced to admit defeat: 'The sun of our fortunes seemed to be setting. We had been six months in America and were no nearer in achieving our ambition. Our creditors were pressing us; we were so poor we had not even loose cash in our pockets to buy a meal.'[4]

Unable to pay their bill, they were forced to leave the Roosevelt Hotel and seek cheaper accommodation. Keith Anderson began to talk of returning to Australia, and Smithy too, but Charles Ulm refused to give up.

> My job therefore was to track from interview to interview, from oil company to aircraft builder, from Jew to Gentile, seeking monetary backing for a project which nobody in the world thought was possible. For month after month it went on . . . month after month of staving off small creditors . . . of a nightmare existence in second-rate hotels, whose credit clerks watched us with suspicious eyes. Of actual hunger; of days when there was not even a cigarette to smoke. Our clothes began to advertise our circumstances.[5]

A concerned Locke Harper watched Ulm struggle, but there was little more that he could do.

> They were continuously pressed for funds and very often I gave them a ten or twenty dollar bill so they could buy something to eat . . . Ulm walked the streets of San

Francisco so much in an attempt to interest local industries . . . that he wore holes in the soles of his shoes. He refused outright to let me buy him a new pair; however, he finally agreed to let me have them re-soled.

Ulm was a remarkable individual. He had a tremendous command of the English language and had the ability of dashing off a proposal . . . regardless of the confusion surrounding him . . . When dealing with the various companies, he absolutely insisted on going to the top and he invariably accomplished this. General managers, vice-presidents etc. meant nothing to him and he was just as much at home in the office of the president of an outfit as he was in his bare hotel room.[6]

Smithy and Ulm flew *Southern Cross* to Los Angeles to try to sell it to Union Oil Company, so that they could pay off their debts. As an inducement, they offered to fly her across the Pacific to promote the company's products. After a glimmer of interest, Union Oil passed on the deal. Totally depressed, Smithy flew back to San Francisco, where Anderson announced that he had decided to return to Australia.

When he heard the news, Ulm was furious and returned at once to San Francisco on the overnight train. He was so broke that Locke Harper had to wire him the fare.

At a meeting in Harper's office the next day, they agreed that the situation looked very bad: their debts were now US$16,000 and the New South Wales government had ordered them to sell *Southern Cross* and abandon all plans to fly the Pacific.

Smithy told them he was sorry that things hadn't worked out. He reminded them that he was an airman; all he wanted to do was fly aeroplanes. The business side—the endless wheeling and dealing—bored him to tears, and he didn't want to know about it. For him, all the fun and excitement of the venture had evaporated. When Ulm suggested that they sell *Southern Cross* and buy a single-engine aeroplane, his eyes momentarily lit up, but Anderson wouldn't hear of it. He wanted to go home, where his fiancée was waiting.

That night, Ulm spent several hours with Anderson in their cramped hotel room, trying to talk him into changing his mind. But Anderson was adamant; he was going home. Finally, Ulm drew up a document for Keith to sign, agreeing to the sale of the *Southern Cross*. One clause read: 'It being understood that should any such sale or disposal of the said monoplane result in our partnership being employed or engaged to fly said monoplane to Australia or New Zealand, I (Anderson) shall be one of the pilots.'

Ulm's reasoning is puzzling. He had never had a high opinion of Keith Anderson, regarding him as a lightweight ever since their first meeting in the office of Interstate Flying Services. He had not wanted Anderson to come to America, and yet now he was pressing him to stay. Why?

In Ian Mackersey's opinion, it was because Ulm and Kingsford Smith both realised that a Pacific flight, if it happened, would need two pilots. One of these would be Smithy, and Ulm didn't want the co-pilot to be an American, especially George Pond, whom he had come to dislike. He wanted it to be an all-Australian affair.[7]

After Anderson returned home in February 1928, there was talk in the newspapers of a Kingsford Smith–Pond world flight in *Southern Cross*, but it came to nothing. By now Ulm and Smithy were virtually homeless, bedding down in airport offices and hangars, and scrounging meals wherever they could. They lost weight and, with their threadbare clothes, began to look like characters from a Steinbeck novel.

They had one last desperate card to play: a letter of introduction to a Dr Read, a surgeon, who lived in the countryside north of Los Angeles. Shocked by their appearance, Read and his wife took them in, fed them, housed them, prescribed some serious rest and recuperation, and then set about trying to find someone to sponsor their Pacific flight. They were not successful, but the Californian sunshine and country air soon restored the Australians' health.

Smith and Ulm still had to dispose of the aeroplane, and work out some way to refinance their debt, so Ulm arranged a meeting with Andrew Chaffey, president of the California Bank. He could not have made a better choice, because the two men found common ground at once. Chaffey had lived for a time in Australia, at Mildura, on the Murray River, where his father had been an engineer working on a large irrigation scheme. They parted on friendly terms, and the next day Ulm and Smithy gave Chaffey a guided tour of *Southern Cross*.

As they showed him around the aircraft, Chaffey detected the light of ocean conquest still glimmering in their eyes and it set him thinking. Short term re-financing was not the solution. On the other hand, the money that would flow following a successful crossing of the Pacific Ocean would resolve their problems immediately. He arranged for them to meet a fellow director who was also an experienced maritime navigator, and a wealthy man.

Captain George Allan Hancock was indeed extremely rich. His family had owned a property known as the Rancho La Brea, in the foothills of the Santa Monica mountains. The young Hancock had not been particularly interested in the land for its agricultural potential, but rather for the mineral wealth that lay beneath.

Borrowing money from his mother to finance the venture, Hancock had started drilling, tapping into rich deposits of gas, oil and tar. His mining enterprise had expanded quickly and he had diversified into real estate, at one stage owning a sizable piece of Hollywood when it was still covered by orange groves. He had then moved into shipping, serving his time at sea and becoming a master mariner, eventually commanding his own vessels on scientific expeditions to the Galápagos Islands and the Arctic. He was a qualified pilot. And, somehow, he had also found the time to establish the California Bank.

Andrew Chaffey knew in his bones that Allan Hancock would identify with Ulm and Kingsford Smith. There was no one else better placed to help them achieve their dream.

71

Although he appreciated Chaffey's interest, Ulm was not overly excited; he had been knocked back too many times before. The best that he hoped for was that Captain Hancock would buy their aeroplane to fly between his mining interests.

Ulm and Kingsford Smith met with Hancock at Rogers Field airport. He was, to their surprise, 'a short, stocky, serious and softly spoken man in his early fifties, with receding black hair and glasses', not at all like the popular stereotype of a multimillionaire.[8] They showed him over the *Southern Cross* and took him for a short flight over Los Angeles. It was the kind of thing they had done many times before. The questions that Hancock asked were perhaps a little more incisive than usual, but, as he drove away in his Cadillac, there was nothing to suggest that they would ever hear from him again.

They were wrong.

To their surprise, a few days later they received an invitation to join Hancock and other guests on a 12-day cruise to Mexico and back on his luxury yacht *Oaxaca*. They were delighted, then intrigued, then dismayed; a wonderful opportunity to impress had presented itself, but they looked like a couple of hobos. Their clothes were rags.

> We decided we would have to hire trousers to replace the unshapely and shoddy garments in which we stood up. To board a millionaire's yacht in patched pants would be bad prestige and damaging for pride . . . Both pairs were

of identical size. We had to reef up one pair for Smithy and let the other down for me.

As the *Oaxaca* cruised down the coast on the 1600-kilometre journey to Mazatlán, where Hancock had large tomato farms, he quizzed Ulm and Smithy about their plans. Ulm had no expectation other than that of being well fed for a while: 'I hardly dared to hope that he would seriously entertain our financial proposals. When one has faced disappointment after disappointment and listened to mile after mile of "ifs and buts" one's funny bone becomes paralysed, and one gets cynical.'[9] Nevertheless, Ulm shrewdly guessed that if he were to have any chance at all with the millionaire, he would have to be frank, and tell him the whole state of their financial affairs. But he did not have the nerve to ask Hancock directly if he would be prepared to buy *Southern Cross*.

It appears that Smithy took little part in the proceedings: 'more or less resigned to apparent failure, and grateful for the unexpected comfort which kindly providence had showered upon us, [Smithy] prepared to settle down comfortably for a while and leave the business to me. The respite from bitter arguments and petty squabbles, from evasions and subterfuge, from differences with potential navigators and persistent creditors, from the gossip of airports, was indeed comforting.'[10]

The *Oaxaca* was fitted with the latest navigation equipment, and during the run down the coast Ulm and Smithy took the opportunity to hone their skills, plotting their position using their own sextant, and comparing the results obtained from the ship's instruments. It was valuable experience.

At Mazatlán, they enjoyed Hancock's hospitality for a week—touring his plantations, swimming, lying in the sun and racing around the harbour in a speedboat.

> The happy days passed with discussions on navigation and aviation as the sole reminder of more serious issues. Never a word was spoken, however, concerning the one thing which was necessarily uppermost in my mind—money. But Fate was playing a whimsical hand.
>
> A few days before the yacht was due in our home port Hancock turned to me with one question which, in a flash, opened immense possibilities.
>
> 'How much money,' he said, 'is required to put you boys on the right side?'
>
> I gulped. My tongue stuck to the roof of my mouth. The query came as a shock. Then I told the frank truth: $16,000.
>
> 'I'll buy your machine for that sum,' said Captain Allan Hancock. I fought down my mad desire to dance around the chart room. I tried not to look excited but in thirty seconds or less the whole world had changed. Our battles, struggles and anxieties were not to be in vain, and the Pacific would be flown for the first time in the history of the world.

In this dramatic account, written years later for publication in *The Herald*, Charles Ulm would have us believe that in this vital interchange, he and Hancock were the only players. Kingsford Smith was probably present, but Ulm was happy to take all the credit.

When they disembarked in Los Angeles they were quickly brought back to reality: the *Southern Cross* had been seized by creditors, pending its sale. But the crisis was short-lived: after settling the debt, Captain Hancock became the legal owner of the aeroplane. At long last they were able to buy new shoes and new clothes, and sit down to a decent meal.

They also repaid Locke Harper in full.

One pressing task remained: as their legal partner, Keith Anderson was entitled to know of their good fortune.

There were no telephone links between the United States and Australia in 1928, so on 6 April Charles Ulm sent a cable to Anderson via the office of Bon Hilliard's father, Arthur Hilliard, a solicitor and Anderson's putative father-in-law:

UTMOST SECRECY IMPERATIVE STOP FINANCES COMPLETELY
ARRANGED TO EVERYONES SATISFACTION HENCE ESSEN-
TIAL KEITH RETURNS FIRST STEAMER ADVISE LEAVING
DATE CHILLACHAS[11]

Telegraphic cables were of necessity short and to the point, because they were charged by the word. But this message, sparse and dramatic, contained little specific information, so after discussion with Hilliard Anderson cabled back:

NO FINANCIAL HELP HERE. REQUIRE DETAILS WHAT MACHINE WHO OWNERS DATE DEPARTURE ROUTE CREW MY STATUS EXPLAIN POND SMITH WORLD FLIGHT YOU FURNISH MY FARE TAHITI SAILING NINETEENTH ANDERSON

After more than a week's silence, Ulm replied:

DEBTS PAID NEW SKIN WING RECONDITIONED IMPERATIVE IMMEDIATELY KNOW KEITHS MOVEMENTS REPLY PETRO-LEUM LOSANGELES CHILLACHAS

This did not answer any of Anderson's questions, and in fact posed new ones, so Keith cabled again. This time Ulm's response was unmistakably terse:

STATUS COPILOT PERSONALLY URGE YOU TO COME TAHITI FAILURE TO DO SO NATURALLY LOSES YOUR INTEREST WHICH I WILL CONSIDER TREMENDOUSLY DISLOYAL CHARLES

Anderson's return cable, probably worded by Hilliard, was succinct and unambiguous:

FOR ULM HAVE NO CASH WILL YOU REMIT STEAMER FARE COULD CATCH NIAGRA MAY THIRD INSPECTION AERO-DROME SUVA ANDERSON

During his time in San Francisco, Anderson had been despatched to Hawaii by steamer to find an airfield suitable for an overloaded take-off, and had found one, at Barking Sands. Now he was offering to do it again at Fiji, on his way back to America. It was a reasonable proposal, but Ulm's blunt reply completely ignored it:

CANNOT FURNISH YOUR FARE OUR CABLES EXPLICIT REPLY ARE YOU COMING PER TAHITI OR NOT NO REPLY BY NINETEENTH APRIL CONSIDERED AS YOUR TOTAL WITH-DRAWAL CHILLACHAS

At first glance, one could perhaps attribute this series of acerbic exchanges to the limitations of the telegraphic medium. However, Anderson's cables were concise, but polite. In stark contrast, Ulm's were terse and seldom addressed the questions that Anderson had asked. Why? Had the differences in telegraphic style somehow led to misunderstanding?

Charles Anderson and Arthur Hilliard apparently thought not. It's likely that Hilliard began to suspect that Ulm was being devious; deliberately withholding the information that Anderson needed, at the same time urging him to return, and repeatedly threatening that Keith's failure to do so meant the end of the partnership.

As a lawyer, Hilliard also probably believed that with all their debts relating to *Southern Cross* now settled, Ulm and Smithy had entered into a new legal relationship. That relationship involved

Charles Ulm, Charles Kingsford Smith, and the aircraft's new owner, Captain George Allan Hancock. There was no place for Keith Anderson.

But Hilliard reminded Anderson that he was still a partner, and he could prove it, by virtue of the document that Ulm had coerced him into signing before he returned from America. To Anderson, it was the around-Australia flight all over again; Ulm was once more the cuckoo in the nest, trying to squeeze him out.

And once more, Smithy had concurred.

Keith Anderson saw red. On 20 April, he fired off another cable:

> PRESUME YOU NEGLECT ANSWER FULLY JUSTIFIABLE
> ENQUIRIES MY CABLE TWELFTH MEAN MY PARTICIPATION
> IN FLIGHT UNDESIRED I THEREFORE REQUIRE COMPENS-
> ATION MY THIRD INTEREST AND CLAIM AS CREDITOR
> STOP WILL TAKE THIRTEEN THOUSAND DOLLARS IN FULL
> SATISFACTION OTHERWISE I REFUSE TO WITHDRAW AND
> HOLD YOU BOTH PERSONALLY RESPONSIBLE ANY ACTION
> PREJUDICIAL MY INTEREST ANDERSON

This new-found aggression caught both Ulm and Smithy off guard and, after thinking about it for a couple of days, they replied in a more conciliatory tone.

> TRYING EVERYWHERE BUT NOT HOPEFUL RAISING YOUR
> FARE TRY HARD YOURSELF ADVISING US CHILLACHAS

Anderson ignored this cable, and on 23 April Ulm cabled again, at last providing a modicum of useful information. Significantly, it was not signed CHILLACHAS this time, but more formally, SMITHULM.

> MORTGAGEE GRABBED PLANE SAME LATER SOLD SIXTEEN THOUSAND WITH YOUR SANCTION STOP WE SINCE REPURCHASED FROM PRIVATE BACKING PERSONALLY SECURED AND OFFER YOU THIRD OUR INTEREST PROVIDED YOU COME FIRST STEAMER PAYING OWN FARE OR WORKING PASSAGE AS WE CANNOT RAISE FARE STOP HONOUR DEMANDS REPLY IMMEDIATELY STATING COMING OR NOT THIS IS OUR LAST WORD SMITHULM

Although Anderson had no means of knowing it, the assertion that Ulm and Smithy could not raise his fare was probably untrue. The cost of a first-class steamer passage was insignificant in the context of the budget for a trans-Pacific flight, and Captain Hancock would almost certainly have stumped up the money. It is doubtful whether Ulm and Smithy ever asked him.

On the other hand, did Keith really want to go? Nobody in Australia was prepared to advance him his fare and he was not at all enthusiastic about working his passage. There was pressure to stay from family and friends; after having her son survive the Great War, his mother did not want him to risk his life again flying across an ocean; and Bon, his fiancée, the woman whom Smithy had once regarded as *his* girlfriend, simply wanted to get married.

Ulm received no further communication from Anderson for almost three weeks, so he cabled him once more.

FAILURE REPLY OUR LAST CABLEGRAM AND FAILURE CATCH NIAGRA CONVEYS YOUR NON ACCEPTANCE OUR OFFER THIRD INTEREST STOP UNLESS CATCHING STEAMER AS FLIGHT COMMENCES VERY SHORTLY HENCE WE NOW WITHDRAW PREVIOUS OFFER SMITHULM

On 16 May 1928, Ulm wrote a three-page letter to Anderson, covering the history of their endeavours in the United States in considerable detail. The penultimate paragraph read:

It isn't much good to try and cover the whole situation in a letter—recrimination is useless, you know the facts and we know the facts, but we feel that in justice to ourselves we should point out that we once allowed you to join us in our first effort as a third member having equal rights. This endeavour by the three of us failed and as you know not by any action of ours or yours. We have offered you a third interest in our newly organised flight on the same basis, and whilst we could not for one minute suggest that you have taken the risks into consideration, we feel that you have been influenced against coming back, and as you are not coming back you cannot possibly suggest that you should be given a one-third interest in the new flight, the organisation and financing of which you have had no part in and the risks of which you are not prepared to undertake. We would like you to believe that we are both sincerely sorry that you are not coming back and your failure to return has put us to great trouble and considerable expense for we both believed you would return and planned accordingly.

After our return to Australia we would very much like to see you and go over the whole matter fully . . .[12]

By the time Keith Anderson received this letter, Ulm and Smithy had flown the Pacific.

CHAPTER 6

After the third arrest . . .

When it became clear that Keith Anderson would not be returning to San Francisco, Ulm and Kingsford Smith were faced with the task of selecting a co-pilot for the long, arduous and undoubtedly dangerous flight that lay ahead. There were few pilots with experience on the big Fokker trimotors, so their choice was limited. As they still wanted it to be an all-Australian affair, Hubert Wilkins was their first choice, but he had his sights set on other adventures and wasn't interested. George Pond was well qualified, having spent many hours beside Smithy in the *Southern Cross* during the world endurance record attempt, but he was an American and, in any case, Ulm didn't like him.

It is not clear how Charles Ulm found himself in the right-hand seat, but it is highly likely that he made the suggestion himself. Once again, he would supplant Anderson, but this time he would not be a passenger in the rear cockpit of a Bristol Tourer. This time he would be up front, beside Smithy, and would be expected to take his turn at flying. The prospect did not daunt him. He had been involved with aeroplanes for nine years and knew his way around a cockpit. His war wounds had prevented him from obtaining a pilot's licence, and he had not deemed it important to keep a log book, but by his own estimation he had spent about 200 hours at the controls.

Flying the *Southern Cross* was not a simple matter. The controls were heavy, and the aircraft lacked elevator, rudder or aileron trim, requiring constant inputs by the pilot. In turbulence, it often demanded the combined strength of two men. There was no automatic pilot.

Course-keeping was another issue. On a long flight over a featureless ocean, with no landmarks to crosscheck against his chart, a pilot had to keep the aircraft on the correct heading with only the compass as his guide. This was a challenge, because even experienced pilots had a tendency to wander off course. It was essential to check the compass constantly as part of a routine instrument scan. Even the smallest deviation, if not quickly detected and corrected, could ultimately result in failure to make good their track to their island destinations.

When taking off or landing, in heavy turbulence, or in cloud, rain or fog, it was understood that Kingsford Smith would fly the aircraft. While he was a brilliant instinctive aviator, with an uncanny ability to communicate with an aeroplane through the feel of the controls and the sound of engines and airflow, Smithy knew that in poor visibility, with no horizon visible for refer-ence, it was foolhardy to rely on 'seat of the pants' flying. To do so would almost certainly lead to an inadvertent stall and spin. In such conditions a pilot had to ignore his senses and trust his instruments instead.

By modern standards, *Southern Cross* possessed a rudimentary instrument array: just a compass, an altimeter, an airspeed indic-ator and their only gyroscopic instrument, a turn-and-bank indicator. There was no artificial horizon yet, amazingly, in zero visibility Smithy could keep the aircraft on an even keel at a constant height and airspeed, and heading in the right direc-tion, for hour after hour.

It was airmanship at its highest level.

They called themselves co-commanders, a catchy job title that Ulm thought might appeal to newspapermen. Considering the wide disparity in their flying skills, at first glance it would seem that he was drawing a long bow, almost to the point of arrog-ance. But it was in fact accurate. By tacit agreement, Kingsford Smith had absolute authority in the air, but on the ground, when it came to their business and administrative affairs, Ulm held the reins. They were a two-man team, playing to their strengths, and they were very effective.

One of the conditions attached to Hancock's support was that they engage both a professional navigator and a wireless oper-ator for the flight. Despite their attempts to master the art, they had scant knowledge of celestial navigation, and knew even less about airborne wireless. Captain Hancock was paying, so they were more than happy to oblige.

There was no such thing as a specialist air navigator in 1928, so they had to make do with the marine version instead. They could not find a fellow Australian to fit the bill, so the head of the San Francisco Hydrographic Office suggested an American, Captain Harry Lyon, a first-class navigator and well qualified to guide them across the Pacific.

Lyon was considerably older than Smithy and Ulm, of average height, thickset but well-built, with an open, friendly, weather-beaten face, bushy eyebrows, a high forehead and a luxuriant head of hair. He also had a penchant for bow ties.

His accent revealed his origins: he had been born into an upper-class Maine family, entered the Annapolis Naval Academy, where he failed all his exams, including navigation, and then attended an Ivy League university for just one term before going to sea.

In the years that followed he had travelled the world, rounding the Horn before the mast on a full-rigged sailing ship, and working as a lowly deckhand on tramp steamers that took him to exotic places. He had been in his share of fistfights, witnessed an armed mutiny, survived fires at sea, a U-boat attack and a fall overboard from a yardarm. In 1924, he had been caught up in a revolution in Mexico, captured, sentenced to death, and reprieved at the last minute. Somehow, despite his tumultuous life and poor academic record, he had qualified as a navigator, and now held a master's certificate. He had commanded vessels in the merchant marine and the US Navy.

Harry Lyon had done a lot of living in his 45 years.

They talked for several hours and Lyon was impressed by the Australians' earnestness, their meticulous preparation and their confidence that the Pacific flight would be a success. He told them frankly that he had flown only a few times and that he had a lot to learn about celestial navigation conducted from the air. Nevertheless, recognising a fellow adventurer, Ulm and Smithy made him an offer. They would take him on as navigator and pay him weekly, on the understanding that his engagement would last only as far as Suva. Beyond Fiji, they were confident they could make landfall on a broad target like Australia without his assistance. When the *Southern Cross* arrived in Suva, Lyon would receive a bonus payment of US$500, and a first-class steamship ticket back to California. There would be a further US$500 once the aircraft safely reached Australia.

After thinking about it overnight, Lyon accepted and, the next day, as he shook hands with the two Australians, he was happy with what he believed was a gentlemen's agreement.

He started work immediately. He was shown over the *Southern Cross* and introduced to the bubble sextant. This instrument was similar to its marine equivalent, with the addition of a spirit level marked with a line representing the natural horizon. In the air, when the natural horizon was obscured by cloud, the navigator was still able to take celestial sightings by adjusting the instrument until the image of the heavenly body was resting on the artificial horizon. While it was a variation on a familiar theme, Lyon realised that mastery of this new technique would require some effort.

> I began to practice taking sights with this instrument, and when possible had a man along with a sextant, and at the same time I took altitudes with the artificial horizon or bubble, he took altitudes with the natural horizon for a matter of comparison. Along the beach outside of San Francisco is a long stretch of road following the water. We used to go out there and he would station himself a mile or two away from me and choose a star which he would keep on the horizon as best he could. I would be in a high-powered open car with someone driving and we would go on tearing down the road. I would stand up and observe the same star as I passed my helper, then we would compare. The effect of the fast-moving car, the bumps, etc., had the same effect as taking an observation from a plane.

It was demanding work, tempered by Lyon's wry sense of humour: 'We got in quite a bit of practice at this, but after the third arrest, it became too expensive.' (They were repeatedly pulled over by the police.)

He also practised executing the arithmetic necessary to work the sights while travelling at speed. 'After taking the sights I used to lean over, using the dash lights to see by, and try and see how fast I could work them, the car still bumping about. In fact, I made myself as uncomfortable as possible, and it was good practice for when we started on the trip.'

For more realism, Kingsford Smith borrowed a Swallow biplane and he and Lyon went up a number of times while Harry practised. 'The controls were in the after seat, and so when I took a sight, Smithy had to put the bus in some awful banks so I could get the object clear of the top wing. We had a lot of practice at this.'[1]

It was easier in the *Southern Cross*, which had a sliding hatch in the cabin roof to give the navigator an uninterrupted view of the sky. There was also a pelorus for checking bearings. This instrument had markings similar to those on a mariner's compass, but without the magnetic needle. It was used to take bearings relative to the lubber line—in the case of *Southern Cross*, the centre line of the aircraft. There was a drift sight mounted near the cabin door: by aligning this device with the white cap of a wave breaking astern, the navigator could detect and measure any drift that could be causing the aircraft to deviate from its course. At night a 'bomb', containing a chemical which ignited upon contact with water, was used.

Lyon also advised the Australians on the purchase and installation of the compasses. *Southern Cross* had four: a master aperiodic compass mounted on the floor beside the navigator in the cabin, two standard magnetic aviation compasses in the cockpit, and an earth inductor compass on top of the fuselage. This had a setting device at the navigator's station and an indicator needle on the instrument panel for each pilot. For its day, it was a sophisticated set-up.

Ulm and Smithy were still searching for a radio operator, so Harry Lyon recommended Jim Warner, an old shipmate from the Atlantic convoys during the Great War. They invited him in for a chat.

On first acquaintance, Warner was unremarkable: slightly built, with pointed features, a short-back-and-sides haircut and a well-trimmed moustache. Born in Kansas in 1891, Warner had suffered an abusive childhood. His parents had divorced when he was four, and he had endured time in an orphanage, a foster home, and on a farm where he was forced to work long hours and regularly beaten. At 14 he ran away, wandering about and picking up any work that he could find, until he found refuge in the US Navy in 1911. He became a wireless operator, serving aboard USS *St Louis*, where he met Lyon.

He had never been up in an aeroplane, but Ulm hired him anyway, on terms similar to Lyon's, with his engagement ending at Fiji. He was an acknowledged expert in his field and would be a key player in the flight that was to come. Pleased to have a job, Warner started at once to familiarise himself with the radio gear.

The radio equipment aboard the *Southern Cross* represented state-of-the-art electronic communication. It was lightweight and capable of transmitting and receiving Morse code on several wavelengths via aerials that trailed behind the aircraft. The longer of the two aerials was about 140 metres. It was wound in before landing and frequently tangled. The most important feature of the receiver was its ability to receive signals from land-based radio stations that provided the pilots with an accurate course to steer. This capability had already proved its worth during the Dole Race when it had enabled rescuers to locate aircraft that had come down in the sea. In addition to the main units, a battery-powered emergency transmitter in the wooden wing was capable of sending messages for eight hours, even when completely submerged, using an antenna borne aloft by a kite. If the *Southern Cross* came down in the sea, the plan was to use a hacksaw to cut off the two outboard engines, and take refuge on the buoyant wooden wing. They would then deploy a kite to raise the aerial and broadcast a distress signal, at the same time trying to avoid being swept into the sea. It was wishful thinking.

The transistor was not in widespread use in 1928 and the radio equipment aboard *Southern Cross* utilised fragile thermionic valves. Although rubber mountings gave a measure of protection to the valves' glowing filaments from the pounding vibration of the engines, they often failed, so as well as being a dab hand on a Morse key, the operator had to be capable of making running repairs in flight. Power for the radios was provided by batteries charged by streamlined, wind-operated generators mounted on each side of the fuselage.[2]

The *Southern Cross* had three engines and, at normal weight, if one failed, it could continue to fly on the power delivered by the other two. But on the Pacific crossing, when at times it would be grossly overloaded with fuel, the loss of an engine would mean a slow, inexorable descent into the sea. It was Smithy's worst nightmare. Everything depended on those engines, and although the Wright Whirlwind had an excellent track record, and their engines were brand-new, Ulm and Smithy hired Cecil 'Doc' Maidment, a Wright engineer and world authority on the Whirlwind, to give them a thorough inspection, just to make sure. Doc came to California and gave them the all-clear.

Charles Ulm kept up a steady flow of press releases to the Sydney *Sun* and the San Francisco *Examiner*, and all four crew members were often in the headlines on both sides of the Pacific as they embarked on a series of shakedown flights out of Mills Field, now the site of San Francisco International Airport.

The *Southern Cross* was not a comfortable aircraft in which to fly for any length of time. The cockpit was located beneath the leading edge of the wing, which gave Smithy and Ulm a measure of protection from the elements, and there was a windshield, but it was open on both sides. When it rained, they got wet and cold. They were very close to the engines, which had open exhausts, so the noise was deafening.

Lyon and Warner sat at workstations in the rear cabin, which was a box-like, wire-braced structure of welded steel tube with a plywood floor. Amazingly, their wicker seats were not fastened down, and there were no seatbelts. The cabin walls gave illusory protection from the hostile outside world, little more than a millimetre away on the other side of the doped fabric covering. From the cabin the name *Southern Cross,* painted on the side of the aircraft, could be seen in reverse through the thin cloth.

They were physically separated from Smithy and Ulm, because the area immediately behind the cockpit was occupied by a massive fuel tank. This posed a serious problem, because efficient communication between the pilots and the navigator and radio operator was essential for the safe conduct of the flight. The shattering engine noise rendered speaking tubes and telephone useless, so they tried a system of ropes and pulleys to convey written messages back and forth, but the ropes kept getting tangled. Finally, driving to the airfield early one morning, Locke Harper came up with the idea of a broom handle with a nail at each end, upon which the message slips could be spiked. They couldn't find a hardware store open at that hour, so Smithy borrowed a fishing rod from somebody at the airport. It was an inelegant solution, but it worked a treat and served them well all the way across the Pacific.[3]

As well as working with the crew as a team, Smithy practised instrument flying. With George Pond in the right-hand seat, he plunged into cloudbanks to fly the *Southern Cross* in total whiteout, ignoring his senses and relying solely on what the dials on the panel told him.

While Smithy was honing his skills aloft, Ulm busied himself with more mundane affairs on the ground. There was a lot to organise, many cables to be composed and sent. Since their arrival in San Francisco, they had made contacts in the US Navy and now, at Ulm's request, Admiral Peebles arranged for the *Southern Cross* to be permitted to land at Wheeler Field, near Honolulu. Here, the US Army Air Corps would take charge and prepare her for the next stage of the flight, the long stretch to Fiji. Keith Anderson had already recommended that after landing at Wheeler, they re-position the aircraft, lightly loaded, to Barking Sands on the island of Kauai, about 180 kilometres west of Oahu, where a vast expanse of beach was available for an extended take-off. The bulk of the fuel would be taken on board there.

Because Ulm had chosen to ignore Anderson's offer to check out the landing grounds in Suva, they knew very little of the facilities that would be available to them there. Fiji was a British colony, which was helpful, and two old mates from Smithy's wartime Flying Corps days, who lived in Suva, advised them that they could possibly put the *Southern Cross* down safely on the Albert Park Sports Oval. They offered to put out brightly painted markers and the local authorities agreed to remove telegraph wires and cut down three large trees.[4] Even with these measures, a successful landing at Albert Park was far from certain.

Smithy and Ulm tried to condition themselves to go for long periods without sleep. They drove a car for 12 hours, then flew for a few hours, ran for an hour or two, then drove and flew again, until they had been awake for 35 hours. They repeated this in close succession several times until they were reasonably confident that sustained fatigue would not overwhelm them.

With the day of the flight approaching, they flew the *Southern Cross* across to Oakland where the bay at the end of the runway provided an unobstructed path for a heavily loaded aeroplane clawing for height after take-off. They were provided with a car and accommodation at a good hotel.

Here, without warning, Ulm presented legal documents which he asked Lyon and Warner to sign, confirming the conditions under which they were to be employed. Harry and Jim were taken aback; as far as they were concerned, they already had a deal. They had shaken hands on it.

But a gentleman's agreement was not sufficient for Charles Ulm; he wanted it in black and white. As he pressed them to sign, Harry Lyon ran a suspicious eye over the wording. The original terms to which he and Warner had agreed were there, dressed up in legal language: weekly pay, US$500 in bonus payments and a boat fare. But Ulm had added additional clauses that were clearly designed to prevent the Americans from sharing in any further rewards that might accrue from the flight. The agreement prohibited them from giving interviews or writing articles without written permission, and, furthermore, by signing they indemnified Ulm and Kingsford Smith against any claim in the event of death or accident.

As he read, Harry Lyon felt his anger mounting. To him, a handshake was as good as a signature, but this document revealed a mercenary, ruthless side to Charles Ulm. Harry didn't like it, but he had a come-what-may approach to life. This promised to be a real adventure, and he wasn't inclined to back out now. He signed.

Jim Warner did likewise, although during the shakedown flights he had discovered that he was scared of flying. But he had told his friends that he was going and didn't want to appear yellow.

On the evening before the flight, a cable arrived for Kingsford Smith and Ulm:

> YOU HAVE BEST POSSIBLE MACHINE. IF YOUR COMPAN-
> IONS' SKILL EQUALS YOUR DETERMINATION YOU WILL
> SUCCEED. GOOD LUCK. REGRET FAILURE FURNISH MY FARE
> ENSURING MY PARTICIPATION WAS NOT FIRST CONSIDER-
> ATION. EXPECT A LITTLE JUSTICE AND COMPENSATION
> UPON YOUR ARRIVAL HERE. ANDERSON.[5]

His best wishes were no doubt sincere, but the implication was also clear. They had not heard the last of Keith Anderson.

CHAPTER 7

Exceedingly famous

The morning of 31 May 1928 dawned bright and clear at Oakland Airport, with just a trace of mist drifting across the bay. It was a lovely day for flying. The *Southern Cross* stood near the end of the runway, its name standing out white against the deep blue fabric of the fuselage. The massive plywood wing, doped gleaming silver, would soon be required to lift a staggering four tons (over 3500 kilograms) of fuel into the air.

A short distance away, several hundred members of the general public were gathered behind a rope barrier. They were wellwishers attracted by the newspaper publicity, hoping to be a part of history in the making, although a ghoulish few were no doubt secretly hoping to witness a spectacular crash.

Beside the aircraft, friends and family stood with the aviators for final photographs. Kingsford Smith and Ulm were instantly recognisable; both were dressed for the business at hand, sporting flying caps and stylish riding boots, but the effect was somewhat diminished by Ulm, who was also wearing jodhpurs and a tie. Warner and Lyon, on the other hand, could have blended in with the expectant crowd. Warner, in coat, tie and patterned jumper, looked more like an office worker than a radio operator, and Harry Lyon, sporting a casual sweater and bow tie, could have been about to embark on a drive in the country.

The man whose money had made it all possible was there too, but behind the rope barrier, mingling with the onlookers. Captain Hancock preferred to keep a low profile.

Shortly before nine, it was time to start up and, under the impulse of the inertia starters, the Wright Whirlwinds coughed into life, one by one. Smithy allowed them to idle for several minutes to warm up, then gently eased the throttles open. The note of the engines rose in response and the slashing propellers instantly created a maelstrom of whirling air and stinging grit, scattering spectators who happened to be standing behind the tail.

For a second or two, nothing happened. Then, slowly, the wheels began to turn as the straining engines overcame the inertia of the heavy load.

Finally, the *Southern Cross* was lined up, ready to go. Smithy eased all three throttles forward, and the aircraft began its take-off roll. Not surprisingly, acceleration was agonisingly slow, but even so, keeping the aircraft running straight was no simple matter as the rudder was ineffective at low speed. As the airspeed built up, Ulm took over the throttles, keeping them hard up against their stops to get maximum revs out of the engines.

Suddenly, when they had covered only 200 metres, the central Whirlwind stopped. Pulse rates in the cockpit soared; without power from all three engines, take-off was impossible. The take-off was aborted.

Smithy spotted the trouble before they had rolled to a stop: the altitude control had jammed, causing the engine to cut out. Fortunately, the remedy was simple: shut down the other engines, reset the control, and start all three again.

Several hundred metres away, the watching crowd were no doubt mystified to see the big silver bird come to a halt, stop its engines, then start them again, but in the heat of the moment it is doubtful that anybody on board, even the publicity-conscious Charles Ulm, gave them a second thought.

They had only used a fraction of the available runway, so Kingsford Smith elected to continue the take-off without returning to the starting point. This time all engines kept running, delivering 1800 revolutions per minute, steadily accelerating the *Southern Cross* to 76 knots (140 kilometres per hour), when Smithy, sensing that she was ready, eased her into the air.

They were flying, but only just, and dangerously close to their stalling speed as the end of the runway flashed past. They were over the water, supported by the ground effect, the cushion of air between the wing and the surface of the sea. To climb, their airspeed would have to increase further, and under Smithy's gentle hands it did, but two minutes after take-off, they had reached only 80 knots and 100 feet.

Five minutes later they were at 1000 feet and climbing, still at 80 knots, surrounded by a gaggle of light aircraft carrying photographers and newsreel cameramen. On their port quarter, the skyscrapers of San Francisco were poking above the haze, which was by now stained by banks of brown smog. They had some height, so Smithy eased the throttles back to 1775 revolutions per minute to give the engines a rest. He and Ulm shook hands. They were off!

To mark the occasion they placed a small Australian flag, a gift from a wellwisher, above the petrol gauges. It had taken Ulm eight long years, a great deal of energy, a lot of money, damaged relationships and possibly even the loss of friends to get to this point, but at last they were on their way. For Smithy, who lived for flying, a great aerial adventure lay ahead, but Charles Ulm's ambitions went further than that. Deep down he knew that for him, this flight was but the first step in a very long journey.

They were slowly climbing, but still heavy. For several more hours, until they had burned some fuel, the failure of an engine would put them in the sea. It was of no use to dwell on that possibility, so they settled down into the routine they had established during the shakedown flights. Warner wound out his radio aerials and began to search for the signals being broadcast from the radio beacon at Crissey Field, near San Francisco, that delineated their course to Hawaii.

There were two overlapping beams. If the aircraft was left of the desired course, he heard a continuous repetition of the letter A (*dit dah* in Morse code) in his headphones. If the *Southern Cross* was to the right of the course, he heard the letter N (*dah dit*). When the aircraft was on course the two beams merged into a repetitive series of long tones, the letter T (*dah*). Warner would advise Lyon, who would pass the course corrections to Smithy via the message stick.

The signal from the beacon was coming in, loud and clear, as Ulm passed back the first of many messages.

> Charles Ulm to Harry Lyon
>
> I checked us off the ground at 8.54 P.C.T. and out Golden Gate at 9.06 P.C.T. How are both of you back— enjoying the scenery, eh!
>
> Or what have you.
>
> Chas.
>
> Send out our D.R. position half hourly now, I suggest.[1]

The DR position was their deduced, or dead, reckoning position. As the hours passed, Lyon used his sextant to establish their position, checked it against the course marked on his chart, and passed the coordinates to Warner, who transmitted them to ground stations. Constantly checking and updating the DR position was vitally important; if they were forced to land in the sea, rescuers would know roughly where to look. Despite this precaution, if they came down they all knew that help would be a long time coming; so far they had not sighted a single ship.

They were cocooned in a flimsy airframe above the wide Pacific. It was a lonely feeling.

—·—· —— ·—·—· ··—— ·—··· ——

Lonely, but not alone. Whenever Jim Warner tapped out a message, he knew that at least one person in the outside world was listening, and logging every word. An old shipmate named Charlie Hodge, a radio operator aboard USS *Omaha*, a light cruiser docked at Pearl Harbor, had agreed to tune in whenever the *Southern Cross* was in the air. Hodge would be as good as his word, staying awake, and on listening watch, for more than 30 hours.

Charles Ulm had contracted to supply the San Francisco *Examiner* and the Sydney *Sun* with progress reports and, as the flight progressed, a constant stream of handwritten press releases made their way back via the message stick. As he tapped them out, Jim Warner knew they were breaking new ground: this was the first time that news organisations had received news reports from the air in 'real time', as an event was actually unfolding. Twelve thousand kilometres away in Sydney, the editor of *The Sun*, delighted to be the beneficiary of cutting-edge news-gathering technology, published them with little embellishment.

> 10.00 a.m. We are 100 miles west of the Golden Gate.
> The weather is perfect. Our engines are working splen-
> didly and everything is going fine.

10:40 a.m. We have seen no ships. Everything is okay. The altitude is 2000 feet and we're having very decent weather.

11.15 a.m. The engines are functioning perfectly. We are in the best spirits and have travelled nearly 200 miles.

1 p.m. We are fully 200 miles south-west of San Francisco. The weather is getting cloudy. At present speed is 73 knots. We have dropped to an altitude of 1850 feet because of the low clouds. The visibility is excellent as long as we keep under the clouds. The engines are working without the slightest show of trouble. Tell our Australian friends we feel we are sitting on top of the world.

At 1:15 p.m. the estimated speed was 87 miles an hour. Early this afternoon the fliers reported that they were slightly off the course, 400 miles out. The conditions were favourable.

1:30 p.m. A message address to all ships said, 'We are all doing fine. The engines are doing 1675 revolutions per minute at an altitude of 2500 feet. The oil temperature and air pressure are normal.'

3 p.m. The Matson liner 'Wilhemina' reported that the 'Southern Cross' was having trouble with the radio messages from Crissey Field. Kingsford Smith had been in communication with the 'Wilhemina' for nearly an hour now trying to get his exact bearings. The fliers, however, are making good headway in the meantime.[2]

Unfortunately, in striking what he thought were exclusive deals with *The Sun* and the *Examiner*, Charles Ulm had seriously underestimated the power of radio broadcasting and the international interest in the flight. In 1928, radio, or wireless as it was then called, was firmly established as the premier medium of mass entertainment, particularly in the United States. The wireless set was an imposing piece of furniture and often the centrepiece of the family living room. Most news and entertainment programmes were broadcast on medium frequencies, but by turning a dial, listeners could also tune into the short-wave band and eavesdrop on the arcane world of Morse code. In the early days of June, as they twisted their dials slowly back and forth, those in the know were searching for a specific target: the unique combination of dots and dashes that spelled out the letters KHAB, the call sign of the *Southern Cross*.

Within Australia, interest in the flight was so intense that, by special arrangement with *The Sun* and Amalgamated Wireless of Australasia (AWA), radio station 2BL began to re-broadcast Warner's messages into living rooms, making them available to a general audience. Fading in and out, and at times completely obscured by the hiss and crackle of static, the dots and dashes were totally incomprehensible to most people, but listeners nevertheless felt a sense of participation in a great adventure and, to Ulm's chagrin later, Warner became regarded as the 'voice' of the *Southern Cross*.

Once Warner committed a press release to the ether, Charles Ulm lost control of it. The message became available to anyone who understood Morse code and in the United States some enterprising souls began to transcribe Warner's transmissions and sell them to rival news organisations such as the Associated Press. Eric Cullen Ward, the editor of the *Examiner*, naturally objected to his property being hijacked in this way, and sent a message to the *Southern Cross*, accusing Ulm of breaking their agreement.

Charles quickly professed his innocence.

ONLY MESSAGES SENT ADDRESSED EITHER QST OR S ARD[3] AS ARRANGED HENCE NO VIOLATION OF OUR AGREEMENT STOP IF AP SAYS WE SENT THEM DIRECT MESSAGES THEY LIE STOP PERSONAL TO ERIC CULLEN WARD STOP WE DONT BREAK OUR WORD OR VIOLATE CONTRACTS STOP SORRY YOU WERE TROUBLED BUT SAME BEYOND MY CONTROL STOP WILL LOYALLY SERVE EXAMINER UNTIL CONTRACT ENDED STOP GEE ITS GREAT OUT HERE BUT APPARENTLY BUSINESS WORRIES EVEN REACH ME HERE STOP SMOKE TWO CIGARETTES AT ONCE ONE FOR ME SMITHY AND I BOTH CRAVE THE ODD SMOKE LOVE AND KISSES CHEERIO CHAS[4]

All four men aboard the *Southern Cross* were heavy smokers, but Kingsford Smith had banned cigarettes. They happily complied, because from time to time petrol fumes pervaded the cabin, and fire in the air was an aviator's greatest fear.

As well as smoking, other creature comforts were limited. There was no toilet, so they urinated into empty lemonade bottles and dumped the contents overboard. At one stage, Warner, peering through an open window, noticed the warmth of tropical rain upon his face, only to discover that Smithy was emptying his bottle from the cockpit, immediately upwind. This was not the only indignity suffered by the radio man; while the other members of the crew were able to defer their bowel movements until they were back on terra firma, Warner could not wait (probably because of anxiety) and was forced to squat over a newspaper.

When they were about 600 kilometres out from San Francisco, they lost the radio beacon. It had served them well, establishing them decisively upon their course for the Hawaiian Islands, still more than 3000 kilometres away. Towards the end of the flight they hoped to pick up signals from the beacon at Wheeler Field, near Honolulu, to guide them in. The weather continued to be favourable, and Lyon kept them on track with regular celestial fixes and drift sightings, as Smithy flew at low altitudes to minimise their fuel consumption.

The main problem they had to face was the monotony. As the day drew to a close, banks of cloud began to slide beneath them, obscuring the sea. They had sandwiches and coffee and Ulm passed a message for Warner to transmit to Sydney:

900 PM AT 3800 FEET ABOVE ENDLESS MILES OF CLOUDS STOP NO STARS OR MOON VISIBLE YET STOP PERFECTLY CLEAR UP HERE HENCE NO NECESSITY TO GO HIGHER YET STOP MOTORS HAVENT MISSED A BEAT THANKS TO MAIDMENT STOP SMITHY MUST BE IN LOVE I CANT MAKE

HIM EAT STOP HES HAD 3 TO MY 10 SANDWICHES TO
DATE STOP STARS JUST COMING UP NOW STOP WILL SEND
MORE LATER[5]

Anxious to maintain control of the information emanating from the *Southern Cross*, Ulm had forbidden Lyon and
Warner from sending personal messages, but aware that the
'co-commander' could not possibly know what was happening
in the rear cabin, Harry Lyon asked Warner to send a cable to
Betty Warren, one of the women in his life, back in San Francisco:

SORRY TO LEAVE SO ABRUPTLY STOP ARE NOW 400 MILES
OUT AND GOING STRONG STOP ALL WELL STOP LOVE
HARRY LYON[6]

Had Ulm found out, he would have been furious, but Lyon
no doubt enjoyed thumbing his nose at the rules. Despite the
superficial levity of their banter, he found Charles pompous and
overbearing.

Although they were confident that they were on course, they
were keen to confirm their position with a ship. The chance came
when Warner made contact with the *Maliko*, which was able to
give them a radio bearing that indicated that they were a short
distance north of their great circle route. To get back on course,
Smithy flew towards the ship. When the *Maliko*'s lights appeared,
Ulm took the controls and flew the *Southern Cross* around her
in a wide circle, while Smithy flashed the letters KHAB with the

106

signal lamp. They did the same thing with another vessel, the *Manoa*, 40 minutes later.

They were more than halfway to Honolulu.

As the sun rose, Lyon took yet another sight, and they found that they had picked up a tailwind during the night, and now had a groundspeed of more than 100 knots (180 kilometres per hour). With the islands about 600 kilometres away, Lyon, whose bubble sextant had been giving him trouble, began to lose confidence in the accuracy of his navigation. They tried unsuccessfully to pick up the radio beam from Wheeler Field to guide them in, but one of their wind-driven generators had broken down, and they could not charge the batteries for their receiver and short-range transmitter. Tension mounted.

Shortly after nine o'clock, Ulm saw what appeared to be a series of rocky cliffs rising abruptly out of the sea off their port bow. They had been airborne for 24 hours and he was tired. Maybe he was seeing things. He looked again. The cliffs were still there. Smithy saw them too, and changed course to head in their direction.

Had they made landfall? Was this Hawaii?

Harry Lyon's confidence was shattered. He had been serving on trading ships around the Hawaiian Islands for years and knew them well. If this indeed was landfall, it was much too soon and in the wrong place. The only rocks that remotely resembled the cliffs that he could now see through his window should be 250 kilometres away, beyond Kauai at the western end of the Hawaiian group. The situation was very confusing. If he could not establish their position definitively, and very soon, they could miss the islands altogether and fly on to vanish into the wastes of the Pacific.

Jim Warner eyed his colleague warily, sensing that something was very wrong.

As they flew closer, the cliffs suddenly transmogrified into clouds and drifted away. Smithy turned back on to his original course. His colleagues were disappointed, but Harry Lyon was secretly very pleased that the quality of his navigation had been vindicated. But more 'cliffs' appeared and each time, to Lyon's concern, Kingsford Smith altered course and flew towards them, only to have them vanish once more into thin air. The constant deviations from the course so carefully marked on his chart thoroughly confused Harry, who could not keep track. As he hunched over his chart table, trying to make sense of it all, Jim Warner passed him a note asking him if he was lost.

Despairingly, Lyon scribbled back, 'Yes.'

Panic-stricken, Jim Warner immediately informed the world, causing great consternation.

GUESS WE ARE LOST

Finally, with the batteries for his long-range receiver almost completely flat, Warner managed to make contact with the powerful radio transmitter at Hilo, on Hawaii, the largest island in the group. The operator there used his direction-finding loop to provide a bearing line, which Lyon marked on his chart, projecting it to intersect the great circle course. This gave him a dead reckoning position, which he immediately confirmed with a sun shot. After hours of confusion, wandering about in the mid Pacific, he now knew exactly where they were. He plotted a new course and sent the heading to the cockpit via the message stick. Much relieved, Ulm replied immediately, 'Damned good work Harry, old Lion, keep on doing your stuff.'[7]

Lyon attached a reply and sent it back. 'If we get a cigarette and cup of coffee we'll feel like flying back—ha, what, Old Top.'[8]

They were back on course, but dwindling fuel now became a concern, because they did not know exactly how much remained in their fuselage tank.

There was enough. The unmistakeable, snow-capped form of Mauna Kea appeared above the clouds on the horizon, and an hour later they were flying over Honolulu. They had spent 27 hours and 25 minutes in the air. The *Southern Cross* was not the first aeroplane to make the crossing from San Francisco, but they received a rousing welcome anyway. Fifteen thousand people were at Wheeler Field as they landed.

They had endured the unrelenting hammering of the motors for so long that when Kingsford Smith shut them down the sudden silence was unnerving. As soon as the propellers clicked to a stop, the *Southern Cross* was surrounded by people. Flashbulbs popped, newsreel cameras whirred, the press crowded around seeking comments. Bleary-eyed, unshaven, deafened, lei-bedecked and totally exhausted, Smithy, Ulm, Lyon and Warner were driven under police escort to the Royal Hawaiian Hotel at Waikiki.

In Australia, Jo Ulm had spent a restless night, waiting for news. She had been married to Charles Ulm for ten months, but they had spent all but a few days of that time on opposite sides of the Pacific. Although her job as a teacher had kept her busy, she missed Charles very much and was looking forward to having him back again.

Cables phoned through to her from the San Francisco *Examiner*, which was handling all personal messages from the *Southern Cross*, had been disturbing. The flyers had reported being off course, then totally lost, then back on course again. Then they had announced that were running out of fuel. After that, nothing.

The telephone rang again.

'Boys arrived safely. Very tired but happy. Went straight from field to hotel.'9

It was 5.50 a.m., but Jo didn't care. Charles was safe and that was all that mattered.

The crew stayed for a little over a day in Honolulu, resting. At the Royal Hawaiian, after a shower, a shave, a decent meal, more than a few drinks and a long revitalising sleep, the four aviators met for a briefing prior to the longest leg of their flight. Smithy had some sobering news. After carefully measuring the fuel that remained in the tanks after the long crossing from San Francisco, he had been able to calculate that with all tanks brim full, in still air, the *Southern Cross* had a range of 4590 kilometres, without reserves. It was 5070 kilometres to Fiji.

On paper, they could not make it. On paper, they would come down in the sea, 480 kilometres short of Suva.

But he was nonetheless optimistic. A following breeze would increase their range significantly, he told them and, in any case, it was too late to back out now. They should go. The US Navy offered to lend them a rubber dinghy, complete with paddles and inflation bottle, but Smithy declined with thanks; it was too heavy. Still buoyed by their recent triumph, they all concurred. They would cast their fate to the winds.

But Charles Ulm was not prepared to rely entirely on the vagaries of the weather. At the Bernice P. Bishop Museum in Honolulu, he sought advice on islands along their track where they could land should their fuel run out. The curator suggested two places and provided sketch maps. Canton Island, among the Phoenix Islands of Kiribati, was a coral atoll with a narrow rim surrounding a lagoon. Enderbury Island was uninhabited, covered by palm trees and outcrops of coral rock. There were several open sandy areas on Canton where an aircraft might possibly be put down.[10] Ulm did not relish the prospect of having to make a forced landing at either place in the middle of the night, but he was at least satisfied that he had done his best to cover every contingency.

The next day they flew to the island of Kauai, about an hour west of Honolulu. Here, Keith Anderson had recommended the

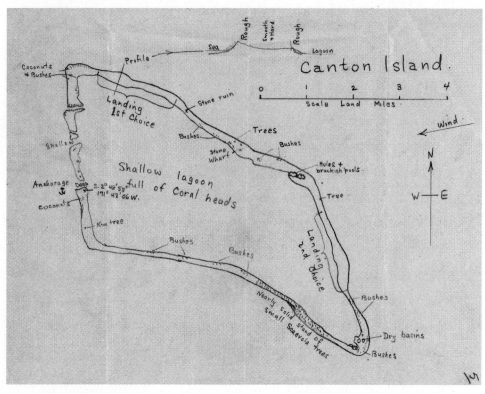

The sketch map of Canton Island, one of two possible emergency landing places should *Southern Cross* run short of fuel on the long sector to Fiji. A diversion would almost certainly have resulted in a crash landing. Mitchell Library, State Library of NSW

long expanse of Barking Sands as the best place for an over-loaded take-off and, at Ulm's behest, the Air Corps had graded the beach, creating about 1500 metres of level sand. Drums of fuel had been brought in by boat and, when the aircraft had been towed into position at the downwind end of the beach, the long process of refuelling commenced.

The *Southern Cross* was not the only aircraft at Barking Sands. A three-engine Fokker from the US Army Air Corps, and two other machines—the *Aloha* and the *Woolaroc*, which had both made the crossing from San Francisco during the Dole Race—had been flown in to lend support.

The press attention was unrelenting and Kingsford Smith found himself at the centre. He didn't seek the limelight, but he dominated the headlines nevertheless.

Busy attending to the details of the next leg of their flight, Ulm didn't seem to mind, but Kingsford Smith was embarrassed and attempted to set the record straight in a cable to *The Sun*.

MY PARTNER CHARLES ULM WHO WRITES THE STORY OF OUR FLIGHT SEEMS TO NEGLECT MENTIONING HIMSELF STOP LET ME SAY THAT FLIGHT COULD NOT HAVE BEEN EVER COMMENCED WITHOUT CHARLES STOP HIS PREPARATORY ORGANISATION OF FLIGHT HAS BORNE FRUIT AND OUR PLANS MOVE AHEAD WITHOUT ANY HITCH STOP HIS EXPERT KNOWLEDGE OF EVERY DEPARTMENT CONNECTED WITH FLIGHT AND HIS TIRELESS EFFORTS ARE GREATLY RESPONSIBLE FOR ANY SUCCESS WE ACHIEVE AND I COULD NOT WISH FOR A BETTER MATE AS RELIEF PILOT ON TOMORROW'S LONG HOP[11]

At about a quarter past five the next morning, Charles Ulm sat in the co-pilot's seat listening to the three Wright Whirlwinds ticking over. Above his head in the wing tanks, and in the cabin behind him, was the heaviest load of fuel that they had ever asked the *Southern Cross* to carry; enough to keep them in the air for at least 33 hours; enough, they hoped, to take them to Fiji. More than a kilometre of freshly graded sand stretched ahead, and Ulm knew they would need every centimetre of it.

Kingsford Smith gave her some power. The engines snarled in response, and the tyres bulged under the load as the wheels began to turn. Acceleration was sluggish, and it seemed to take ages to reach forty knots. Smithy concentrated on keeping her straight while Ulm maintained pressure on the throttle levers. Sixty-five knots. Seventy. The wing was beginning to do its work, partly relieving the undercarriage of its load.

The end of the beach was approaching. Smithy eased her off gently, and she obeyed him, but *Southern Cross* was not yet ready to fly. She rose briefly and touched down again. The undercarriage legs flexed alarmingly and bounced her back into the air. She sank again. There was no sand left now . . . just thin air, a short drop.

Then, the sea.

But as she sank, she gained a few precious extra knots of airspeed and the formula of flight at last began to work. The wing assumed its burden and held her as the wave tops flashed by beneath the spinning wheels.

Ulm breathed a sigh of relief and noted the time of take-off for his log: 5.22 a.m. on 3 June 1928. They were airborne on the longest non-stop overwater journey yet attempted, through skies that had never known the sound of aircraft engines.[12] He and Smithy shook hands.

The *Southern Cross* was very heavy; in the first five minutes they were able to climb only 250 feet. The air was bumpy, further stressing the overloaded wing.

At first they headed south from Kauai to intercept the radio beam from Wheeler Field, which had been turned towards Fiji for their benefit. Warner unwound his aerial to pick up the signals, but they were so low he was concerned it might hit the sea. At his request, Kingsford Smith coaxed *Southern Cross* up to 500 feet, when the A signals from the beam came in loud and clear. Guided by messages from Warner, Smithy began a gentle turn to intercept the beam and put them onto the course for Fiji.

It took them almost four hours to reach their planned cruising altitude of 3000 feet, where the north-east trade winds nudged them along at a useful groundspeed of almost 90 knots (170 kilometres per hour). About three hours into the flight, the port generator failed again, leaving them dependent upon the starboard unit, which on its own could not deliver enough power to operate the aircraft's radios and charge the receiver batteries.

Then the charging circuit blew. The resourceful Warner took the unit apart and spread the components out on the cabin floor, trying to find the fault, but to no avail. Finally, with the batteries completely flat, they were no longer able to receive. They lost the beam. This was disturbing, but they were not entirely cut off for the remaining generator was still delivering enough power for them to transmit, and Warner kept up a constant stream of messages advising concerned listeners around the world of their progress.

At twelve o'clock, and about 1000 kilometres from Honolulu, a smudge appeared on the horizon, denoting a change of weather. They were entering the notorious inter-tropical zone where prevailing winds from the northern and southern hemispheres meet in a ferocious swirl of storm clouds, violent turbulence and torrential rain. Its terrors had been known to mariners for centuries, but in 1928 few men had dared plumb its depths in an aeroplane.

As the *Southern Cross* droned serenely on, the smudge became a wall of cloud. The air grew stiflingly hot, and Lyon and Warner stripped to their underwear in an effort to keep cool. Soon the massive scale of the system became apparent and they found themselves confronted by towering cumulonimbus cloud stretching from horizon to horizon. It was awe-inspiring. The tops, shaped like anvils, reached into the stratosphere, well above the altitudes that *Southern Cross* could achieve. The cloud base hung low above an ink-blue, heaving sea, the surface of which was riven by curtains of driving rain.

They could not go around this weather. They could not climb over it and they could not sneak under it. The only way to get to Fiji was to fly through it, come what may, and this is what Kingsford Smith elected to do.

Her engines blaring defiantly, the *Southern Cross* plunged into the cloud, to be instantly enveloped in a maelstrom. Unseen forces went to work, picking them up, dropping them, catching them, dropping them again, tossing them from side to side, making them nauseous, confounding their senses until there was no up and no down, just a dazzling whiteout, a violent, whirling, shapeless, endless void.

Without seatbelts, they clung to anything they could grab onto. Seatbelts would have been of no use anyway, because the seats themselves were not secured to the floor. Everything loose became a missile. It was terrifying. Nobody on board had ever been called upon to endure such turbulence, but somehow, using only his rudimentary instruments, Kingsford Smith was able to keep them from spinning out of control into the waiting sea. The strain on the airframe was enormous, but the Fokker's massive wooden wing was immensely strong and saw them through.

After several hours of struggle, it was over. Without any warning, they emerged from the clouds to find themselves in clear air. The turbulence ceased. *Southern Cross* was cruising above a calm blue sea.

They had no idea where they were, so Harry Lyon took a sun shot and soon had them back on course. At 5.30 p.m. he estimated they had flown 1240 miles, one-third of the way to Fiji.[13] They still did not know if they would have enough fuel to allow them to complete their journey; when they reached the Phoenix Islands they would have to decide whether to put down at Enderbury Island, which lay close to their track, or to press on.

At dusk, another weather front loomed ahead, this time presenting an even more menacing prospect, the clouds pulsing with lightning. Not wishing to subject the *Southern Cross* to such demonic forces again, Smithy turned away in a steady, circling climb; this time they would try to fly over the weather. They were expending fuel without advancing towards their destination, but it was the price of survival.

At 8000 feet he levelled off. This was as high as they could go. Smithy turned once more towards the weather front. Cumulonimbus still towered above them. They had no choice but to plunge into it. This time they had to endure the turbulence in darkness, punctuated by blinding flashes of lightning. The windshield began to leak and Ulm and Smithy were soon wet through. At 8000 feet it was bitterly cold.

Once again, Kingsford Smith's phenomenal flying skills prevailed and by eight o'clock they had left the worst of the weather behind. Ulm made a note in his log: 'Sighted the good old Southern Cross above our Port Bow. Moon up also. Alt 8000. Above impenetrable clouds.'

They were now in the southern hemisphere and the significance of this was not lost on Charles Ulm. 'Stars are popping out all over the Heavens. But our group of Heavenly bodies the SC looks best to us.'

Now that the flying conditions had improved somewhat, he was able to relieve Smithy at the controls: 'Both had a refreshing doze—one doesn't really sleep when off duty on a job like this but even 10 mins shut eye is helpful.' Their instrument dash light failed so they used a hand torch.[14]

At midnight, Lyon sent a note forward advising that they were over Enderbury Island, although he could not see it in the gloom. It was clear to him, as navigator, that it was time for Kingsford Smith and Ulm, as co-commanders, to make a decision. A forced landing at Enderbury would almost certainly end in a crash. Even if somebody picked up their SOS, help would be a long time coming, and there would be no possibility of taking off again. Their dream would amount to no more than a pile of coral sand. The alternative was to take an enormous chance and go for fame and fortune.

For Smithy and Ulm it was a no brainer: they would press on for Fiji.

Although the decision had been made, Kingsford Smith became increasingly worried about their fuel. According to his reckoning, they had enough to take them, at most, 400 miles (650 kilometres). Fiji was more than 700 miles (1100 kilometres) away. Unless they picked up a good strong tailwind, they were going to come down in the drink. To make matters worse, they didn't know exactly where they were; high clouds had made it impossible for Harry to take a star sight. Smithy sent an anxious query aft via the message stick: 'Harry, can't you get a star position at all? Or can't Jim get a radio bearing? Getting pretty serious if we don't get one in a few hours.'[15]

At dawn, when they used the hand pump to transfer the last of their fuel from the tank in the cabin, they discovered that they had more than they thought.

Fate had smiled upon them. The winds had been favourable. They could reach Fiji!

Lyon sent a message forward to Ulm: 'Chas, when Jim Warner and I get back to U.S. we sure are going to try to have Smitty made president.'[16]

There was an embarrassing moment for a stressed Jim Warner during the final hours. Already stripped down to a one-piece undergarment in the steamy tropical heat, he was squatting over a newspaper once again when they hit some turbulence. The floor dropped violently, then lifted. The consequences were messy, and he spent the rest of the journey stark naked.

They made landfall at Vanua Levu, the second largest island in the Fiji group, and flew on for the town of Suva on Viti Levu, over a deep blue ocean studded with myriad islands, palm-fringed beaches, aquamarine lagoons and waves breaking white on fringing reefs. Ulm passed Smithy a note: 'The rest is easy. It's hard to realise it's over and that, at the moment, we are exceedingly famous.'[17] Indeed they were, for the whole world had been listening to Jim Warner.

One small task remained: Smithy had to put the *Southern Cross* down safely on an area the size of a postage stamp.

CHAPTER 8

An act of sportsmanship, an act of grace

The governor had declared a public holiday in Suva, to enable as many people as possible to witness the historic landing, and Fijians, Indians and Europeans had turned out in their thousands, many excitedly anticipating their first encounter with an aeroplane. As the *Southern Cross* circled the capital, Ulm was relieved to see that, as he had requested, uniformed police had erected rope barriers at Albert Park to contain the crowd, and white flags had been placed to indicate the longest available landing run.

Kingsford Smith, however, took one look, thought the whole thing highly problematic, and flew away in search of a beach. What he needed was a long stretch of hard sand, but the tide was in and he couldn't find one so, with fuel dangerously low, he headed back to Albert Park. He had no alternative now. After 34 hours in the air, he had to summon the energy to put the *Southern Cross* down, and bring her safely to a stop, in the length of a couple of rugby fields. The brakes had been removed back in San Francisco because Kingsford Smith had decided that they were too heavy. This was going to be one of the most difficult landings that he had ever made.

On their final turn over the bay, Ulm caught a glimpse of the government launch *Pioneer* that he had requested to stand by in case they came down in the water. At such times he was acutely aware of his subordinate position in the right-hand seat. He had done everything he could to organise things on the ground; their fate was in Smithy's hands now.

The park was situated on the beachfront and bordered on its other sides by rising ground, tall palm trees and stately colonial buildings. The only feasible approach was from the sea and even this was partially obstructed by a road and the Grand Pacific Hotel. To stand any chance of stopping in the available length, Smithy needed to approach at the lowest possible airspeed, just above a stall, so he ordered Warner and Lyon to move to the tail to change the balance of the aircraft. This was easier said than done, because the plywood floor did not extend the full length of the cabin. The navigator and wireless operator, one in his underwear, one stark naked, left their workstations and clambered aft to cling like monkeys to the tubular framework in the tail. A slip would mean disaster, because the fabric floor would not support a man's weight.

Kingsford Smith brought the *Southern Cross* in low and slow, cleared the hotel, crossed over the road, and put her down decisively on the grass. She bounced once and ran on, slowing, but it soon became clear that she was not going to stop before the fence at the top of the park. At the last moment, with a bootfull of rudder and a burst of power, Smithy neatly ground-looped her between two trees. The aircraft ran into a soft patch and came to an abrupt stop.

The tail rose, dislodging Warner, who lost his handhold and fell clean through the fabric. He hit the ground hard and lay in a heap like a rag doll. The tail came down and, as Smithy opened the throttles to taxi away, the tail skid missed the unconscious, naked radioman by centimetres. Aghast, a nursing sister in the crowd broke through the barricade to render first aid. He was soon on his feet again, her cape around his waist to preserve his modesty.

It would not be Jim Warner's last unconventional arrival during this long journey.

Colonial officials in pith helmets guided them to their parking place and, as Smithy cut the engines, the crowd surged forward, forcing the police to link arms to keep them back.

Charles Ulm scribbled a cable for transmission to *The Sun*. Only a portion has survived, but it makes fascinating reading.

ATTEMPT TO SAVE HER STOP SHELL CRASH THE PITY OF IT TO COME 3000 MILES AND THEN CRASH THAT GLORIOUS SHIP STOP SHES INTO THE HILL AT WHAT

A HELLISH SPEED HES TURNING HER SHE WILL GO ON
HER NOSE HE IS GETTING HER ROUND WHAT A GROUND-
LOOP HE IS ROUND THANK GOD HE IS ROUND WHAT
A WONDERFUL EFFORT HE HAS STOPPED HE IS CLEAR
OF THE TREE BY A FEW FEET STOP THANK GOD STOP
I NEVER WANT TO SEE ANOTHER LANDING LIKE THAT
OLD MAN IT IS TOO MUCH AT THE END OF 33 HOURS
OF WAITING[1]

Obviously composed while the adrenaline was pumping, and written in the present tense, the cable evokes the immediacy and urgency of a live radio broadcast, even though it was intended to be reproduced in print. It is a testament to Ulm's natural flair for publicity.[2]

Despite their fatigue, the crew of the *Southern Cross* were exultant. They had just spent a day and a half in the air, travelling more than 5070 kilometres in the longest continuous over-water flight ever made.

They emerged from the aircraft to a rousing welcome. Although deafened, unshaven, grimy, ravenous and totally exhausted, they had to endure the anticipated round of speeches delivered by local dignitaries eager to bask in the reflected glory.

News of their arrival in Suva was quickly cabled around the world and the story filled front pages on both sides of the Pacific. As the pilot of the *Southern Cross*, Charles Kingsford Smith naturally attracted most of the attention. His modesty, ready smile and laid-back manner quickly established him as a favourite of the press and public alike. Somewhat embarrassed that he was attracting more than his fair share of the limelight, Smithy sent a cable to *The Sun*:

PARTICULARLY REQUEST YOU REPORT MY APPRECIATION OF MAGNIFICENT ORGANISATION AND PREPARATION BY MY COCOMMANDER ULM STOP HIS INDEFATIGABLE WORK AND PRACTICE WITH ME RELIEVING AT CONTROLS HAS HELPED IMMENSELY STOP SPECIALLY PROTEST RECEIVING SO MUCH INDIVIDUAL CREDIT[3]

Lyon and Warner quickly became popular too, because of their readiness to make jokes with the press and bystanders. But Charles Ulm did not smile easily and came across as intense and businesslike. When somebody in the crowd asked whether their next stop would be Brisbane or Sydney, he snapped, 'Give us a chance. We do not know yet.'[4]

Ulm's irritability was understandable for he had a lot on his mind. Firstly, they had to find a beach suitable for take-off. The final stage of their journey would be the shortest of the trip, about 20 hours, so they would not need full tanks, but the *Southern Cross* would still require a substantial stretch of good hard sand. The beach at Naselai had been suggested and Smithy would have to go there to check it out. If it was suitable, Ulm would arrange transport for their drums of fuel. Then they would fly the *Southern Cross* there at low tide, when the sand was firm. They would need men standing by to haul her up the beach before the tide came in, and then, as it ebbed, to move her back. They would then have just a few hours to refuel on the hard sand and take-off before the tide turned yet again.

These were all operational matters and would be resolved in due course. But a more difficult problem was emerging: what to do with the Americans?

Under the terms of their contract, Harry Lyon and Jim Warner's employment was due to end at Fiji and passages had been booked on the *Aorangi* for their return to the United States.

But circumstances had changed. Because of the wide media coverage, the general public regarded the crew of the *Southern Cross* as a four-man team and, when it was rumoured in the press that the Americans would be returning to the United States by sea, there were rumblings about disloyalty. In Australia, questions were even asked in federal parliament.

When he read about it in the paper, Smithy's father, William Kingsford Smith, was concerned too. In his opinion, if the rumours were true, such behaviour was distinctly un-Australian and not worthy of his son. He sent a personal message to Smithy. The actual cable has not survived, but Tom Warner, Jim's son, told aviation historian Ian Mackersey that the message was blunt: 'Unless you bring the Americans, don't bother coming on to Australia.'[5]

The public disquiet worried Ulm. While he was the first to admit that Lyon and Warner had done a first-class job under very difficult conditions, in his eyes they had done so as employees, not partners, so it was within his rights to pay them off. He could see nothing wrong with it.

He would not miss Lyon, whose natural charm, upper class American accent and dry sense of humour tended to draw more than his share of media attention. He was an excellent navigator, but they could get by without him on the next stage: Australia was a wide target.

Ulm viewed Jim Warner in a different light. Since they left San Francisco, Warner had done more than merely receive and transmit messages and tune radio beacons. Warner had emerged as his conduit to the press and Ulm was beginning to realise that he was indispensible to effective public relations. He began to entertain the possibility of taking him on to Australia.

He was not happy about it. It was his cherished dream that the *Southern Cross* would complete the journey with an all-Australian crew and that their ultimate arrival in Sydney would be an all-Australian triumph. But now it seemed that public opinion was about to dictate otherwise.

Thoroughly enjoying his role as intrepid aviator—the centre of attention at a seemingly never-ending succession of social gatherings in Suva—Smithy was in an expansive mood. He told Ulm that he could see no reason why Lyon and Warner should not both come with them to Australia. They had shared the risks, why should they not share the limelight? Ulm did not agree and he had a final card up his sleeve.

When all four men met the following evening, he announced that Harry and Jim would be coming to Australia, but by sea.

It was a delaying tactic, the same ruse that he had employed to prevent Anderson and Hitchcock sharing the triumph of the around-Australia flight.

But Harry Lyon saw through Ulm's subterfuge. He quickly realised that by the time their ship docked, the arrival in Sydney of the *Southern Cross* would be old news. The fanfare would be over. Ulm and Kingsford Smith would have taken the lion's share of the glory and he and Jim would be yesterday's men left with the crumbs.

That afternoon, at a civic reception, he had heard Ulm say, 'I am telling you on behalf of myself and Smithy that we would have been cold meat but for the aid of our two American friends.'[6]

For Harry, such blatant hypocrisy was the last straw. He had been drinking and his dislike for Charles Ulm, which had been simmering for some time, suddenly exploded into blazing anger. He leaped up, slammed Ulm hard against the wall and held him there with an elbow to his throat, brandishing a clenched fist under his nose. Sensing that blood was about to be spilt, Smithy jumped to his feet and pushed them apart. He ordered Harry to settle down and announced that Harry and Jim would both be flying with them to Australia.

As always, Smithy had the final say.

The next morning, Ulm engaged a local solicitor to draw up a new agreement for Lyon and Warner to sign. William Hunt, a retired aeronautical engineer who had known Lyon well, told Ian Mackersey that he had seen the agreement.[7] It was an intimidating document that went to inordinate lengths to ensure that Lyon and Warner would not benefit in any way from the rewards of the flight. It declared that Kingsford Smith and Ulm, as 'owners' of the *Southern Cross*, had 'incurred a personal liability of upwards of $50,000 to mount a Pacific flight in the interests of aviation and for the promotion of amity and communication between the United States of America and the Commonwealth of Australia'. This was misleading, at best: Captain Hancock was the legal owner of the *Southern Cross* at that time. The document further stated that Lyon had already been paid $1767, and Warner $1267. (Presumably Warner had been paid less because he commenced work after Lyon.) These payments terminated all the owners' current obligations.

In tortuous legal language, meticulously drafted to close all possible loopholes, the agreement made it absolutely clear that Lyon and Warner were in no sense partners in the Pacific venture, but paid employees. As such, they could not expect to share in any rewards that might eventuate.

Furthermore, to 'foster good feeling between the USA and Australia', the Americans were invited to proceed to Brisbane, but no further, as an 'act of sportsmanship'. On arrival in Brisbane, Lyon and Warner would each be paid a further $500, as an 'act of grace'.

The final clause really rubbed it in: 'The said Lyon and Warner hereby record their appreciation of the generous performance of the owners . . . and of the owners' sportsmanlike act in inviting them to proceed in the *Southern Cross* to Brisbane.'

While he no doubt found the language patronising and offensive, Jim Warner, who had been in master–servant relationships all his life, signed the document.

But as a man who knew the difference between leadership and coercion, Harry Lyon would have found Ulm's attitude very disappointing. In his eyes, all four men aboard the *Southern Cross* had faced great danger together and had won through. Now they were on the verge of completing the first flight across the Pacific Ocean. When completed, it would be a magnificent achievement and they should have been eagerly anticipating a triumphant arrival in Sydney. But Ulm's mercenary, legalistic approach had taken the sheen from the whole enterprise.

Harry signed anyway.

Charles Ulm almost certainly saw the situation differently, for the previous months of struggle would have affected him more than he knew. In his eyes, unless a man had shared his privations, unless he too had pounded the pavements of San Francisco seeking funds, unless he had suffered the hunger pangs and high anxiety, unless he had endured cold, sleepless nights in draughty hangars, there was no way that he could ever hope to participate in the rewards. Not Harry Lyon. Not Jim Warner. And certainly not Keith Anderson.

CHAPTER 9

'This is no ordinary aeroplane!'

The *Southern Cross* took off from Naselai Beach on Friday, 8 June 1928, for the last stage of their epic flight. This was the shortest stretch—2700 kilometres—so they were not carrying a full load of fuel.

They were all in good spirits. The sky was blue, the winds were fair, and the nose of the *Southern Cross* was pointed towards Australia.

As they settled into their familiar routine, Charles Ulm reached for his notebook and began to draft a message.

Well, here we are on the way again! Everything is O.K. In 19 or 20 hours we will be in dear old Aussie again. Landing at Brisbane will be the culmination of 10 months' hard work and the realisation of our ambition to be the first to really cross the Pacific by air.

Smithy is at the controls with a sandwich in one hand, Ulm is writing you a radio, while our two efficient, loyal and alert colleagues are a few feet behind us, each at his job.

When we actually started the flight at Oakland we wondered whether Australia would want to kiss or kick us on our arrival, in view of so much adverse criticism against out undertaking. But we have been so overwhelmed with kind congratulatory cablegrams and wireless reports that we feel our fellow Australians agree that we were right in sticking it out and completing our self-appointed task.

It was time to tell the world about their benefactor.

Now that we are sure of success we wish to announce to the world that we could never have made this flight without the generosity and wonderful help given us by Captain G. Allan Hancock, of Los Angeles, California. For months we had fought against our difficulties, giving up all hope, but we were practically counted out when we met Captain Hancock, who then, in the most unselfish manner, saw us through, details of which cannot be given here. But we take this opportunity of publicly thanking him in the most modern manner, that is, by radio, from the first aeroplane crossing the Pacific Ocean.[1]

Soon after nightfall the weather changed and storm clouds once more built up ahead. Bitter experience had taught Smithy the futility of attempting to surmount massive banks of cumulonimbus and they could not fly under it as the cloud base sat low upon the sea. There was no alternative but to tackle it head-on. The *Southern Cross* had done it once before, she could do it again.

For the next two hours they endured the worst weather of the trip. It was yet another violent roller-coaster ride, this time with turbulence so severe that Harry Lyon feared the wing would collapse under the strain.[2] Their flying suits were soon wet through and Smithy was concerned that the torrential rain could penetrate the magnetos and stop the engines. Powerful updrafts carried them as high as 9000 feet, where it was bitterly cold, and several times they dropped 400 feet in downdrafts.

Ulm sent an urgent message back to Warner: 'Jim, don't report this terrific storm we are in. It would worry our people to death. Will tell you should things become very serious.'[3]

In response, Warner screwed his Morse key down. Concerned listeners who understood such things found the ensuing continuous screech reassuring: while the *Southern Cross* remained *on* the air, they knew it was still *in* the air.

Finally, in the early hours of the morning, they left the storm behind. Ulm let *The Sun* know what they had just survived. 'Smithy and I are wet through but as soon as the moon comes up and blind flying ends for the night we will sit and have a spot of our emergency ration of whiskey. I am too cold to write more. We have no gloves.'[4]

After hours spent hunched over his instruments, Smithy passed a weary note to Ulm: 'If anybody hereafter suggests to me that I go practise blind flying, I'm going to caress them gently on the skull with a pisspot.'[5]

They had no idea where they were, because in the confusion of the storm it had been impossible for Harry Lyon to plot the many course changes. His best estimate was that they were a long way south of their intended track. To complicate matters, the port generator decided to maintain its reputation by failing again and, without battery power, Jim Warner could not pick up signals from radio beacons.

He could still transmit and the message that he sent caused some concern:

EXACT POSITION UNKNOWN[6]

This was not as dire as it sounded: Lyon decided that the best course of action was simply to head due west, and after making landfall, follow the coast to Brisbane.

At about eight o'clock, a thin grey line appeared on the horizon.

Realisation dawned. Australia!

They had done it! They had flown the Pacific!

In the cockpit, Smithy and Ulm shook hands and, after they received the welcome news via the message stick, Warner and Lyon did likewise.

As they drew nearer, the coastline took on more detail and Smithy identified the small town of Ballina, 180 kilometres south of Brisbane—by happy coincidence, Jo Ulm's home town.

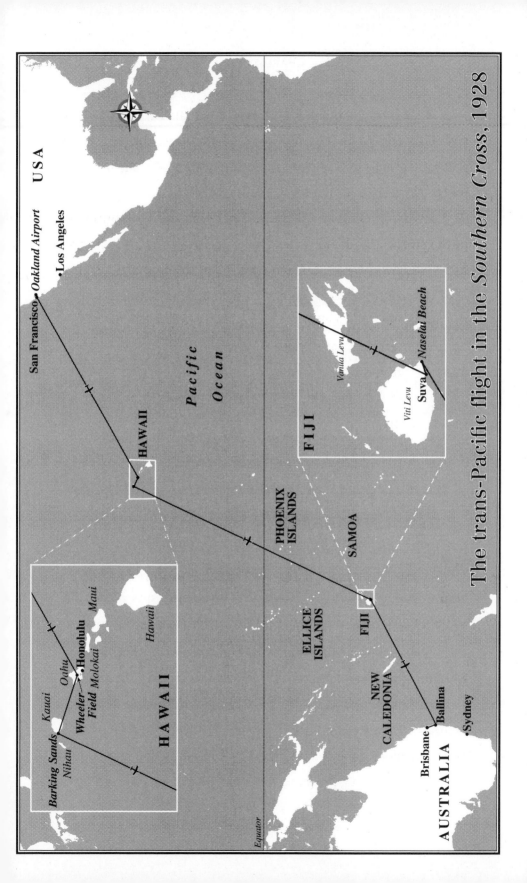

The trans-Pacific flight in the *Southern Cross*, 1928

They had expected a warm reception in the Queensland capital, but the welcome that awaited them was beyond their wildest dreams. A flight of seven biplanes came out to meet them and fell into formation around the *Southern Cross* like bees around their queen. As they approached the airport at Eagle Farm, a few kilometres from the city centre, they were amazed to see the morning sunlight glinting upon the roofs of hundreds of parked cars. The surrounding paddocks were jam-packed with vehicles and traffic on the approach roads was at a standstill. On the airfield itself, a large crowd was gathered behind a rope barrier and, as Smithy banked, the aviators looked down onto a sea of upturned faces and a forest of waving arms. Although those aboard the *Southern Cross* couldn't hear them, fifteen thousand people were cheering themselves hoarse.

They had gathered there on that frosty morning of Saturday, 9 June 1928, largely because of Charles Ulm's natural ability as a publicist. As the *Southern Cross* had made her way across the Pacific, he had penned the press releases and Jim Warner had tapped them out. All over Australia millions of people had been listening, missing meals, missing sleep, even missing work to keep track of their progress. It was a stunning demonstration of the power of radio broadcasting and it engendered a response that would not be seen again until people gathered around their television sets to witness the first landing on the moon 40 years later.

The *Southern Cross* had completed a journey of 11,950 kilometres in a flying time of 83 hours and 50 minutes. By any standard, it was a magnificent achievement and, at 10.15 a.m., as Kingsford Smith brought the big Fokker in for a perfect landing, car horns honked in salute and the cheering began anew. They completed their landing run and, as Smithy taxied back, excitement reached fever pitch.

The flimsy rope barrier gave way and the crowd began to spill out onto the airfield. Fearing that somebody could be decapitated by the whirling propellers, a uniformed inspector attempted to arrest the human tide, waving his arms and shouting, 'Get back! Get back! This is no ordinary aeroplane!'[7]

They completely ignored him.

It was utter chaos.

And then a strange thing happened. Some distance down the runway, the *Southern Cross* came to a stop. The cabin door opened, two men climbed out, and then, with a burst of throttle, the aircraft moved on towards the advancing throng.

Harry Lyon and Jim Warner were left standing on the grass.

They were smartly attired in brand-new dinner suits, brightly coloured bow ties, and Warner was wearing a Panama hat. They did not look at all like intrepid, ocean-conquering aviators, and at first they were mistaken for officials. But Norman Ellison, the aviation correspondent for Sydney's *Daily Guardian* newspaper, had seen them disembark and guessed who they were. He sensed a story. Why did they leave the aircraft prematurely? Elbowing his way through the milling onlookers, he introduced himself to the Americans and sought answers.

Harry Lyon's explanation was simple: this was an Australian affair and he and Warner were keeping out of it. As Ellison tried to convince them to change their minds, somebody in the crowd heard their American accents and the decision was taken out of their hands. Lyon and Warner were hoisted onto burly Australian shoulders and carried off to join Kingsford Smith and Ulm and the waiting dignitaries. The man carrying Jim Warner called proudly, 'Have a look at him! He's the boy that worked the keys!'[8]

As he watched them go, Norman Ellison's curiosity remained unsatisfied. He resolved to speak with Lyon and Warner again.

The four aviators were driven in an open car through streets lined with cheering people to the Brisbane Town Hall, where the Queensland premier, William McCormack, told the assembled audience that Kingsford Smith, Ulm, Lyon and Warner had completed one of the most amazing feats in history. 'It has done something very material, I believe, to bring closer together the English-speaking peoples upon which, after all, civilisation depends.'

A message was received from the Australian prime minister. Addressing his remarks to Charles Kingsford Smith, Charles Ulm and their 'gallant comrades', Stanley Bruce had written, 'We are grateful that in this achievement you have been associated with two citizens of our great sister democracy beyond the Pacific.

I ask you and your companions to accept a cheque of five thousand pounds in recognition of your epoch-making flight.'[9]

The rewards had started coming in.

Speaking in reply, Kingsford Smith said,

> This is a very big moment in our lives. It is the fulfilment of my life's greatest ambition. Mr Ulm is an equal co-leader in this expedition with me. We are very much overcome with emotion for the magnificent reception and the munificent donation by the government. This is a very wonderful thing indeed. We are particularly delighted and honoured to have our two Yankee friends come through with us. The flight was not an individual thing. It was the magnificent co-operation between four people who understood each other and worked together for the common good.

In the space of a few hours, Charles Kingsford Smith's prowess as a pilot, together with his modesty, easy-going manner, ready smile and craggy good looks again made him the focus of media attention. In contrast, Charles Ulm, in the words of a reporter from the Brisbane *Courier*, was 'the businessman of the party with a brusque, direct manner':

> He speaks with the curt rapidity of the machine gun. A suggestion that Captain Kingsford Smith should issue a message of greeting to the people of Queensland, to which the pilot showed signs of compliance, was instantly

vetoed by Mr Ulm who vouchsafed the information that the fliers were bound by newspaper contracts not to divulge any information concerning their flight.

It was becoming clear to the Australian media that, on the ground, Charles Ulm called the shots.

Early that evening, at Lennon's Hotel, there was a knock at Ulm's door as he dressed for a formal dinner. An official from the local aero club, who was acting as a liaison officer, informed him that a journalist named Norman Ellison wanted to see him and Smithy on an urgent matter. Ulm raised a dismissive hand, but the official persisted. Ellison had been talking to Lyon and Warner and had a few questions. Were Lyon and Warner flying on to Sydney? If not, why not? Had he and Harry Lyon had a falling out in Suva? What were the terms of their contract?

Ellison had also asked the official to deliver a message: if the plan was to leave Lyon and Warner behind in Brisbane, Ellison's paper, the Sydney *Daily Guardian*, would charter an aircraft and fly them to Sydney independently. They would time their arrival to coincide with that of Ulm and Smithy.

Warning bells sounded for Charles Ulm. Because *The Sun* held exclusive rights, the *Daily Guardian* had been denied access to any of the press releases that Warner had broadcast during the flight. But here, on the ground in Brisbane, Ulm realised that he could no longer control news stories relating to the *Southern Cross* or its crew. Norman Ellison was free to publish anything that he could dig up.

Best to cut this off at the pass.

A short time later, Ulm called a press conference at which he announced that, contrary to the rumours that were circulating, Harry Lyon and Jim Warner were not leaving the team. Tomorrow, they would fly in the *Southern Cross* to Sydney.

Meanwhile, on the other side of the Pacific, Captain Allan Hancock was also speaking to the press. Addressing reporters assembled aboard the *Oaxaca*, he announced that he intended to make a gift of the *Southern Cross* to Kingsford Smith and Ulm in recognition of their magnificent achievement. In addition, he would settle all outstanding debts relating to the Pacific crossing.

He said, 'Give me no credit for the successful flight. I merely saw an opportunity to advance the science of navigation in the air. Aeronautics have been advanced many years by their success.'[10]

CHAPTER 10

Rog

On the morning of Sunday, 10 June, 200,000 residents of Sydney converged upon Mascot aerodrome to witness the arrival of the *Southern Cross*. They came by car, by tram, and on foot, bringing traffic on Botany Road to a standstill.

The better vantage points were soon taken, and latecomers were forced to spill out into the market gardens that bordered the aerodrome. It had been raining and they found themselves ankle-deep in mud fighting off hordes of flying insects. It was a long, uncomfortable wait.

Shortly after three o'clock there was a stir, and then a chorus of excited shouts, as sharp-eyed onlookers caught their first glimpse of the big Fokker.

Instead of heading directly to Mascot, Smithy made a triumphant progress up the harbour from the heads, surrounded by an entourage of welcoming light aircraft. The sun glinted silver off the wing as he banked over the city centre and headed south to bring her in for a smooth landing.

The crowd pressed forward as the *Southern Cross* taxied in, but the New South Wales police, no doubt aware of the shambles at Brisbane, had mustered sufficient manpower to maintain control and the welcoming ceremony went ahead without incident. The flyers were then driven through cheering crowds to their hotel.

The Atlantic Union Oil Company, which had supplied the petrol and oil used on the flight, had reserved a suite of offices for Ulm and Kingsford Smith at their headquarters in the *Herald* Building at 66 Pitt Street in the heart of the city. Here, on the following day, they were introduced to a slim, smartly dressed young woman, Ellen Rogers, secretary to the managing director of Atlantic Union, who had been deputed to look after them.

Twenty-one-year-old Ellen could not believe her luck. She had made the pilgrimage to Mascot, but had been impeded by the crowd. By the time she had reached the airfield, it was all over including the shouting and the aviators were long gone. She had not even caught a glimpse of them. Now they were shaking her by the hand!

She did not have much time to think about it, because within hours Smithy and Ulm were scheduled to attend a civic reception at the Sydney Town Hall.

The place was packed with the good and the great, while those who could not find seats crowded the entrance lobby and spilled out into George Street. Kingsford Smith received a standing ovation when he rose to speak, but he kept his remarks short, confining himself to tributes to his parents, and expressions of gratitude to all those who had made the flight possible, before handing over to his co-commander.

Charles Ulm began by thanking *The Sun* and the Los Angeles *Examiner*, and then Alan Hancock. 'You probably don't know what the gift by Mr Hancock of the *Southern Cross* means to Smithy and me,' he said. 'It means nineteen thousand dollars, or four thousand pounds.'[1]

He then quite pointedly turned his attention to Keith Anderson:

> I also have a feeling of regret that Andy was not able to accompany us. It was he who suggested the name *Southern Cross* for the plane. I am very proud that he was associated with us in the early stages of the venture.
>
> What can we do in return? I think we can respond by, in some little way, furthering the cause of aviation. Aviation is more needed in Australia than in any other part of the world. We have long distances and small populations. I believe that the lesson of our flight will make Australia more air minded. We have the finest flying country in the world.

He reminded the audience of an article that he had written for *The Sun*, after the around-Australia flight, in which he had expressed his concerns about the security of Australia's vast and sparsely populated north. A well-organised enemy force, he believed, could 'in some months establish an inland flying base, so that it could attack every capital without anyone knowing where the attacks came from. The *Southern Cross* flight has shown that I was right. A plane with 5,000 miles' [8000 kilometres] range, carrying four or five tons of bombs, could do these things.'

It was something for people to think about.

Finally, he paid a carefully worded tribute to their navigator and radio operator. 'We lose our friends, Lyon and Warner on Thursday, and we regret losing them, but business engagements in America make it imperative that they go as soon as possible. Hearst Newspapers . . . is making a nation-wide appeal for them, and they must go there. If they get all the money in America it will not be enough for them.'

He neglected to say that Warner and Lyon had already been offered 'business engagements' in Australia, in the form of sponsorship deals, and that he had insisted that they refuse under the terms of their contract. Warner and Lyon appealed to Ulm, asking him to relax the terms of their contract, but he ignored them for ten days, by which time they were aboard ship on their way to America. Delay was a tactic that he used repeatedly.[2]

Despite his repeated fulsome praise for his colleagues at almost every public function that he attended, in private Ulm remained stubbornly resolute: within Australia, the spoils belonged to him and Kingsford Smith. As far as the general populace knew, all four aviators were participating in the financial rewards of the flight and he did nothing to disabuse them.

After speaking with Lyon and Warner in Brisbane, Norman Ellison no doubt knew the full story, but the *Daily Guardian* never published his article. In 1928, newspapers tended to treat celebrities more respectfully than they do in the twenty-first century. Ulm and Kingsford Smith were national heroes and to publish an article that was highly critical of Ulm was probably deemed unwise.

The money was rolling in. Apart from the award from the federal government, New South Wales Premier Bavin had guilty second thoughts and coughed up £4500, as originally promised, followed by an additional £2500. Readers donated £2500 to an appeal for the aviators in the pages of *The Sun*. A gala benefit performance of the stage show *Rio Rita* at the St James Theatre resulted in a packed house and £1000, with the aviators rewarding donors by making a personal appearance in the VIP box. Private donations from wealthy Australians also came in.

It is estimated that in all, Charles Kingsford Smith and Charles Ulm benefited from the flight of the *Southern Cross* across the Pacific Ocean to the extent of £30,000, the equivalent of AU$430,000 in 2018.

As well as money, there were tributes. From San Francisco, Locke Harper and Sidney Myer cabled:

> We who have been intimately associated with Ulm and Smith and know of their great mental and physical suffering here feel privileged to again send them our warmest congratulations and had it not been for Ulm's remarkable ability and tenacity Smith would never have had the opportunity of showing the world what a marvellous pilot he is.[3]

Frank Jordan, the Secretary of State for California, added his voice:

> We in California who have intimately known Smith and Ulm wish to express our great admiration for the flying ability of Smith and the untiring efforts of Ulm. No credit can be taken from Smith, but without the remarkable ability of Ulm the expedition would not have left our shores. Both are invincible.[4]

Lord Wakefield, the owner of the English company that manufactured the world-renowned Castrol Motor Oils, sent a cable to Smithy:

> Hearty congratulations to self, Ulm, and crew upon completing hazardous epoch-making flight America to Australia. Courageously conceived intrepidly completed combining sheer pluck and efficiency.[5]

Within a few years Lord Wakefield would prove to be a friend in need.

Many other official functions followed. Despite their celebrity status, the hectic pace and her heavy workload, Ellen Rogers enjoyed working with Kingsford Smith and Charles Ulm. Smithy was friendly and easygoing, but it soon became clear that he did not like the confines of an office. Apart from dealing in a desultory fashion with the fan mail that was pouring in, he avoided paperwork, preferring to spend his time entertaining visiting relatives and friends.

By contrast, Ulm was brisk and businesslike. As well as making innumerable phone calls, he kept Ellen busy taking dictation, typing up letters and dealing with people seeking interviews. She was very efficient, which was exactly what he liked, and they quickly established an excellent rapport. Miss Rogers became Rog, although she continued to call him Mr Ulm. It was the beginning of a close and respectful relationship that would last for the rest of his life and, touchingly, beyond. Charles Ulm would later write a thank-you note to Ellen Rogers praising her 'remarkable qualities': 'No words of mine can express adequately my appreciation of your truly splendid LOYALTY—ability, and energy.'[6]

A week or two after the triumphant return of the *Southern Cross* to Sydney, Bob Hitchcock arrived at the Atlantic Union office and asked to see Ulm and Smithy. He wanted the £1000 that he believed had been promised to him almost a year earlier, before the two flyers left for the United States.

They dismissed his claim out of hand. Kingsford Smith accused Hitchcock of dereliction of duty, in that he had been employed to maintain the two Bristol Tourers while they were overseas and had failed to do so. They were therefore under no obligation to pay him anything. Ulm washed his hands of the whole affair on the grounds that they had all been 'half sozzled' at the time the promise was made.[7]

It was a brief encounter. Hitchcock found himself back on Pitt Street, empty handed, angry, disappointed and determined to seek justice.

When Keith Anderson turned up bearing solicitor's letters they were forced to take him more seriously. Anderson presented two identical documents addressed severally to Ulm and Kingsford Smith, and obviously drafted by Arthur Hilliard, in which he claimed the sum of US$13,000 as a creditor and reminded them that his family had invested at least US$3000 in the Pacific flight.

As usual, Smithy was reluctant to become involved in a business discussion, but Ulm was in his element. He told Anderson in no uncertain terms that as he had ignored all their requests to return to America to participate in the flight, he had forfeited his share in the *Southern Cross* together with any rewards that had accrued. Keith could therefore forget about the US$13,000: the only thing they owed him was a portion of the US$3000 that his family had contributed. Ulm then wrote out a cheque for one third of that amount in Australian pounds, but Anderson, who had been warned by Hilliard not to accept anything but the full US$13,000, refused to take the money and walked out, leaving no doubt that, as far as he was concerned, the matter was far from settled.

A few days later Smithy and Ulm received a letter from Anderson demanding a full statement of accounts relating to the purchase and preparation of the *Southern Cross* for the Pacific flight. Ulm refused.

The legal battle would drag on for months.

CHAPTER 11

A pair of wings

In the euphoric period that followed the Pacific flight, there were calls for Smithy and Ulm to be given knighthoods. Ross and Keith Smith had been knighted after their England-to-Australia flight in 1919 and many people felt that the same honour should be bestowed upon the Pacific flyers. But the government stalled, possibly because Kingsford Smith and his wife were estranged. There was a stigma attached to divorce in those days and, although the state of Smithy's marriage was not widely known, it is likely that the authorities wanted to avoid any hint of a scandal. In the circumstances, a knighthood for Charles Ulm was never a possibility.

They were however both awarded the Air Force Cross and given honorary commissions in the RAAF, Smithy as a squadron leader and Ulm as a flight lieutenant. This caused consternation within the service. The Chief of the Air Staff, Air Commodore Richard Williams, considered it wrong in principle. He believed that as Ulm and Kingsford Smith had never been members of the RAAF, other honours would have been more appropriate. He wrote, 'I would hardly have expected Sir Francis Chichester, who not so long ago sailed a yacht around the world—and was knighted for it—to be appointed to a commission in the Royal Navy.'[1]

The honorary commissions may have displeased him, but, when both Kingsford Smith and Ulm began appearing at official functions wearing pilot's wings, he was outraged, declaring, 'People must never wear wings unless they have earned them.'[2]

Smithy was perfectly entitled to display the prized insignia for he had earned the right in the Royal Flying Corps, but Ulm didn't even possess a private pilot's licence.

Writing in *Aircraft,* Edward Hart, who had not been a fan of Charles Ulm since the days of the Aviation Service Company, fulminated at Ulm's 'effrontery in putting up a pair of wings on a RAAF tunic without the least authority'.[3]

Ulm took them down.

For Ulm and Kingsford Smith, the successful crossing of the Pacific Ocean in the *Southern Cross* had seen a long-held dream fulfilled. The glittering prize that had seemed so unattainable during those late-night discussions at Lavender Bay was now well and truly theirs.

For Smithy, the journey in all probability had been an end in itself, because he lived for flying. But while he also drew deep satisfaction from their achievement, Charles Ulm now had his eyes on another goal: the establishment of an airline linking the capital cities of Australia.

He was well aware that the Pacific Crossing had been in no sense a 'proving flight'. He and Smithy had pushed the *Southern Cross* to the limits of its performance, flying at a level of risk far beyond anything that could be deemed acceptable for regular public transport across a vast ocean. But over shorter distances between Australia's capital cities, where outrageous loads of fuel were not necessary, he believed that the big Fokker, or aircraft like it, had the capacity to operate safely and to earn its keep; in fact he believed that it could make a profit. He and Smithy intended to make a non-stop flight from Melbourne to Perth to demonstrate its potential.

With Lyon and Warner now back in the United States, the flight across Australia would provide them with an opportunity to break in a new navigator and radio operator, because they also had the Tasman Sea in their sights and planned to take the *Southern Cross* to New Zealand.

Harold Litchfield, a navigation officer on the *Tahiti*, had been unavailable for the Pacific flight, but had now agreed to join them. While his job would be relatively straightforward, the shakedown flight would provide Tom McWilliams, their new radio operator, with an opportunity to familiarise himself with their sophisticated equipment. McWilliams was the superintendent of the Union Steamship Company's wireless training school in Wellington and Ulm and Smithy could see the public relations value in having a Kiwi on board.

In the middle of July, a new legal hurdle presented itself. Hearing of their proposed flight across Australia, Keith Anderson petitioned the Supreme Court seeking an injunction preventing the *Southern Cross* from being flown out of New South Wales. He also asked the court to declare that his original partnership with Kingsford Smith and Ulm still existed and demanded that the aeroplane be sold and a receiver be appointed to administer the partnership's assets.

Until the matter was resolved, Smithy and Ulm were effectively grounded.

However, all was not lost. In the first week in August, when the matter finally came before the Supreme Court in Equity, the chief judge ruled that the *Southern Cross* should only be within the jurisdiction of New South Wales when the full case came to trial.

Ulm and Smithy were now free to make their trans-Australia flight, but Anderson wasn't beaten yet. He asked his lawyer to seek an order that he be allowed to participate.

The flyers were appalled. This was madness!

Wisdom prevailed; the judge refused to issue the order on the grounds that if he allowed Anderson to fly, there could well be disruption in the cockpit. He was right, because Ulm would not have vacated the right-hand seat without a fight. The case was then adjourned, pending statements from Captain Hancock, Locke Harper and Harold Kingsford Smith in the United States.

Yet almost at once another hurdle loomed, this time in the shape of a writ from Hitchcock claiming his £1000. They shrugged it off; a decent King's Counsel could easily handle Bob Hitchcock.

After the marathon crossing of the Pacific, the flight to Perth was a relatively simple affair. Taking off from Point Cook in Melbourne, they covered the 3200 kilometres in 23 hours and 24 minutes, flying through the night in freezing rain.

The return flight offered a further opportunity to perfect their teamwork and, back in Sydney, they prepared to tackle the Tasman Sea.

Not to be outdone, Keith Anderson announced that he and Bob Hitchcock were about to leave in an attempt to break the England–Australia record, established by Bert Hinkler, of fifteen and a half days. They intended to use the remaining Bristol Tourer. This caused a stir in the Ulm–Kingsford Smith camp, for Smithy still owned a half share in the aircraft. Anderson had not asked his permission to take the Tourer on such a long and hazardous journey, but he decided not to stand in Andy's way, possibly for old time's sake. Charles Ulm had no financial interest in the Tourer, so he kept out of it. The less he had to do with Keith Anderson, the better.

As the sun set on 10 September 1929, the *Southern Cross* took off from the RAAF Station at Richmond, north-west of Sydney, and headed once more into the Pacific on the 1250-mile (2010-kilometre) crossing to Wellington, New Zealand.

About 500 miles (800 kilometres) out, they flew into a violent, unexpected storm, with torrential rain and violent turbulence. Both pilots were soon drenched and, for the first time, rain penetrated the cabin and partially disabled their radio gear. The trailing aerial was struck by lightning, which burnt out the transmitter, delivering McWilliams an incapacitating shock. He recovered sufficiently to try to improvise some form of rudimentary communication, but the outside world heard only spasmodic fragments of Morse code from the *Southern Cross* for the rest of the flight.

They had learned some lessons from the Pacific crossing. The pilots' chairs were now fastened to the floor and fitted with seatbelts, but, astonishingly, the chairs in the cabin were still completely unsecured. McWilliams and Litchfield struggled to maintain a handhold as the aircraft was tossed about in the turbulence, sometimes surging upwards for 2500 feet, before dropping with a violence that threatened to send them crashing through to the cabin ceiling. There were no workplace health and safety regulations in those days, but by modern standards any lawyer could assert that Kingsford Smith and Ulm were in breach of their duty of care.

And then there was the ice. As they were carried up to 10,000 feet, the windshield frosted over, and ice began to build up on exposed surfaces, adding weight and changing the shape of the wing, diminishing its ability to generate lift. The *Southern Cross* began to sink. The controls became sluggish. The airspeed indicator, which was one of Smithy's primary instruments when flying blind, suddenly went from 95 to zero.

Thinking that they were about to stall, he pushed the nose down. The indicator still showed zero, but a growing, terrifying roar of rushing air and the rapidly unwinding altimeter told him they were descending at breakneck speed towards the sea.

Suddenly Smithy realised what had happened; ice had blocked the Pitot tube, cutting off air pressure to the instrument's mechanism. He was now flying with no outside visual reference, no indication of airspeed, and with only the fluctuating engine rev counters to tell him whether they were climbing or diving. But worse was to come. Ice that had accumulated on the propellers began to break off in chunks, unbalancing them and causing violent vibrations that threatened to shake the engines from their mountings.

Fortunately, such conditions brought out the very best in Charles Kingsford Smith. In the right-hand seat, his co-commander could do little but hang on, white-knuckled, as Smithy's raw courage, steely determination and unparalleled flying ability brought them through.

Shortly before dawn they broke out into clear, warmer air. Almost immediately, the *Southern Cross* shed her load of ice and began to fly properly again. The airspeed indicator came to life. Litchfield took a sighting as the sun came up and to their surprise they found that they were only slightly off course.

Their arrival above Wellington, the nation's capital, caused a sensation, for it was the first international flight ever to arrive in

New Zealand. Despite the early hour, people rushed from their houses to wave and cheer as Smithy made a triumphant circuit of the city.

The airfield at Wellington could not accommodate the *Southern Cross,* so they headed south to Christchurch, which had the largest aerodrome in the country. More than 30,000 people were waiting to greet them and, in scenes reminiscent of their arrival in Brisbane, the crowds ignored the police and broke through the barriers to surround the aircraft as it taxied in. As they climbed down from the cockpit, Smithy and Ulm were seized and carried off shoulder high.

In the midst of their triumph they learned that Anderson and Hitchcock had come to grief. The old Tourer had suffered engine failure near Pine Creek in the Northern Territory, forcing Anderson to make a crash-landing into some trees. He was unhurt, but Bob Hitchcock had suffered a badly cut lip. The aircraft, damaged beyond repair, had been abandoned in the bush. Ulm would not have been surprised at the news; in his eyes, Keith Anderson had always been a lightweight and now he was emerging as a loser.

At a ceremony in Wellington, the prime minister of New Zealand, Gordon Coates, presented Smithy with a cheque for £2000. It was no doubt assumed that the money would be disbursed among the whole crew, particularly as McWilliams was a New Zealander, but this did not happen. Ulm and Kingsford Smith took £1000 each and their navigator and radio operator received nothing. Using the same strategy that he had employed for Lyon and Warner, before leaving Richmond, Ulm had required both Litchfield and McWilliams to sign contracts restricting them to a fee for their services and nothing more. It was all perfectly legal and straightforward. Charles Ulm was by now an old hand at this sort of thing.

They spent a month in New Zealand as honoured guests of the government and were flown around the country in three Bristol Fighters.

People waved as they passed over small towns and crowds gathered wherever they landed. Although the term was not then in vogue, they were treated like superstars and it appears that they behaved accordingly.

In public, their behaviour was impeccable. At official receptions they listened politely to the speeches and responded with modesty and apparent sincerity, even though they had said the same thing dozens of times before. Kingsford Smith had by this time developed a standard patter along with a repertoire of jokes that made him a favourite with the crowd. As always, Ulm played second fiddle and usually spoke in a more serious vein.

In private, it was a different story. There were parties almost every night with long drinking sessions that often resulted in broken furniture. Smithy's womanising became legendary within aviation circles and it was rumoured that he and Ulm had both brought female companions over from Sydney by sea. But the New Zealand press, respectful of their achievements and perhaps overawed by their celebrity, maintained a respectful distance. Few details of their carousing were ever published.[4]

When the time came to leave New Zealand they chose Blenheim, on the north-east of the South Island, as their departure point, to avoid having to fly over the Southern Alps. They were forced to wait for a month for suitable weather and Ulm put the time to good use. The New Zealand Permanent Air Force provided him with some flying instruction.

Now formally qualified, he could at last put up a set of wings and wear them with pride.

CHAPTER 12

Airline interruptus

To avoid the horror of another night above the Tasman, they planned their departure from Blenheim so as to complete most of the journey by daylight, but soon after take-off they encountered a ferocious headwind. It took them 23 hours to make the crossing and, by the time they reached the Australian coast, night had fallen and they were almost out of fuel. To complicate matters Sydney was blanketed by fog and low cloud and they could not locate Mascot aerodrome despite repeatedly asking for a searchlight to be switched on to mark its position.

Finally, through a fortuitous break, they glimpsed the lights of the city and Smithy brought the *Southern Cross* in to land . . . the first aeroplane ever to arrive in Australia from New Zealand. It was midnight in Sydney, yet such was their celebrity that 30,000 people were waiting in the dark to greet them.

Charles and Josephine Ulm had lived apart for most of their married life, but now they looked forward to building a life together in Sydney. Money was no problem and they bought a smart new house in Dover Heights, which Charles named *Kauai* after the island from which he and Smithy had ventured into the unknown during the Pacific flight.

Charles re-established a relationship with John, his seven-year-old son, who was living at Chatswood with his mother and stepfather. To break the ice, he sent the young man a photograph of the *Southern Cross* inscribed, 'To Johnny from Daddy—1928', and followed up by arriving on the doorstep bearing a brand-new Hornby clockwork train.

Josephine Ulm made John very welcome at Kauai, where he met Blackie, an Irish retriever, who was treated as a member of the family. One Saturday morning they all went out in Ulm's seven-metre yacht *Snippet*, which he kept at Double Bay. As they sailed down the harbour, Charles drew John's attention to the billowing sails, pointing out that they acted in much the same way as an aeroplane's wing.

At Middle Harbour, they anchored and put down a fish trap, which yielded a fine catch of leatherjackets. On the way back they encountered the weekend fleet racing up the harbour seeking shelter from a howling Southerly Buster. To John's delight, his father cut across in front of them, provoking howls of rage from outraged skippers.

Back at Kauai, Jo prepared the tiny fish, dissecting them with scissors, then frying them in hot oil. For dessert there was ice-cream cake, cut into slices with a hot knife.

Although John could not remember it, Charles had taken him for a flight in a Sopwith Dove when he was six months old, but now, as a four year old, he flew with his father again, this time in an Avro Avian, held securely by a Sutton Harness in Jo's lap in the second cockpit.[1]

At Kauai, Ulm often entertained wealthy and influential visitors for he and Smithy were seeking support for a new venture. It did not take long to get the money and on 12 December 1928 they were able to announce the formation of Australian National Airways, an airline that would link the east coast capital cities. Registered in Sydney, the new company had a nominal capital of £200,000, subscribed mostly by a group of Sydney businessmen. The chairman and largest shareholder was Frederick Stewart, the governing director of the Sydney Metropolitan Omnibus and Transport Company. Charles Ulm and Charles Kingsford Smith were appointed as salaried joint managing directors. The two fliers did not invest any of their own money in the company, but were each gifted a parcel of £6250 in shares.[2]

Ulm and Smithy quickly established an office at Challis House in Martin Place and Ellen Rogers was headhunted from Atlantic Union Oil Company to become their first secretary. It was not difficult to persuade her to join them.

The minute book of the company still exists, preserved in the Mitchell Library. Once handsomely leather-bound, but now a little dilapidated and dog-eared after almost a hundred years, it provides us with a comprehensive record of the rise and fall of a courageous and far-seeing venture.

The entries in the minute book indicate very clearly that from the day it opened its hangar doors, Charles Ulm regarded Australian National Airways as *his* airline. Although he and Kingsford Smith were joint managing directors, Smithy's name seldom appears in the minutes of the board meetings. The records show that Ulm was the driving force, throwing his intellect and energy into every aspect of the business. He was a budding airline executive and he loved every minute of it.

Kingsford Smith, on the other hand, was rarely about. While Ulm put in long hours at Challis House or at Mascot, Smithy spent his time visiting friends and relations in the country, tearing about Sydney Harbour in his new speedboat, or looping the loop in a Gipsy Moth. Although his advice was keenly sought on matters relating to flying, everybody knew that his main value to the company was his immense celebrity.

In 1929, there were three principal airlines in Australia. From Perth, Norman Brearley's West Australian Airways flew scheduled services to Adelaide carrying mail, passengers and freight. Qantas was well established in western Queensland, carrying mail, passengers and freight between the railheads in western Queensland, and was about to extend its service from Charleville to Brisbane. And Lasco was struggling to sustain a single service between Camooweal and Daly Waters. All three depended upon government subsidies to remain viable.

Ulm was well aware that his proposed service between the capital cities would have to operate entirely without any financial assistance because the government would not subsidise any form of transport that competed with the railways. ANA would have to be totally self-sustaining.

As usual, he had done his homework and his cost and revenue estimates were derived from careful study of other airlines operating within Australia, and also the Dutch KNILM, which had built up an enviable reputation operating the longest route in the world.[3]

The choice of aircraft was crucial if the airline was to make a profit and the trimotor seemed to be the configuration of choice for progressive airlines throughout the world. The all-metal Ford trimotor was in widespread use in the United States, but Ulm believed that, to equip ANA's fleet, he needed to look no further than the *Southern Cross*, a Fokker F.VIIb/3m. The big Fokker was a proven design, sturdy and reliable, and its three engines gave it a good margin of safety. It was already in airline service in the United States. In Australia, it could easily be configured to carry eight passengers between all the capitals on the east coast, and across Bass Strait to Tasmania, with reasonable fuel reserves. Even without a government subsidy, provided they could fill most of the seats, most of the time, they would make a profit.

The F.VIIb/3m was a Dutch design manufactured in Holland. However, in 1929, there was a widely held belief within Australia that the best aircraft in the world were designed and built in Great Britain. Charles Ulm was well aware that purchasing ANA's fleet from anywhere outside the British Empire would be deemed downright unpatriotic. It would be bad for public relations.

Fortunately, an English firm, A.V. Roe and Company (Avro), had acquired a licence to build the F.VIIb/3m at their factory in Manchester. The Avro Ten, so named because it could carry two pilots and eight passengers, was therefore regarded in Australia as a British aircraft. For practical purposes, it was identical to the *Southern Cross*, except it was powered by Armstrong Siddeley Lynx radials, instead of Wright Whirlwinds, giving it 8 kilometres per hour better airspeed.

At the next board meeting, orders were placed with Avro for four aircraft. With an eye to future expansion, Ulm also had discussions with the Clyde Engineering Company about manufacturing additional aircraft in Australia.[4]

Another pressing question was the recruitment of suitable pilots. There were very few pilots in Australia with multi-engine experience, so Ulm placed advertisements for aircrew in the English aviation magazine *The Aeroplane*. Bored with buzzing around Sydney Harbour, Kingsford Smith was looking for a new aerial adventure, so he suggested they fly to the United Kingdom in the *Southern Cross* and interview the shortlisted applicants personally. To add excitement to the exercise, he wanted to try to break the record of fifteen and a half days, set by Bert Hinkler, flying in the opposite direction. Ulm lost no time in selling the exclusive rights to the story to Sun Newspapers, who agreed to pick up the tab for the fuel costs. Herbert Campbell Jones would get very good value for his money.

They could not leave until Keith Anderson finally had his day in court and it was late in February when the hearing resumed before the chief judge in equity, Justice Harvey.

The proceedings did not take long. A great deal of evidence had been presented during preliminary hearings and Ulm and Smithy had hired a King's Counsel to make good use of it. Under the resulting terms of settlement, Keith Anderson was compelled to admit that when he left the United States, prior to the Pacific flight, he did so voluntarily and had thereby abandoned his partnership with Ulm and Kingsford Smith. The partnership consequently dissolved.

The judge ruled that after Hancock bought the *Southern Cross*, from a legal standpoint the Pacific flight was an entirely new venture. Anderson had to admit that Ulm and Kingsford Smith had offered him an opportunity to join them in the new flight and that he had been unable to take part. He also conceded that the defendants had never been under an obligation to pay his fare back to America.

Finally, and perhaps more importantly, he had to admit that he had no legal interest in the *Southern Cross*.[5]

Under the terms of settlement, both sides agreed to pay their own costs, but Ulm and Smithy gave Anderson £1000, contributing half each.

As they still owed him the £600 that his family had subscribed to the partnership while Keith was in San Francisco, this was not as generous as it appeared.

Ulm and Kingsford Smith's lawyer had done his job, but the successful outcome was due in large part to Charles Ulm's clever wording in the cables that had passed back and forth across the Pacific. By failing to respond to each in specific terms, Anderson had played into Ulm's hands.

Bob Hitchcock's hearing, which began on 19 March, ran for just three days. Ulm and Kingsford Smith's counsel, Mr Windeyer KC, adopted a superior tone, constantly emphasising Hitchcock's lowly status as a mere mechanic, to establish that he would have been of no use to the aviators during the flight. Kingsford Smith denied ever offering Hitchcock a role in the flight and further denied that he had ever offered him £1000. Hitchcock's claim was dismissed.

With their legal problems behind them, Ulm and Smithy could now make preparations to leave for England. Ulm once more engaged Harold Litchfield and Tom McWilliams, as navigator and radio operator, under contracts similar to those of Lyon and Warner.

Unlike the Pacific crossing, most of the flight would be over land, beginning with a 3000-kilometre leg from Richmond to Wyndham. From there, they planned another long hop to Singapore, thence a series of shorter stages through Burma, India and the Middle East.

The newspapers, as always, had a field day and published interviews with Smithy highlighting the dangers the airmen would have to face en route. Charles Grey, the editor of the British aviation magazine *The Aeroplane*, was prompted to write:

Mr Kingsford Smith has in interviews in Sydney done his best to make people's flesh creep by visualising all sorts of hidden dangers in the flight. He says the heavy rain at Wyndham *might* delay the start, that there is a *possibility* of meeting much rain and tropical storms over Java, that it will be necessary to be wary in dodging mountain peaks in this region, that there is a *probability* of worrying storms until they reach Calcutta, and so on.

Now there are no more routes to pioneer the principal function of the long-distance flyer is to demonstrate the safety, comfort and speed of aerial travel. Talking about problematic heavy rains, worrying storms, tropical rain, etc., savours too much of the 'intrepid birdman' in search of personal glory at the expense of the reputation of aerial travel for comfort and safety.[6]

But all was not well. Kingsford Smith was ill, suffering from flu-like symptoms that often seemed to plague him when he was under stress. Smithy would develop a pathological fear of being forced down into the ocean. Prior to several over-water flights he came down with acute flu-like systems, which were quite likely of psychosomatic origin. On a future flight from New Zealand to Sydney in the *Southern Cross,* he would become incapacitated by fear and have to rest in the cabin, leaving his co-pilot to fly the aircraft.

Meanwhile, Ulm was much occupied by the affairs of their new airline and, after a long run of successes, both men were perhaps becoming a little complacent. Whatever the cause, they let their standards slip.

On 30 March 1929, with minimal preparation, the joint managing directors of the Australian National Airways took off from Richmond air base. Their destination was Wyndham, but they vanished instead into the wilds of north-west Australia.

Their embryonic airline had yet to operate a single service.

CHAPTER 13

Coffee Royal

The disappearance of the *Southern Cross*, and the series of events that followed, which became known as the Coffee Royal affair, marked the beginning of a change in the public perception of Charles Ulm and Charles Kingsford Smith. People would begin to question their credibility and their competence. Their image as infallible and intrepid aviators would start to tarnish.

The flight did not begin well. Twelve minutes after leaving Richmond, as Litchfield opened a cabin window to obtain a drift reading, he accidentally bumped the release mechanism for McWilliams's trailing receiver aerial, which rapidly unwound to its full length, broke away and was lost overboard. The *Southern Cross* could no longer receive any radio messages.

They had covered only 30 kilometres and it would have been a relatively simple matter to return to Richmond, replace the aerial and start again. But it would have meant dumping more than 3000 litres of fuel, and Smithy did not want to do that. He decided to fly on.

It was a fateful decision, because they had no up-to-date knowledge of the conditions at their destination. A senior official of the Atlantic Union Oil Company had been sent to Wyndham to locate suitable landing grounds and, before the *Southern Cross* left, he had cabled that prolonged monsoon rains had inundated the whole area. The cable further stated that, although the weather was now fine, the landing grounds were probably still too soft for a landing. The official had promised to check the condition of the surface personally and report back later in the day.

Kingsford Smith, in a hurry, had decided not to wait. This was unfortunate, because the next cable reported that the conditions in Wyndham had deteriorated further. But by the time it was received in Richmond, the *Southern Cross* was incommunicado and on her way.

The flight across the continent, although bumpy, was uneventful, but at about 7 p.m. Ulm, who had begun sending regular reports to *The Sun*, reported that they were flying blind in thick cloud. In the early hours of the next morning it began to rain heavily. As morning dawned, after a long night of instrument flying, Smithy eased the *Southern Cross* down. They came out of the cloud at 50 feet above rocky and desolate country. It was difficult, dangerous flying, but it was essential to keep the ground in sight if they were to locate the coast. Shortly before 10 a.m. it appeared, but they could not match the scanty detail on

171

Litchfield's small-scale maps with the terrain that was unfolding below. He had three pages from *The Times Atlas*, which were small scale, with limited detail, and two small-scale Admiralty Charts, of 'lower' and 'upper' Australia, designed for seafaring and with no detail inland from the shoreline. All were virtually useless for Litchfield's purpose. They flew about for hours, hopelessly lost.

At one stage they circled a small settlement and dropped a message asking for directions to Wyndham. They flew off in the direction indicated by a man on the ground, but after several hours, with still no sign of their destination, they decided that their message had been misunderstood.

They had been in the air for almost 25 hours when further signs of habitation appeared. Once again they circled the tiny cluster of roofs and dropped a note asking for the direction and distance to Wyndham. This time an arm pointed unequivocally to the east, and somebody traced the numerals '150' in sand upon a sheet that had been laid out on the ground.

Ulm and Smithy held a hurried conference, scribbling notes to each other on the windshield. Fuel was running low. There were mudflats nearby, but to land there would mean ignominy. It was not yet time to give up on Wyndham. The *Southern Cross* climbed away and headed east.

An hour later they had second thoughts and turned back, but they knew that they had little chance of finding the settlement again. Finally, with their fuel gauges on empty, Ulm sent a last message to the *The Sun*.

Have been hopelessly lost in dense rain storm for ten hours. Now going to make forced landing at place we believe to be 150 miles from Wyndham in rotten country. Will communicate again as soon as possible.[1]

One hundred and fifty miles from Wyndham. East, west or south? They were over swampy coastal country, with mangrove-lined rivers snaking their way between low, rocky hills on their way to the sea. It was a most inhospitable place, but Smithy spotted a level surface at the edge of a mudflat and put the aircraft down. It was a heavy landing, and the surface was soft. The wheels sank into the mud and, under the rapid deceleration, the tail came up, threatening to bury her nose. She came to a stop and the tail sank. They were down. Lost, in the middle of nowhere.

Although they didn't know it, they were actually quite close to the settlement they had sighted hours before. It was a Presbyterian mission named Port George IV, only 20 kilometres away to the north, but they could not see it because the swamp where they had landed was surrounded by tall grass and low hills.

When the adrenalin ceased pumping they emerged from the aircraft and climbed one of the hills to get their bearings. They had landed in an estuary of some kind, an intricate patchwork of mudflats, salt pans and swamps, through which a large tidal river, bordered by mangroves, snaked away to the south. The *Southern Cross* stood out quite clearly against the landscape, like some alien craft from another world, which indeed she was.

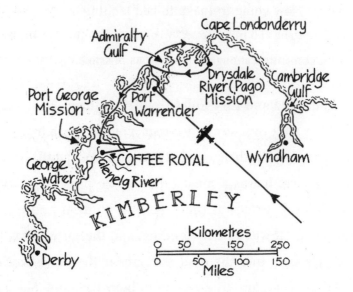

⇀COFFEE ROYAL 1929⇀

The approximate track of the *Southern Cross* as Kingsford Smith and Ulm, lost in bad weather, searched desperately for a landmark that would lead them to Wyndham. They were eventually forced to land on a mudflat that would become known as Coffee Royal. Map by Bronwyn Searle

Back at the aircraft, they assessed the situation. The wheels had not penetrated deeply into the mud, which had been made soft by a recent spring tide. After examining the surface, Smithy was confident that in a few days, when the high tides were lower and the mud had dried out, the *Southern Cross* would be able to take off again quite easily. All they needed was fuel.

In the meantime, they would have to survive and it quickly became apparent that they were in dire straits. Their store of emergency rations, which was usually stowed in the wing of the aircraft, was gone. In their hasty preparation Ulm had not bothered to check that it was there. All they had to eat were seven stale sandwiches, and some tins of baby food that they had been taking to a sick child in Wyndham. They had very little water. They did however have a bottle of brandy, which they mixed with the remains of their coffee and drank to celebrate the fact that they were still alive. They named the place Coffee Royal.

When night fell, they were attacked by millions of mosquitoes, which sought out every square centimetre of exposed skin. To keep them at bay they put on gloves and long-sleeved clothing and stewed in their own sweat in the tropical heat.

They were totally cut off from the outside world. When McWilliams tried to rig up a replacement for their receiver aerial, there was another shock: most of their tools were missing. They didn't even have a hammer or a small axe, which were normally kept aboard the aircraft. Once again, Ulm had omitted to check.

Nevertheless, McWilliams persisted and soon they were listening to Morse messages passing back and forth between people far and wide, all of whom were deeply concerned by their disappearance. Confident that search aircraft would soon begin sweeping the area, they resolved to light signal fires at the earliest opportunity.

Their radio transmitter was powered by a wind-driven generator, which operated only in flight. As this device also charged the receiver's batteries, it was vital to get it operating again. They removed the vanes from the generator and, jacking up one of the Fokker's big wheels, tried to improvise a belt drive. Without proper tools, it was easier said than done.

As soon as the sun was high, Litchfield used his sextant to establish their position. Hampered by the lack of detail on their maps, they could not positively identify any settlements in their vicinity, but they were confident that they were a little south of Port George IV Inlet and close to a stream that they thought could be the Glenelg River. It was vitally important to tell this to the world, so that aircraft could begin searching with good prospect of success.

They knew it was possible to convert their battery-powered short-wave receiving set into a transmitter. In fact, since they had been reported lost, instructions on how to do this had been broadcast several times to them by Sydney radio. But, for some inexplicable reason, McWilliams was reluctant to attempt it. Whether this was due to lack of confidence in his ability or for fear that he might irreparably damage the apparatus in the process will forever remain a mystery.

Had he succeeded, two men may not have lost their lives.

In 1929, Australia had no central body to coordinate and control search-and-rescue operations. The Australian Maritime Safety Authority, which today covers both the maritime and aviation sectors, would not be established for 60 years. Consequently, when the *Southern Cross* went missing, initial attempts to locate her and to rescue her crew were largely the result of individual and uncoordinated efforts.

Herbert Campbell Jones of the *The Sun* was the first to make a move, no doubt anticipating yet another sensational and exclusive story. Hearing a rumour that the *Southern Cross* may have put down near the Drysdale River Mission, he decided to check it out. The normal method of contact with Drysdale was to send an Aboriginal runner from Wyndham, the nearest European settlement, who took three days to get there. (The mission was so remote that the monks did not hear about the end of the First World War until 1920.) Campbell Jones chartered a DH.50 biplane instead. There was nowhere to land at the mission, so the aircraft circled overhead, dropping questions together with descriptions of gestures to denote the answers. The monks caught on to the system immediately and the pilot learned that the *Southern Cross* had indeed flown over the mission before heading off in a south-westerly direction.

The board of Australian National Airways were naturally concerned that both of their managing directors had gone missing, but the recently formed airline did not yet own a single aircraft to join the search. The best it could do was to charter a DH.50 from West Australian Airways.

In Canberra, the federal government did nothing. The RAAF had no aircraft in the vicinity and, in any case, the defence department, which was dominated by the army, declared that the *Southern Cross* would not be found from the air. Their advice to the prime minister was that the most effective method would be to mount a ground party.[2] How long that would take to organise was anybody's guess. And where would they begin looking?

Finally, in Sydney, one of Kingsford Smith's friends decided to act. John Garlick, the city commissioner, formed the Citizens' Southern Cross Rescue Committee to raise money and initiate its own search. The public response was magnificent and the committee was quickly able to charter the *Canberra*, a DH.61 Giant Moth single-engine biplane. Its pilot and co-owner was the experienced Captain Les Holden, who had flown in the First World War. Unfortunately, by the time the *Canberra* arrived in the Kimberley, the *Southern Cross* had been missing for nine days.

Help also came from an entirely unexpected quarter. Keith Anderson was approached by Jack Cantor, the publican at the Customs House Hotel at Circular Quay where Kingsford Smith was a regular drinker. Cantor offered Anderson £500 to take his aircraft to the Kimberley and join the search. Anderson had just fitted his Westland Widgeon monoplane, the *Kookaburra*, with long-range tanks so he was well equipped for the flight, but, after his shameful treatment by Ulm and Smithy, and his subsequent public humiliation in court, Anderson had many eminently justifiable reasons to refuse point-blank.

Amazingly, he agreed.

Apart from the money, the reasons behind Anderson's acceptance of this dangerous mission are not clear. Ian Mackersey thinks that by putting Kingsford Smith in his debt by saving his life, Anderson hoped to re-kindle their friendship. He perhaps also hoped it could win him a job as a captain with Ulm and Smithy's new airline. Jack Cantor believed it was simply good old-fashioned Aussie mateship. 'He undertook the flight from a spirit of sympathy and fellowship with Kingsford Smith,' he told the newspapers.[3]

Whatever his reasons, Keith Anderson pocketed the £500, hired the long-suffering Bob Hitchcock as mechanic, and took off in his tiny aeroplane to look for Smithy. Everything went wrong. Low cloud forced them down in a paddock, damaging the tail-skid. At Broken Hill, somebody stole their tool kit, which had been stowed on the floor of the front cockpit. Anderson took off without noticing the loss and the consequent change in the magnetic field upset the compass, taking him more than 300 kilometres off-course. At Oodnadatta, they had engine trouble, but pressed on to Alice Springs, where Hitchcock sought medical attention for an infected wound in his leg.

Here, Anderson made a fateful decision. Ignoring advice to take a circuitous route to the Kimberley, across country that would provide at least a reasonable chance of survival if their engine failed, he decided to save time by flying direct to Wyndham. At Woodford Springs, he turned the *Kookaburra* away from the reassuring landmark of the overland telegraph line, and headed north-west. He had neglected to have his compass re-swung. They were soon hopelessly lost amid the arid, feature-less wastes of the Tanami Desert.

At Coffee Royal, after several days in the wilderness, and with the baby food all gone, the crew of the *Southern Cross* were doing it tough. There was plenty of fresh water lying around after recent rains, but the only protein they could find was in the form of small snails that lived in the mangrove swamps. They collected hundreds of these, smashed the shells and boiled them. The taste made them nauseous, but the *escargot* kept them alive. They also ate small beans, which grew on a type of grass.[4] With such a limited diet they grew weaker by the day, making even simple tasks an ordeal. They thought about making spears to catch fish in the river, but to reach the water they had to wade through thick mud, using a lot of energy and sinking waist deep in the process. And always there was the threat of crocodiles, just below the surface, stalking them, waiting to strike.

They decided that fish was off the menu.

They were all smokers, and when their tobacco ran out they began to feel the effects of nicotine withdrawal. They tried smoking dried leaves, but hated it and gave up in disgust.

Kingsford Smith finally got his improvised generator working using a wooden friction drive, but cranking the massive wheel took a lot of energy. In their weakened state they could only operate it for ten or fifteen seconds at a time, while McWilliams tapped out their position. Their messages were never heard.

They could, however, listen to the nightly news reports, which told of aircraft searching the country near the Drysdale River. This was understandable, as the *Southern Cross* had indeed flown over the mission. But the swamp where they had come down was a long way to the south-west. Ulm and Smithy knew that with just one brief Morse message the searchers would have arrived at Coffee Royal within hours, but without a transmitter they were mute.

Aircraft did in fact fly over them on a couple of occasions and, believing that deliverance was at hand, they eagerly heaped damp grass on their signal fires to put up smoke. But to their dismay the pilots did not see them and were soon gone. They found out later that the crews were not actually searching at the time, but had in fact been in transit, heading for the main search area south of the Drysdale Mission, further east. It was all extremely frustrating.

When the days passed without result, it finally became apparent to Colonel Horace Brinsmead, the Controller of Civil Aviation, that searchers were looking in the wrong place. After making a detailed plot of the radio messages received from the *Southern Cross*, he became convinced that the aircraft had come down somewhere south of the Port George IV Mission. The *Canberra*, flown by Captain Les Holden, was directed to search the area.

Ulm's diary gives the impression that time was running out for them at Coffee Royal.

> The spring tides had covered the large mud flats to our south, completely cutting off our main food supply of mud snails, the few adjacent water holes in the foothills were dried up and we were far too weak to climb to our best water supply, and even this was fast drying up. We had a supply of the bean weeds handy but the sun was fast drying even them up.

Our faces, hands, arms and legs were lacerated by grass and bramble cuts and the flies were poisoning these sores rapidly. A painful death by starvation and thirst was not more than 3 or 4 days away.

Mac heard the Canberra first and called listlessly 'Charles, there's another plane about, I think.' I replied, 'I can't hear him—anyway he'll pass away to the north-east, like the rest.' A few seconds after, I heard him, and soon saw him.

When Les Holden eventually turned towards us our last ounce of strength discovered itself and calling to Mac I struggled over to our fire and heaped on damp grass to make a smoke fire.[5]

After circling a few times, Holden decided not to attempt a landing, but dropped some supplies. To the stranded aviators, it was manna from heaven.

We were mad with excitement. Smithy and Litch came staggering down and when Les dropped the food we were like wild beasts, tearing open the packages and eating Bully Beef with one hand and raisins and jam with the other. We forgot everything but food, and the fact that we were saved.

The hour that the Canberra flew over Coffee Royal was one of the most memorable in our lives, for without any exaggeration we were just on the final point of complete starvation and utterly exhausted.

Before Les Holden flew away he dropped a note saying that he would probably return the following day with more food.

We then settled down to some steady eating. We tried hard not to overeat the first day, but eventually the four of us ate 6 tins of Bully Beef, drank 4 tins of Café au Lait, and 2 bottles of beef extract, sundry chocolate, raisins, jam, etc., before going to bed that evening, and then we still felt hungry.

The next day Les Holden flew out again with more supplies, and early in the afternoon another aircraft appeared. It was a DH.50 from West Australian Airways and, after making a careful examination of the mudflat from the air, the pilot, Bertie Heath, decided to attempt a landing. The surface had not yet completely dried out, but the DH.50 was a smaller and lighter aircraft than Holden's and Heath put it down without incident.

As well as more supplies, Heath brought a passenger, a reporter named Tonkin from the *West Australian* newspaper, which had chartered the aircraft. As the first journalist to reach the scene, Tonkin knew that he had a scoop of national importance on his hands, but, conscious of their contractual obligations to the Sydney *Sun*, Ulm and Smithy were reluctant to answer anything but the most basic questions.

The *West Australian* was not in direct competition with *The Sun* and Ulm was anxious to provide Herbert Campbell Jones with a firsthand account of what would soon be called the Coffee

Royal incident, so he and Tonkin did a deal. Ulm handed Tonkin his diary notes of their experience on the mudflat, together with permission to publish them in the *West Australian*. In return, the reporter agreed to cable the contents of the diary, in full, to *The Sun* and the Melbourne *Herald*. Tonkin also took a number of photographs.

The DH.50 almost came to grief as Heath and Tonkin attempted to take-off, but they managed to get airborne, carrying a request from Smithy for 75 gallons (280 litres) of petrol. On the way back to Derby, Heath flew over Port George IV Mission and dropped a note giving the exact whereabouts of Coffee Royal, and the missionary George Beard and some Aboriginal companions immediately set out to reach the landing site on foot. It was only about 20 kilometres as the crow flies, but it took them almost two days to get there.

The publication of Ulm's diary caused a sensation. *The Sun* sold a record number of papers; the 'colossal figure' of 335,000 copies, the newspaper boasted. 'Laid end-on the ribbon of paper would have just stretched from Sydney to the mudbank near Port George, where the *Southern Cross* was found! . . . Not since the war has there been such universal interest in any incident as the disappearance of Squadron Leader Kingsford-Smith, Flight Lieutenant Ulm, their companions, and their plane.'

Edward Hart, the editor of *Aircraft*, found such blatant commercial grandstanding deplorable and questioned Ulm's motives.

A stunt it was, and a newspaper stunt at that. The damage which the cause of aviation has suffered in consequence of it is well-nigh incalculable.[6]

The Bulletin took a wider, but equally critical, view.

> ... when private adventurers take foolhardy risks it is very questionable if they have the right to expect that valuable lives shall be hazarded and essential services disorganised in an attempt to retrieve the result of their folly.
>
> The stunt involving unnecessary risks is a public nuisance however gallant the stunters, and it is time the fact was realised.[7]

Meanwhile, back at Coffee Royal and unaware of the growing furore, happy that his account of their adventure was front-page news, Ulm continued his diary.

> Sunday 14th April—7 PM. Our 14th day at Coffee Royal and a wonderful day too. I am writing now by candlelight under my mosquito net which I have slung in the starboard side of the fuselage under the tail plane of the 'Southern Cross'. It is now 7 PM p.m. (local time) and all four of us are in our beds. The flies are terrible all day but regularly at 6 p.m. they leave and the mosquitoes arrive in hordes.

Kingsford Smith was badly affected by the flies, which attacked his eyes. Fortunately, a first-aid kit had been dropped with their emergency supplies and they were able to bathe them regularly. Ulm and Smithy both had heartburn and indigestion, as a result of their poor diet, and their legs were sore and swollen from grass cuts and insect bites. Despite these afflictions, Ulm was confident that they would all be fit in a few days. 'Another week in the open here and I'll be fitter than I have been in years.'

He went on to record some impressions of their experience.

Firstly is the knowledge of how much abuse the human frame can stand up to without breaking down altogether and here I pay tribute to my comrades' wonderful efforts. None of us are by any means physically perfect—three of us normally weigh about 10½ stone each and yet at the end of 12 days of almost total starvation, one of us, Litchfield, was still capable of hard physical work under the most trying conditions. Smithy, the smallest in stature and lightest of us all, only caved in during the night of the 11th day, but prior to this he certainly worked more strenuously than any of us. His energy was truly astounding.

One of my most lasting impressions will be our landing here. It was to me final proof (not that I needed one) that in really skilled hands a large machine can be landed in very small and most unsuitable grounds without accident. This forced landing was undoubtedly Smithy's masterpiece.

He was worried about Anderson and Hitchcock:

> If they flew a direct course from Alice Springs to
> Wyndham and had a forced landing away from habita-
> tion they will be in a far worse plight than we were. We
> had water here—they will probably have none, and no
> possible means of communication. Every night we eagerly
> await news of them for we know from experience the
> terrible suffering they may be experiencing. We hear that
> R.A.A.F. planes[8] are commencing a search for them and
> if they are not successful before we get out we'll condi-
> tion the Southern Cross immediately and search until
> we find them.

From his earliest days in aviation, almost everything that
Charles Ulm wrote, diaries and memoirs included, had been
composed with an eye to eventual publication. But he was about
to learn that the media can also turn around and bite the hand
that feeds it, for the next day a Bristol Tourer landed on the
mudflat carrying another reporter.

John Marshall already knew Ulm and Kingsford Smith: two
years earlier he had been a passenger on Smithy's unsuccessful
attempt to set a new record time for a flight between Perth and
Sydney. Marshall worked for *Smith's Weekly*, which was widely read
and notorious for its sensational reporting and scandal mongering.

Sir Joynton Smith, the proprietor, was incensed. Coffee Royal
was big news Australia-wide, and yet the only paper able to

publish anything worth printing was *The Sun* because of its exclusive contract with Charles Ulm. Joynton Smith had decided it was time to cut Ulm out of the loop. John Marshall was at Coffee Royal to sniff around and report back firsthand.

The overall mood of Marshall's subsequent articles, which were published in *Smith's Weekly* and the *Daily Guardian*, also owned by Joynton Smith, was one of scepticism. The crew of the *Southern Cross* were quite close to Port George IV Mission; why they did they not attempt to go there? Why had their smoke signals been ineffective, even though aircraft flew overhead? Marshall had not been entirely convinced by Ulm's story that they had survived on snails and wild beans, because when he saw them they appeared fit and well. In his opinion, Ulm and Kingsford Smith were 'thrill exploiters'.

The crew of the *Southern Cross* spent six more days on the mudflat after being found, resting and recovering their strength. Smithy inspected the big Fokker and, despite some minor sun damage to the plywood skin on the wing, declared the machine fit to fly.[9]

The mud had by now dried out sufficiently for them to take-off. Two aircraft arrived to evacuate Litchfield and McWilliams, and on 18 April, 18 days after they were forced to land, Ulm and Smithy departed Coffee Royal. After circling over Port George IV to acknowledge the missionaries, they set course for Derby, a small town in the Kimberley, where a curt telegram from Jack Cantor awaited them:

THE BOYS SENT KEITH TO LOOK FOR YOU STOP FOR GODS
SAKE LOOK FOR HIM AND BOB[10]

Ulm and Smithy were taken aback. Although they were not yet sufficiently recovered to spend long periods in the air, they had already declared their intention to join the search. The accusation implicit in Cantor's telegram worried them. What was wrong?

It was not just the tone of Cantor's cable that was puzzling. The people of Derby, although obviously pleased that they had survived their ordeal, had extended a welcome that was polite but reserved. The aviators felt not embraced, but held at arm's length. By now accustomed to being acclaimed as all-conquering heroes everywhere they went, Ulm and Kingsford Smith found this change of attitude baffling, to say the least.

The reason soon became apparent. During their sojourn on the mudflat, and despite their adulation by *The Sun*, the sustained campaign of pointed questions and innuendo mounted by *Smith's Weekly* and the *Daily Guardian* had fanned flames of suspicion that rapidly spread Australia-wide. Small minds and wagging tongues did the rest. There was talk of cutting tall poppies down to size and calls for a Royal Commission.

The clamour on the front pages was so virulent that Eric Campbell, Kingsford Smith and Ulm's solicitor, became concerned that irreparable damage might be done to his clients' reputations. He promptly filed a libel suit against Joynton Smith's newspapers and advised Ulm to have pilots Heath and O'Dea, both of whom had visited Coffee Royal, to sign statements confirming the harsh conditions that the flyers had endured. Ulm sought out both men, brandishing documents that he urged them to sign. Heath flatly refused, and O'Dea, after asking for time to read his 'statement', left Derby without complying. At the time, the Australian aviation community was small; both men, probably aware of Ulm's dealings with Lyon and Warner, were not prepared to play his game.

And then came devastating news. Captain Lester Brain, flying the Qantas DH.50 *Atalanta*, had found the *Kookaburra* in the Tanami Desert. The aircraft stood, apparently undamaged, in the blistering heat. A body lay under the starboard wing, but there was no sign of the other member of the crew. Brain dropped some water, more in hope than expectation, for it was clear that Anderson and Hitchcock had not survived. A search party subsequently confirmed that Hitchcock had succumbed to thirst under the wing and Anderson's body was located 400 metres away. There was fuel in the aircraft's tank, and attempts had been made to clear scrub to prepare a take-off run. It was also evident that the flyers had force-landed with engine trouble and made repairs, but had been unable to become airborne again.

Events then took an even more macabre turn. Rumours began to circulate that the entire Coffee Royal affair had been a hoax; that Ulm and Kingsford Smith had staged the whole thing as a publicity stunt. Some people went so far as to suggest that Smith and Ulm had pre-arranged with Anderson and Hitchcock to descend, like knights in shining armour, to rescue them from the mud.

'Vile attempt to blame dead!' thundered the *Guardian*.

In the circumstances, such accusations were not only in bad taste, they were outrageous, and fuelled not by fact but by commercial and professional rivalry between newspaper proprietors. Joynton Smith's newspapers, who employed Norman Ellison, were the principal offenders.

Edward Hart had always been highly critical of Charles Ulm, and called the flight a stunt, but he now moved swiftly to dissociate *Aircraft* from the conspiracy theorists, and Eric Baume, who was the editor of the *Daily Guardian* at the time, later tried to make things right. He wrote:

> ... because the Sydney 'Sun' and not ourselves had the rights to the story I'm afraid we headed our own matter in such a way that the meaning was ambiguous. 'Ulm's Tale' was our headline and our poster. It was a very wrong one because these two men—one the greatest airman, the other the greatest air organiser Australia has ever known—were above faking a stunt when the whole of their careers in big commercial aviation depended upon a successful flight.

The coverage of the Coffee Royal affair did not reflect favourably on the fourth estate and, for Ulm and Smithy, things would never be the same again. Their honeymoon with the Australian public was over.

CHAPTER 14

A question of credibility

Shortly before ten o'clock on the morning of 20 May 1929, Charles Ulm found himself standing before the imposing Grecian columns of the Darlinghurst Court House, at Taylor Square in Sydney. Many famous trials had been held here and, as he passed between the sandstone columns and through the massive wooden door, he knew that he was walking in the footsteps of some of Australia's most notorious criminals.

The historic building was not to be the setting for criminal proceedings today, however, and he would not be in the dock, but Ulm felt apprehensive nonetheless. He was acutely aware that although they were not facing a court of law, in a sense he and Kingsford Smith were on trial, for they were the central figures in an inquiry set up by the prime minister to examine the Coffee Royal incident. A great deal was at stake, for he knew that an adverse finding would have a profound effect on the fortunes of their new airline.

Stanley Bruce had not considered the matter sufficiently important to warrant a Royal Commission, but instead had appointed a three-man committee to look into the circumstances surrounding the entire episode. While the Air Inquiry did not possess the powers of a Royal Commission, witnesses were sworn, and the proceedings were to be conducted with all the *gravitas* of a court of law. At first glance, the brief seemed straightforward. The committee was to inquire into, and report upon:

1. The flight of the *Southern Cross* from Sydney on 30 March 1929; particularly the adequacy of the provision of equipment, accessories, food and other supplies, having regard to the possible contingencies of the flight.
2. The reason why the position of the *Southern Cross* after its forced landing on 31 March was not known in the outside world until 12 April 1929.
3. The reported deaths of Lieutenant Anderson and R.S. Hitchcock, and the forced landing of the *Kookaburra*.
4. The loss of the RAAF DH.9A sent to search for the *Southern Cross*.
5. Further precautions that could be adopted in relation to long-distance aeroplane flights in the interest of pilots, passengers, crew and the community generally.

After his experience with the Anderson and Hitchcock trials, Ulm was no stranger to a courtroom and, as one of the stars of the Smithy and Ulm Roadshow, he was by now a confident and competent public speaker. But as he waited to be called to the witness stand, he felt increasingly nervous, smoking cigarette after cigarette. This morning he would be addressing not an admiring throng, but a perspicacious and expert tribunal. Of the three-man committee, two were pilots: Geoffrey Hughes, a solicitor and president of the Aero Club of New South Wales, and Cecil MacKay, a businessman and president of the Aero Club of Victoria. The chair, Brigadier-General Wilson, was a Brisbane lawyer of wide experience and highly experienced in the conduct of military courts-martial.

Smithy had already appeared before the committee and things had not gone well. He had not been able to provide a reason for leaving Richmond without an updated weather forecast, apart from saying lamely, 'We were in the position of pioneers, and pioneers have to take risks. We don't pretend to be supermen, and we are not.'[1] When asked why they had not returned after they lost their receiver aerial, Smithy had replied that McWilliams, their radio operator, would soon have been deafened by engine noise and, consequently, the loss of their ability to receive messages was of no great import. Ulm knew that this was drawing a long bow, for on the Pacific crossing Jim Warner had been able to hear messages after 24 hours in the air. The truth, that Smithy had been unwilling to dump 3000 litres of precious fuel and risk the heavily overloaded take-off from Richmond again, would not have been palatable to the committee.

Things had come to a head when a member of the panel asked Smithy if he and Ulm had become deliberately lost for publicity purposes. Kingsford Smith had exploded, shouting from the witness box, 'That is an absolute, deliberate and malicious lie, and I'm very glad that you have given me the opportunity of saying that publicly!'[2] The world-famous aviator had emerged from the hearing battered and bruised and thoroughly demoralised. Not only his airmanship, but also his integrity, had been called into question.

Charles Ulm took another deep draw on his cigarette.

When he finally took his place on the stand, he quickly proved to be an articulate witness. As he had been the organising mind behind the flight, and as his so-called diary had been quoted widely in the newspapers, there was plenty to talk about.

Hammond KC, one of two counsels assisting the committee, was interested in the missing emergency rations. 'When did you last see those emergency rations?'

'To the best of my knowledge and belief, I saw them last in the machine some ten or twelve days before we left.'

'Did you take them out?'

'No.'

'Did you change their position?'

'No.'

'Was the plane kept locked up?'

'It was locked up in a hangar, but hundreds and hundreds of people had access to it.'

'Did you not make any special inspection before you left to see whether [the rations] were still there?'

'That is when I say that I must have seen them, although I honestly cannot recall the actual incident. I know that I would not have left without them, and I believed that they were there.'

Hammond then turned his attention to Ulm and Kingsford Smith's decision not to carry the emergency wireless set that had been aboard the *Southern Cross* on the trans-Pacific flight. 'And you say that the emergency wireless would have been of no use to you?'

'I fully believe it would have been of no possible use. I say that after consultation with experts. After our return from America, Warner, who was then our wireless man, told us that this emergency wireless that we were carrying was so much junk, it was of little or no value.'

Hammond then read a passage from *The Great Trans-Pacific Flight: The story of the Southern Cross,* which Ulm had written, ostensibly with the assistance of Kingsford Smith: 'Our biggest safety factor was a special emergency radio transmitter, which was completely watertight.'

'Was that intended to convey to the public that, as an added precaution, you had an emergency wireless in the machine?' Hammond asked.

'It was an added precaution.'

'But now you tell me that the added precaution was quite useless.'

'Yes, but may I explain something about it?'

'Yes.'

'When the book was written, Kingsford Smith and I were not on oath. We had received support from wireless people in other parts of the world, except Australia, to make the flight possible. Those wireless people did their best to turn us out something which might possibly save our lives; and we did not intend, when we came back here, to turn around and perhaps do them some injury in their business by saying that their equipment was no good.'

'Even to the length of representing to the public that a thing was of use to you when it was absolutely useless?'

'It was never called upon to be of any use to us.'

'But you told me that your wireless expert had told you it was useless; that it was so much junk?'

'That was his term.'

Later, Hughes KC switched the committee's attention to Ulm's logbook, which had been widely quoted in the newspapers.

'About your logbook: I think you said yesterday that it was accurate as far as regarded the flights and the entries at Coffee Royal?'

'Accurate, but by no means complete.'

'Is the Committee to take this diary as a somewhat graphic account of your adventures written in retrospect, or as an absolutely accurate statement of what occurred at Coffee Royal?'

'I do not understand quite what you mean by "graphic account"; that diary is true.'

'That is what I want to get at. Is it accurate?'

'That diary is true.'

'It is accurate, although it was not actually written day by day?'

'Some of the entries would be on the same day and some a day or two afterwards.'

'But they purport to be entries on the day.'

'Yes. My answer is that the diary is true.'

'It is absolutely true?'

'Yes.'

Charles Ulm spent a lot of his time in the witness stand on the back foot, defending his credibility, but he nevertheless displayed a knowledge and understanding of the state of Australian civil aviation that set him apart from the other witnesses. Asked by Hughes whether he thought that steps should be taken to regulate long-distance flights within Australia, Ulm replied, 'I think that question is too general. If the Department [of civil aviation] assumes control of all pioneering work, such pioneering work is liable to cease. If Drake had to wait until a battleship was built, perhaps half the world would not have been discovered. There will always be pioneers, and there will always be casualties among them.

'A few years ago, every man, woman and child practically in Australia thought we were lunatics, and "stunt" flyers, and everything in the world, to try to fly the Pacific Ocean. Leading authorities, including the Controller of Civil Aviation, Air Commodore Williams, Chief of the Air Force in Australia, and many other experts in Australia, have since our return apologised to us for their statements concerning our so-called "stunt" flights and have said that our pioneering flights across the Pacific and Tasman and elsewhere have done more for the future of aviation in Australia to anything else.'

Ulm then launched into a long discourse, during which he described the measures that could be taken to improve the safety of long distance flights within Australia.

When he had finished, Hammond attempted to summarise: 'So far, you have given me three things—improved wireless, radio beacons, and lastly, a survey?'

'Yes, but not in that order. I would put them in order of probability. It would be useless to recommend to the country that they expend money on radio beacons when you know very well that they will not do it at this stage, and it is not warranted at this stage.'

'Then I take it that aviation is in the pioneering stage as far as long-distance flights are concerned?'

'Yes.'

'And therefore it cannot be recommended as a passenger-carrying means?'

'Yes, it can.'

'Although the passengers may have the same experience as you had?'

'No, they would not. You're just mixing up two things.'

'How would you prevent them having that experience?'

'Look here, no passenger service would be run on a non-stop flight from Sydney to Wyndham, if I had anything to do with it, unless the sciences of aviation, wireless telegraphy, and everything else had reached a stage which they will reach very soon. Machines will be built to carry possibly twenty or thirty passengers over that range, and the business or whatever organisation is running it will be such that it will enable them to have, either from the Government or their own resources, those beacons and other aids that are necessary; but we cannot immediately do that. But I believe that the time will come when aeroplanes will fly over the route we covered on the Pacific.'

'The position is that the risks you took will continue to be taken until the services are developed?'

'Pioneering work is necessary in everything. We still have, in every branch of service, men who take risks—such as radium and X-ray. We have tried to emulate these men in aviation.'

Hughes bowled the next ball. 'In connection with this pioneering work, does it occur to you that possibly the very fact that these pioneering, hazardous flights are taken on gives a somewhat false impression to the public as to the safety of flying?'

'No. I believe that our flights have done more to create public confidence in aviation in Australia than anybody else. Any reasonably-minded person would say that our last flight was probably our greatest achievement, and the greatest proof of the safety of aviation, in that we had a forced landing in what has been described as the worst flying country that could be experienced anywhere. The machine landed in the most horrible place to get into. We are back in Sydney, and not one of the four is hurt. It proves pretty well that, in capable hands, aircraft are safe things to travel in.'

Hughes sent down the last delivery. 'But does not the man in the street, to take up aviation, need to be convinced first not only that he will not be killed, but that he will get where he is going with reasonable certainty?'

Ulm parried it with a straight bat. 'And we have proved that pretty well.'

Although the members of the Air Inquiry did not acknowledge it, they all knew that they were in the presence of a master of spin.

In an attempt to establish whether there was any truth behind the suggestion that the Coffee Royal incident may have been the result of a conspiracy between Anderson, Ulm and Kingsford Smith, the committee interviewed a number of journalists who had written articles suggesting such a plot. Each man testified that he had merely been repeating rumours; there was no evidence to back it up. Edward Hart told the committee that 'there was not the slightest suggestion that it was a disreputable flight, in any sense reprehensible'.[3]

Despite Hart's assertion, and the lack of any supporting evidence, the controversy was not over yet. As the proceedings moved towards their conclusion, several new witnesses came forward.

Jim Porteus, the Sydney advertising manager for Shell Oil, told the committee that, in 1927, Ulm had requested a meeting to discuss the possibility of Shell sponsorship for the around-Australia flight. During their negotiations Ulm had suggested that 'there were other ways of focusing attention for publicity on the plane and one was to install a wireless on the machine and get lost in central Australia. I treated it more or less as a joke. I said we weren't interested in anything like that.' Recalled to the stand to respond, Ulm denied making the suggestion, adding that he had decided not to give any advertising to Shell as he did not trust Porteus, who was quite likely bearing a grudge.

S.W. Lush, the New South Wales manager of the Neptune Oil Company, testified that Ulm had made a similar proposal to him, saying, 'There are lots of stunts we could bring off for publicity. One would be to get lost in the wilds somewhere or other. That would be a good stunt.' Lush told the Inquiry that in his opinion, Ulm was not joking, and that he had replied, 'It would not be much of a stunt if you were using my oil.' Ulm told the Committee that Lush's statement was 'a complete fabrication'.

A last-minute witness was the *Tahiti*'s navigator William Todd, whom Ulm had fired in San Francisco. Todd testified that he had heard Ulm say that if his plans for getting lost in Central Australia on his around-Australia flight had been carried out, there would have been sufficient money to finance the trans-Pacific venture. Ulm denied that he had made such as suggestion, even as a joke, adding that Todd was 'a great big lump of a fellow and much given to drunkenness'.

'Can you have forgotten it, even if it was a casual joke?' asked the chairman.

'It is possible,' Ulm replied. 'But I cannot think of any possible reason why I should mention it, even as a joke.'[4]

The Committee sat during May and June 1929 and the voluminous official record is now kept in the National Archives of Australia in Canberra. Witnesses gave depositions in Sydney, Melbourne and Adelaide, yielding 904 pages of typewritten transcript. There are also more than 80 exhibits, which include logbooks, diaries, legal documents, photographs, telegrams and correspondence. The Committee sought submissions from the public and the response was interesting, covering subjects as diverse as the use of pigeons to carry distress messages from aviators stranded in remote areas, to the distillation of water from desert soil.[5]

Their 15-page official report, which was released on 24 June 1929, was critical of the crew's failure to obtain up-to-date weather reports before the *Southern Cross* left Richmond, and of Ulm's failure to check the tool kit and emergency rations. It completely rejected the suggestion that the loss of the receiving aerial was unimportant and that deafness would soon have prevented McWilliams from hearing subsequent messages. McWilliams was criticised for not converting their wireless receiver into a transmitter.

But, importantly, it found that Kingsford Smith and Ulm had not conspired with Keith Anderson, or with each other, to become lost in north-west Australia.

However, their findings cast doubt on Ulm's truthfulness. They found that he probably made jokes about deliberately becoming lost and acknowledged that his remarks had not been intended as serious business proposals. They took a dim view of it all:

This opinion, together with the misleading evidence regarding wireless reception in the area, causes the committee to regard the evidence of Flight Lieutenant Ulm with some suspicion, and particularly so in the matter of his diary, which contains internal evidence that it was not a daily record, but was obviously written for publication. In fact portions of the diary which purport to be written on the day to which the entry refers were not written until several days later. The committee considers that Flight Lieutenant Ulm's account of the weakness of the crew during the first few days after landing is exaggerated.[6]

Charles Ulm's credibility had been questioned and found wanting. Unfortunately, some of the mud from that swamp in north-west Australia would stick to his reputation forever.

As the Air Inquiry Committee was completing its work, a large six-wheeled van returned to civilisation after recovering the bodies of Keith Anderson and Bob Hitchcock from the Tanami Desert. Hitchcock was buried in Perth, while Keith Anderson was interred in Rawson Park, overlooking Sydney Harbour, with full military honours.

Charles Ulm and Charles Kingsford Smith were not there, for they had resumed their journey to England in the refurbished *Southern Cross*.

They did not send a wreath.

CHAPTER 15

The fork in the road

Although they had engine problems along the way, the flight to England was largely uneventful and Smithy managed to cut three days off Bert Hinkler's record, flying almost 20,000 kilometres in 12 days and 18 hours.

They arrived at Croydon Airport to an official welcome from the country's most senior aviation dignitaries and a message of congratulation from the King. It appeared that half a world away from Coffee Royal, their celebrity remained undiminished.

The usual round of official engagements followed and, as usual, Smithy was the focus of attention. Charles Ulm dutifully played his part as the other half of the famous duo, but his mind was on other things.

At the Avro works in Manchester, four new airliners were in the final stages of construction, and he and Kingsford Smith made the journey north by train to inspect them, and to arrange for their shipment to Australia in time for ANA's first scheduled service, which they hoped would be in January 1930.

They then flew the *Southern Cross* to Amsterdam, where they were greeted by an enthusiastic crowd at Schiphol Airport. The Dutch were justifiably proud of the much-travelled aeroplane and she was completely overhauled, free of charge, at the Fokker factory.

Back in England, Charles Ulm interviewed prospective pilots who had responded to his advertisements. One of the candidates, George Urquhart 'Scotty' Allan, a serving officer with 58 Squadron of the Royal Air Force, later recalled that his job interview with Ulm was absurdly brief:

'Can you fly at night?'

'Yes.'

'Are you a good pilot?'

'I suppose so.'[1]

In fact the interview was just a formality, for Ulm knew a great deal about Allan before the two men met. Through the Secretary of State for Air, he had gained access to the service records of every RAF officer who had applied for the job and had picked only the best. Scotty Allan was exactly the type of man he was looking for. Rated as an exceptional pilot, Allan was experienced in flying large, heavy aircraft in bad weather and was also a trained navigator. At Ulm's request, the Air Board agreed to release him, together with another 58 Squadron pilot,

J.A. 'Paddy' Sheppard, to travel to Australia and fly for ANA for a period of six months 'for the good of the Empire'.

His new airline had yet to operate a single service within Australia, but Ulm already had ambitions to extend its operations overseas. At a meeting with Sir Sefton Brancker, Air Vice Marshal and Director of Civil Aviation, he outlined a plan for ANA to fly from Australia to connect with the Imperial Airways service that terminated at Karachi. It was a bold initiative, and not without precedent, for the Dutch airline KLM was already flying all the way to Batavia in the East Indies. But the timing was not right. Despite Ulm's achievements, the air vice marshal no doubt regarded the brash Australian as an upstart, punching well above his weight, and nothing came of it.

When the time came for them to return to Australia, Kingsford Smith dropped a bombshell by announcing that, when the reconditioned *Southern Cross* emerged from the Fokker works, he and Ulm intended to fly her across the Atlantic, and then the United States, to San Francisco. When they touched down once more at Oakland, the circle would be complete. His beloved 'Old Bus' would have circumnavigated the world. He and Ulm would then return to Australia by sea.

It was a nice idea, but the board of Australian National Airways would have none of it. In their view, Ulm and Kingsford Smith had been lucky to emerge unscathed from the swamp in north-west Australia and it was pointless and downright foolhardy to risk their lives yet again in the tempestuous skies above the North Atlantic. As joint managing directors, they had responsibilities back home in Sydney and Frederick Stewart ordered them both to return to Australia by sea.

His chairman's blunt directive made Charles Ulm stop and think. While the prospect of accompanying Smithy on yet another aerial adventure had lost none of its appeal, he realised that their partnership, which had brought so many rewards, had been but one step on the road towards his ultimate goal, an airline linking the Australian capital cities. That airline was now a reality, newly formed and highly vulnerable, waiting for him back in Sydney. It was time to re-order his priorities.

He booked a passage immediately.

Charles Kingsford Smith viewed the situation differently. Intensely patriotic, he shared Ulm's dream of an Australian airline and was happy to lend his name and his skill to such a venture. But in his heart, he knew that he was an aviator, not an airline executive. He liked taking risks and breaking records, not attending board meetings and dictating letters to Ellen Rogers.

Smithy defied Stewart's directive. He notified the board that he would be home in time to test-fly the Avro Tens before they entered service in January. Meantime, he was going to fly the 'Old Bus' over the Atlantic and on to San Francisco.

The co-commanders had reached a fork in the road, and their paths would henceforth diverge. Ulm and Kingsford Smith had made their last record-breaking flight together.

Both men were joint owners of the *Southern Cross,* but they agreed that for practical purposes it would be better if Smithy owned the 'Old Bus' outright. They therefore did a deal under which Smithy became the sole owner of the aircraft, in exchange for which he handed Ulm his parcel of ANA shares. The deal would come into effect immediately once the *Southern Cross* became airborne over the Atlantic. They had a gentlemen's agreement that Smithy would make the Fokker available for service with ANA whenever it was available, but it was no doubt an emotional wrench for Charles Ulm to sever his ties with the aeroplane in which they had shared so many adventures.

Back in Sydney, Ulm embarked enthusiastically upon the task of getting his airline into the air, aided in no small part by Ellen Rogers. There was a great deal to be done. Engineering and administrative staff were hired and fuel supplies organised. A Studebaker parlour car was purchased to transfer passengers from ANA's offices at Challis House to Mascot, where a new hangar had been erected to accommodate the Avro Tens. The bulky wings and fuselages, which had been shipped as deck cargo, were transported to the airfield by road in the dead of night, in order to avoid disruption to traffic. After assembly, each aircraft was test-flown by Kingsford Smith, who had in the meantime arrived back in Australia. He pronounced them all airworthy.

They named the new airliners *Southern Cloud*, *Southern Star*, *Southern Sun* and *Southern Sky*. It was a smart move to associate the aircraft with the *Southern Cross* and it captured public imagination in much the same way as Pan American Airways was soon to do with its famous *Clippers*.

Suitably experienced pilots were in short supply, but eventually, as well as Scotty Allan and Paddy Sheppard, the line-up included Eric Chaseling, James Mollison, Jerry Pentland, Pat Lynch-Bosse, E.J. Stevens, Pat Hall, R. Beresford and T.W. Shortridge. Ulm paid his pilots good money and, once the scheduled services had been established, it was his intention to invite selected RAAF pilots to join ANA on secondment so as to gain experience on large three-engine aircraft. Engineering apprentices also sometimes occupied the right-hand seat.

To introduce the Avro Tens to the public, Ulm organised joy-flights over Sydney Harbour. Keen to ride in the giant new airliners, and perhaps to catch a glimpse of Kingsford Smith, people flocked to Mascot. This created a problem, because ANA's new pilots had little or no experience with the big Avros either.

Scotty Allan's conversion course was almost as brief as his job interview.

I had never seen an Avro Ten before. I met Kingsford Smith out at Mascot. He was taking six passengers for a joyride in the 'Southern Star' and the engines were already running. He didn't bother to walk me round the aeroplane or brief me on the way it handled. He just said, 'Hop in.' I went up into the co-pilot's seat and off we went. He didn't even talk me through the controls. There was no intercom and it was too noisy to hear anything anyway. But as soon as we were in the air he handed the whole thing to me. We did one wide circuit over Sydney and he indicated I should land it which I did. We had been in the air for less than 25 minutes. That was all the instruction I got. I think he just assumed that like himself I could get into any aeroplane and fly it. Two days later he sent me off solo with six fare-paying [joy-riders] aboard. He never checked me out again. Less than one hour's experience on the type and I was an ANA Captain.[2]

Late in December 1929, *Southern Sky* was flown to Brisbane's Eagle Farm airport, where she was officially named by Lady Goodwin, wife of the governor of Queensland. At a similar ceremony at Mascot, Lady de Chair, wife of the New South Wales governor, christened the *Southern Star*.

All was now ready for the commencement of scheduled services between Sydney and Brisbane on 1 January. To mark the occasion, both joint managing directors decided to participate; Kingsford Smith elected to take the *Southern Star* northbound, with Scotty Allan in the right-hand seat, while Ulm would fly the *Southern Sky* down to Sydney. Ulm had yet to obtain a commercial pilot's licence, so Paddy Sheppard would be in command.

The first day of the new year was not a good day for flying. It dawned grey and rainy at both ends of the route, but ANA was offering an all-weather service, so both Avros departed at the scheduled time of eight o'clock. At Mascot, the *Southern Star* lifted off in a shower of spray and headed for Sydney Harbour at about 500 feet; Smithy knew better than to enter the cloud. Above the wave-lashed Heads, he eased the aircraft into a gentle left-hand turn until the misty shoreline was sliding steadily past the wing; an infallible guide, taking them to Brisbane. It was the long way. Six hours later, they splashed into the mud at Eagle Farm.

Lacking Kingsford Smith's experience, Sheppard unwisely chose to fly a faster inland route, which led them over the McPherson Ranges to Grafton, thence to Sydney. Cloud lay heavily upon the mountaintops, and they soon became totally lost in what Ulm later described as 'the thickest weather I've ever seen'. Eventually they found themselves trapped in a valley, dangerously low above a partially cleared paddock, which was littered with ring-barked trees. Heavily timbered mountains rose into the cloud on all sides. To climb into the cloud would be to court disaster, so Sheppard elected to make a forced landing. The aircraft touched down safely, but over-ran the field, through a fence and into some logs, which ripped off the undercarriage. Fortunately, nobody was injured.

They found that they had come down on a property near Bonalbo, not far from Casino, in northern New South Wales, from where the unfortunate passengers were forced to complete their journey by train. Summoned to the site of the mishap, engineering staff talked of dismantling the aircraft and trucking it to Sydney, but Kingsford Smith would have none of it. When the weather cleared, he would fly *Southern Sky* out.

Running repairs were made, trees were felled, a fence lowered, and the aircraft was towed to the downwind end of the paddock, where its tailskid was attached to a tree with a stout rope. An axeman was summoned. Smithy climbed aboard, started the engines, raised a hand, and opened the throttles.

The engine note rose from a grumble to a full-throated bellow. The rope straightened, then snapped taut. Smithy dropped his hand. The axe fell. Suddenly free and lightly loaded, the *Southern Sky* leaped forward and into the air. Even so, she barely cleared the trees.

Despite the poor weather, the mishap was due almost entirely to poor airmanship and, as head of flying operations, Smithy sought an explanation from Sheppard, who could easily have followed the coastal route. Sheppard subsequently resigned from the company.

The Brisbane–Sydney run proved popular, particularly among 'first trippers' who were probably attracted to air travel for the glamour associated with Smithy and Ulm, and the big Avros soon became a familiar sight as they droned across the sky. Their cabins were trimmed in blue leatherette and contained eight wicker armchairs, four along each side of a central aisle. The windows could be opened during flight. Every seat had a side pocket containing the daily newspaper, a map of the route with approximate flight times and distances between the main features, an envelope containing cotton wool and a couple of Minties, and a large paper bag. There was a simple toilet at the rear of the cabin. The chairs were not attached to the floor and during turbulence it was common for the passengers to slide up and down the cabin. Not surprisingly, airsickness was common, probably induced as much by fear as by rough air, and many passengers put their paper bags to good use.

Flights departed from each capital city at 8 a.m., arriving at their destination at 2 p.m. The fare was £9 13s 0d single, and £18 17s 6d return.[3] By the end of March 1930, ANA airliners had flown 91,700 miles on scheduled services, carrying 1244 passengers and 1200 kilograms of mail.[4] Letters posted by 6 a.m. at the GPO in each capital city reached their destination the same day.

At the end of its first six months of operation, the directors were sufficiently confident of the future to declare an 8 per cent dividend. Even though he was pleased with the response to his venture, Ulm knew that there was a long way to go before the Australian public accepted the aeroplane as an everyday form of transport, essential for the business traveller. ANA therefore published a slick brochure encouraging people to travel by air. The aim was to dispel myths and engender confidence, and the style of the copywriting makes fascinating reading:

Nothing On Earth Like It!
A message for people who have never flown—and who
THINK they never will
by
'Nervous'
Confessions of a Nervous Man

I am one of those chaps who never admit that anything scares them. I once spent ten minutes of mortal agony in a racing car all through telling the driver that speed to me was the breath of life. I don't suppose I should ever had gone inside a plane if I had not been faced with the choice between going in or looking a fool. In a moment of weakness I had suggested to my firm that days could be saved in a certain business deal if we 'took to the air' to Brisbane. I was merely trying to appear efficient. I had no intention of flying. Judge my horror when the Chief said, 'All right, catch the Australian National Airways plane.'

But I had to go on.

With a sort of wobbly feeling inside I rang up Australian National Airways ('phone number B1600) and, trying to put a bland note into my voice, said I wanted a seat on the next Brisbane plane. In three minutes the matter was fixed.

What Was It Like?

The next day I was back from Brisbane and what I am telling you now is the sincerest thing I have ever written. Air Travel! THERE IS NOTHING ON EARTH LIKE IT! Those Australian National Airways people have just taken all the luxuries of a liner, all the safety of a car, all the comforts of a hotel lounge, and wrapped them up in the world's most reliable aeroplanes.

World's Best And Safest Pilots

The A.N.A. Parlour Coach picks you up at A.N.A. Headquarters, in the centre of the City, and runs you out to the aerodrome. You meet the pilot—one of the men for whom the Company has combed the world; men whose record for safety, caution, and skill has been subjected to the most rigid examination—and then with the rest of the smiling, cheerful group you take your lounge seat in the big, comfortable, all British-built, three-engined 'AVRO TEN'.

Everybody is chatting (some just get in and bury their heads in the morning newspaper) and in a few moments somebody says 'Hullo, we've left.' The 'take-off' is no more a sensation than the starting of a train. One minute you are gliding along the ground, the next you are in the air. Nervous! There is just nothing to be nervous about. You're too comfortable, too pleased with life.

Nothing On Earth Like It

It isn't even an adventure. These big planes take all the excitement out of the clouds—it's just like the difference between a dinghy and a steam-yacht. The Assistant Pilot strolls down the cabin and chats with you. You wonder why on earth you ever hesitated. You are not conscious of height or speed—you just know you are comfortable, safe, and happy.

It 'gets' you! I will make a wager with anybody who flies with A.N.A. that you'll want to go again and again. And when you know that every little detail of the service is watched and controlled by quiet, capable and experienced men; that absolutely no risks are taken, that the ground organisation leaves absolutely no margin of hazard—well, why stick to stuffy, jolting trains and leisurely, rolling steamers?

Fly! There's nothing on earth like it![5]

⁂

Charles Ulm worked hard and expected every member of his staff to do likewise. His message to all employees was, 'We all have to work hard and work together as a team. I don't want any disturbing influences.'[6] It was routine practice for a pilot to arrive at Mascot after flying the 8 a.m. service from Brisbane, have a quick sandwich, and then spend the afternoon teaching people to fly in one of the de Havilland Moths operated by the Kingsford Smith School of Flying (a division of Australian National Airways).

Kingsford Smith flew as pilot-in-command during the first two months of scheduled operations, but his name then disappeared from the roster. He found regular line flying boring and much preferred the challenge of setting new records. He was not particularly interested in the management of the airline either, even though he was a joint managing director. He was often absent from board meetings. Ulm, on the other hand, attended every meeting, except when he was interstate on company business, and his name appears constantly in the minutes as the driving force behind almost every initiative and major decision.

In October 1930, Smithy flew *Southern Cross Junior*, his new Avro Avian, from England to Australia in a new record time of ten days. In December, he married Mary Powell at Scots Church, Melbourne. He had just been promoted to the honorary rank of air commodore in the RAAF and a wedding photograph shows him looking every bit the dashing airman in his new dress uniform. Charles Ulm, his best man, was still a humble flight lieutenant—once again, the other man in the picture.

Although he had never publicly revealed his feelings, Ulm harboured a deep and heartfelt resentment at always having to play second fiddle. Matters came to a head in the second half of 1931 when Kingsford Smith completed his biography *The Old Bus*, which had been ghostwritten by Geoffrey Rawson, a journalist at the Melbourne *Herald*. Smithy left for England without showing the manuscript to Charles Ulm and *The Old Bus* began to appear, in serialised form, in the *Herald* and associated newspapers, no doubt to boost sales when the book was released.

When he read the early instalments of the serial, Ulm was furious. In his opinion, *The Old Bus* completely downplayed his role as Kingsford Smith's partner and co-commander during the Pacific flight. He also felt that Smithy had not adequately explained the reason for his withdrawal from the Atlantic crossing. Outraged, he phoned his solicitor, Eric Campbell.

The result was a legal agreement between Ulm and Kingsford Smith that before any further instalments appeared, the manuscript be changed to acknowledge Ulm's role as co-commander on all the flights of the *Southern Cross*, including the flight to England, and from England to Holland. It was also to acknowledge that Ulm was 'practically solely responsible for the whole of the organisation leading up to the commencement of the flights and the actual organisation of each and every one of the flights en route'. There was to be a definite statement that Ulm's withdrawal from the Atlantic crossing was because the directors of ANA had refused him permission to make the flight.

Finally, the amendments were also to make it clear that Ulm was 'perfectly entitled to share in the profits or revenues or any rights connected with the flights which Smithy and I jointly commanded, and which were undertaken by us in partnership'.[7]

When *The Old Bus* eventually reached the booksellers, all the changes demanded by Ulm had been made. In addition, the dedication read, 'To my old flying colleague, Charles T.P. Ulm, without whose genius for organisation and courageous spirit many flights in the *Southern Cross* could never have been achieved.'

At last, Charles Ulm was receiving a measure of credit where, beyond all shadow of doubt, credit was due. It was a pity that he had been forced to fight for it. Scotty Allan, who knew both Ulm and Smithy better than most, later summed up the situation very well:

> Original flights can only be done by someone of considerable quality. It doesn't just happen. Somebody has to think of it. It was the combination of Ulm and Kingsford Smith that made the combination function. There's no doubt about it that Ulm had the ideas and Smithy had the skill. That was the way it went. They fell out, disagreed, at a later date. It's not surprising, and definitely in the

proportion of things, Smithy was rewarded more of a proportion of the honour than was due to him, whereas Ulm was neglected just because he wasn't a pilot. There was a glamour attached to being a pilot in those days that the newspapers blew up one way or another. Although the honour should have been shared equally between the two, it wasn't.[8]

The two men had reached a fork in the road. Destiny now led them in different directions, but they would remain steadfast friends.

CHAPTER 16

Southern Cloud

On 1 June 1930, ANA extended its services to Melbourne and an additional Avro Ten, the *Southern Moon*, was added to the fleet.

Flights departed Essendon and Mascot at 8.30 a.m. from Monday to Friday, arriving at their respective destinations at 2.00 p.m. It was a more demanding route than the Brisbane run. The weather was more changeable and the aircraft were often forced to fly in cloud, over mountainous country and in icing conditions for most of the journey. In cloud, the descent into Essendon was a critical phase, with the ever-present possibility that the aircraft had not yet cleared the high ground.

Scotty Allan was in command of the inaugural flight, assisted by Pat Hall.

> When we left Sydney it was raining, the clouds were at
> 200 feet, the aeroplane was full of people on the first

flight, and we set off for Melbourne. When I estimated we were passing over Goulburn, at about 9000 feet, the aeroplane was covered with ice. We pursued our way towards Melbourne, in cloud all the way, and when I thought we were approaching Melbourne I steered off to the right, to the west a bit, and when I thought, right, we've cleared the hills now, I went down until I could see some trees. I then pursued my way south until we came to a railway line which was shown on a map, then turned to the left, and going along the railway line we read the name of the first railway station we came to, which was, believe it or not, Sunshine!

I was looking over the side and I said to Pat Hall, where's Sunshine? So he produced the map and said, 'There.' So we proceeded along that railway line . . . it's the main railway line to Adelaide, which passes behind Essendon. And Essendon was half a mile north of the railway line. I turned to the right and flew smack over the top of the middle of the aerodrome, going the wrong way. The visibility would be maybe two or three hundred yards, not more. Did a 180-degree turn, shut off the throttles, came down and landed. When I landed it was so foggy that they couldn't see me from the airport which in those days wasn't very big. And anyway we taxied in and there was a great concourse of people there to meet us.[1]

Ulm and Smithy had good aircraft and a fine team of pilots and engineers. But Ulm was uncomfortably aware that the infrastructure needed for safe scheduled operations—all-weather airports, a meteorological service for aviators, wireless aboard all airliners and the latest navigation aids—was completely beyond their means.

In the United States, aircraft carrying the mail had been guided by an ever-expanding system of lighted airways for almost ten years. In 1930, the system extended from coast to coast, with rotating beacons of 500,000 candlepower at every airfield, and smaller beacons every few kilometres along the route.[2]

Transcontinental Air Transport, under the guidance of none other than Charles Lindbergh, now provided a coordinated air and rail passenger service, enabling passengers to travel from New York to Los Angeles in 48 hours. Weather observers were stationed along the route providing regular updates to pilots by wireless, which was also used in some areas to provide a homing beam similar to the beam used by Ulm and Smithy on the trans-Pacific flight. The importance of infrastructure to the company was reflected in its budget: of the US$3,000,000 that had been spent in 14 months, only US$813,000 had been for aircraft.[3]

In Australia, there was no official meteorological service devoted to aviation, however weather bureau staff cooperated with aviators as much as possible. Each day the Sydney bureau prepared a special report for ANA, but unfortunately it was not available until mid-morning, long after the day's flights had departed at 8.30 a.m. ANA pilots had to rely on the synoptic chart and weather report in the morning newspaper, which had been compiled from data issued by the bureau the previous evening. The information was 12 hours old.

Realising that two-way communication with the ground would enable pilots to receive updated weather information en route, Ulm approached Amalgamated Wireless of Australia (AWA) with a view to having all ANA airliners equipped with equipment that could receive and transmit messages, and also pick up directional signals from homing stations. AWA produced suitable designs and Ulm applied to the Department of Civil Aviation for permission to set up his own network of base stations.

He found support from an unlikely source. Edward Hart, who had always been Ulm's severest critic, wrote in *Aircraft*:

> It will cost no more than £20,000 to install such a system between Sydney and Melbourne, which is the only really bad weather route in Australia. It is not a fair deal to expect the operating companies, which are carrying out their job so well in the face of great difficulties, financial and otherwise at the moment, to provide all the money necessary to equip the air routes of Australia with wireless direction. It should be one of the first and most urgent considerations of the Governments, Federal or State, to consider how best and how soon the air routes can be equipped with wireless systems.[4]

Colonel Horace Brinsmead, the now Director of Civil Aviation, was sympathetic. He had been thinking along the same lines as Ulm for some time and agreed that such a network was highly desirable. But the Department of Defence, which oversaw civil aviation matters, judged that ground stations should be operated by the government rather than by individual airlines, probably with national security in mind.[5] Ulm's application was therefore denied. It was extremely frustrating.

The airports used by ANA were also a cause for concern. While Mascot, Eagle Farm and Essendon were all on crown land, the Department of Civil Aviation was not responsible for their maintenance. Mascot was just above sea level and quickly became a quagmire after heavy rain. Impeded by the mud, the Avro Tens often struggled to lift themselves out of the ooze before they ran out of runway. In such conditions, the wily Scotty Allan sometimes sent his passengers and their luggage in the ANA parlour coach to Richmond, which offered a better surface. He would then take off from Mascot lightly loaded, fly to Richmond, pick up his passengers and continue the journey.

Brisbane's airport at Eagle Farm was often boggy and unusable, forcing aircraft to land at Rocklea on the other side of the city. This happened so frequently that Ulm eventually decided to abandon Eagle Farm and make Rocklea ANA's Brisbane terminus. The site was subsequently named Archerfield Airport.

With Sheppard's departure, then that of another pilot named Beresford, and Smithy's frequent absences, ANA found itself in need of another captain. Fortunately, a pilot had written seeking a position, so Charles Ulm called him in for an interview.

Patrick 'Bill' Gordon Taylor was 34 years old and had served as a pilot with the Royal Flying Corps over the Western Front, where he had been awarded the Military Cross. He informed Ulm that he was still actively involved with flying, and kept a Gipsy Moth seaplane at Bayview, on Pittwater, where his family had a holiday house. His manner of dress, private school accent and easy confidence all spoke of old money. The man was certainly not a run-of-the-mill pilot.

Unimpressed, Ulm bluntly informed Taylor that he considered his application for a captain's position presumptuous: flying a single-seat fighter was entirely different from commanding a large three-engine airliner. A captaincy was therefore out of the question. He would, however, take him on as a second pilot, on probation.

Bill, as he preferred to be known, was taken aback:

> This ruthless dismissal of all the experience I had had up to that time rather shook me and I was on the point of turning down his offer with suitable comment when something stopped me. There was something about this man that I liked. He was ruthless and tough but there was something good about him. He would be equally tough with himself, and there was a swaggering but genuine gallantry about him; and his offer was a challenge. I decided to accept it.[6]

It would prove to be a fortuitous decision.

Both the Sydney–Melbourne and Sydney–Brisbane services continued to be well patronised and on 16 January 1931 the route was extended further with an airmail, passenger and freight service operating from Melbourne to Launceston three times weekly. On the first day of May, it was extended to Hobart.

But the effects of the Great Depression were beginning to be felt in Australia and, in an attempt to reduce costs and fill seats, Ulm reduced both wages and airfares. There were no doubt grumblings in the hangar and the pilots' room, but, despite the dismal economic climate, ANA continued to attract passengers. Businessmen were beginning to accept air travel as the most cost-effective way to travel between Brisbane, Sydney and Melbourne. The concept of a Frequent Flyer was not yet even a twinkle in some marketing guru's eye, but regulars bought season tickets, saving both time and money.

As ANA's services settled into a routine, it had quickly become evident to Ulm and Smithy that, to maintain a daily schedule, a certain amount of 'blind' flying was inevitable. The ability to fly for an extended period without any outside visual refer-ence was a pre-requisite for ANA's captains and Ulm placed the responsibility for operations in marginal weather squarely in their hands. It was company policy that timetables be maintained, but it was also understood that captains were free to take whatever action was needed for passenger safety. Some pilots consequently developed their own highly individual techniques, as Bill Taylor discovered on his first flight with ANA on the Sydney–Melbourne run, with James Mollison as captain.

Without a word to his colleague, Mollison took off, climbed on course for Melbourne and, at 8000 feet, levelled out and synchronised the throttles.

Taylor did not like the look of the weather. Ahead, a great build-up of towering cloud covered the mountains, the tops thousands of feet above the Avro, the base down in the trees on the lower slopes. It was quite clear that there was no way through on their current heading and he waited for Mollison to change course, descend, and make his way to Melbourne via the western plains, keeping the ground in sight. But to Taylor's concern, Mollison just sat there, hands gently on the controls, as the Avro lumbered serenely towards the great menacing wall of cloud that loomed in front of them.

It suddenly dawned on Taylor that Mollison had no intention of altering course. He was going to fly deliberately into a mass of cloud that probably extended all the way to Melbourne and beyond. They had no idea of the state of the weather at their destination and once they lost visual contact with the ground there would be no landmarks to indicate when to come down.

And then they were in the cloud. The Avro hit a downdraft and Taylor felt the floor fall away beneath him. The aircraft dropped until a violent updraft caught her, arrested the fall with a violent jerk, and then carried her upwards like an express lift. She paused, then fell away again. On the instrument panel, the needles of the turn-and-bank indicator swayed madly in response to violent, unseen forces outside.

Taylor glanced at Mollison. Beyond a slight tightening of his knuckles around the control wheel, the man showed no reaction. Taylor thought of their passengers, no doubt scared out of their wits, white-knuckled as they hung on for dear life to their seats. When they had boarded this aeroplane they had expected to get to Melbourne safely and much more quickly than by train. Now, as he watched ice begin to build up on the leading edge of the Avro's thick wing, Taylor wasn't sure that they would get there at all.

They pressed on in this way for several hours. Once or twice, Taylor saw a momentary gap in the clouds, and even caught a fleeting glimpse of trees far below them. But just as quickly, the gap closed and all sight of the ground was gone.

Finally, five hours and 40 minutes after leaving Sydney, Mollison casually reduced power and let the nose go down. Taylor watched the altimeter unwind. Freezing rain streamed around the windshield and through cracks in the cabin and began to drip onto his legs.

Mollison maintained just enough power to keep the engines warm, and Taylor kept his eye on the altimeter as it continued to unwind. He knew that some of the mountains north of Melbourne were 3000 feet high. They were at 3500 now, coming down.

At 2000 feet, just when it seemed that a crash was inevitable, there was a lightening of the cloud blanket. A few wisps flickered by and they were suddenly in the clear at 1500 feet. Below them were green fields, with cattle grazing, and there, straight ahead, was Essendon Airport. Ten minutes later they were on the ground and the exhausted passengers were climbing aboard the airline coach, greatly relieved to be safely back on terra firma.

Bill Taylor was mystified. How had Mollison known when to begin his descent?

Mollison revealed all the next day before they left on the return trip to Sydney. Like Taylor, he too had seen a gap in the cloud, but on his side of the aircraft. By sheer good luck, he had recognised a landmark. It had then been a simple matter to calculate how many minutes they were from Essendon and, consequently, when to start the descent.

Bill Taylor was flabbergasted. He was a beginner in the airline business, but even to his inexperienced eye, to continue operating in this way was to court disaster. The Sydney–Melbourne run was an accident waiting to happen, and he couldn't help wondering how long it would be before ANA's luck ran out.

———

Shortly after 10.30 a.m. on the morning of Saturday, 21 March 1931, Charles Ulm was working in his office when he received a phone call from Harold Camm, the New South Wales assistant meteorologist. It was unusual for the weather bureau to telephone Ulm personally, but Camm wished to convey some worrying information. The weather observations that he had just received from Melbourne indicated that conditions were far worse than had been forecast. The city was being lashed by winds of cyclone force, gusting to 60 knots (over 110 kilometres per hour), with low scudding clouds, rain and snow. On Port Phillip Bay, conditions were the worst they had been for 20 years and the bad weather extended over much of Victoria and into the highlands of southern New South Wales. The meteorologist thought that Ulm would want to know.

It was disturbing news. ANA had regular flights scheduled both to and from Melbourne that morning and, while he appreciated Camm's phone call, Charles Ulm knew that it had come too late. The *Southern Cloud* and the *Southern Moon* had departed from Sydney and Melbourne respectively more than two hours ago. Neither aircraft carried wireless equipment. It was impossible to warn the pilots that the weather conditions had deteriorated. All he could do was wait and hope for the best.

An anxious Charles Ulm was pacing the tarmac as the *Southern Moon* landed and taxied in at Mascot shortly after noon. Scotty Allan's first-hand account of the trip up from Melbourne confirmed Harold Camm's weather report: it had been a fast and wild ride. After take-off from Essendon he had entered cloud almost immediately, and had made no attempt to remain visual, climbing on instruments to 6000 feet when they emerged into broken cloud. The movement of the aircraft, and Allan's experience, told him that they were running before a strong quartering tailwind, so he altered his course to allow for drift. Ice began to accumulate on the wings, struts and engines, so he climbed to 9000 feet to clear the tops, reaching the coast near Wollongong. Ultimately, the ferocious wind had forced him to alter course by an amazing 55 degrees to allow for the drift.

Ulm and Allan agreed that 'Shorty' Shortridge, heading for Melbourne in *Southern Cloud*, would have had a similar problem. He would have been on instruments, and in icing conditions, for most of the trip. But the most worrying factor was the wind. Flying in cloud, in heavy turbulence and bucking a headwind of unknown velocity, it could well have been impossible for Shortridge to estimate his position and, consequently, to judge when to descend. The prospects were quite alarming.

When there were strong headwinds it was common for the Sydney–Melbourne flight to take more than six hours and ANA aircraft often landed at Bowser, near Wangaratta, to refuel before flying on to Essendon. On this Saturday, the Atlantic Union Oil Company's agent was waiting at Bowser with drums of fuel at about 2.15 p.m., but when *Southern Cloud* failed to arrive he was not concerned, assuming that Shortridge had landed further up the route and was waiting for the weather to clear.

In Melbourne, relatives and friends of passengers began to telephone the ANA office in Collins Street, asking when the *Southern Cloud* was expected to arrive. They were told that the flight had been delayed by strong headwinds and not to worry. But as the afternoon wore on, with still no sign of the Avro, the calls became more anxious and the explanations less convincing.

Finally, at half past five, with still no sign of the *Southern Cloud*, ANA's Melbourne manager placed a trunk call to Charles Ulm at his home in Sydney. Ulm, who had spent a wet and windy afternoon sailing on Sydney Harbour, immediately telephoned Kingsford Smith. Disquieted, both men discussed the possibilities. Ulm suggested that Shortridge may have landed at Bowser and decided to stay on the ground until the weather improved. Smithy thought it more likely that he had diverted to the Riverina and had put down on a remote property that lacked a telephone. Both men agreed that while the lack of definite information was alarming, Shortridge had more experience on the Sydney–Melbourne run than any other ANA pilot. The *Southern Cloud* was in good hands. All they could do was wait for his call.

It did not come.

Finally, Ulm telephoned Frederick Stewart, ANA's chairman, and Edgar Johnston, the Deputy Controller of Civil Aviation, to tell them that he believed that the *Southern Cloud* had crashed. It was decided that all ANA services would be suspended to make aircraft available to begin a search at first light. Despite the privations suffered by the crew of the *Southern Cross* at Coffee Royal, the government had yet to establish an official search-and-rescue organisation in Australia, but Captain Johnston immediately took the initiative and began to organise an air search.

At 4.30 the following morning Kingsford Smith took off from Mascot in the *Southern Sun*, carrying a team of observers, to search the Snowy Mountains between Tumut and the Victorian border. A short time later Scotty Allan left Mascot in *Southern Moon* to search along the entire length of the Sydney–Melbourne air route.

When he arrived at Essendon, he reported that the westerlies, although still strong, were slowly abating and, after refuelling, took off once again to search the mountains of south-east Victoria, where he believed that the *Southern Cloud* might have come down. Witness reports that were starting to come in tended to support his view and it was decided to establish bases for search aircraft at Benalla and Wangaratta, where fuel supplies were quickly laid down. Ulm immediately flew to Benalla in an Avian to coordinate the search.

By mid-morning the weather had begun to clear and two Westland Wapitis from RAAF Laverton, together with several private aircraft, began to sweep the ranges north-east of Melbourne.

At Essendon, the ANA telephone did not stop ringing all day and anxious relatives of the *Southern Cloud's* passengers gathered in the hangar, waiting for news. As evening fell, Scotty Allan landed after searching fruitlessly all afternoon.

The mysterious disappearance of an airliner received widespread coverage in the newspapers and on radio, and captured the public imagination. Reports began to come in from people who claimed to have seen or heard the *Southern Cloud* during the Saturday afternoon. Some of these were quite obviously the work of crackpots, but the majority appeared at first glance to be feasible and the search coordinators took them seriously. Supposed sightings from several credible witnesses suggested that the aircraft had come down somewhere between Lake Eildon and Melbourne, while others suggested that *Southern Cloud* had actually overflown the city while in cloud and had been forced to ditch in Port Phillip Bay or Bass Strait. Other reports indicated that it had come down much further east, towards the southern alps. Two stockmen who had been camping on the western edge of the Snowy Mountains reported that they had heard the sound of an aircraft, followed by an explosion, at about one o'clock in the afternoon. Thirty kilometres west of their camp, residents of the hamlet of Tintaldra told investigators that they had seen a column of smoke in the Toolong Range. That evening several people had seen flashes of light coming from the same place, as though somebody was trying to send a signal. The flashes continued at 15-minute intervals until about 10 p.m. Gold prospectors in the Snowy Mountains told investigators that they saw and heard an aircraft fly low over their camp during a blizzard on the day the *Southern Cloud* disappeared.

Although the reports from the Snowy Mountains had come from a significant number of credible witnesses, the search coordinators were sceptical. In bad weather, with low visibility, they knew it was standard practice for Shortridge to divert to the west to avoid the high ground of the ranges. They were therefore reluctant to believe that the *Southern Cloud* had come down so far to the east. Nevertheless, they took the reports seriously and *Southern Sun* was sent to search the area. It found nothing.

As the days passed with no sign of the wreckage of the *Southern Cloud*, searchers doubled their efforts, aware that if anyone had survived the crash, time was running out. Scotty Allan, James Mollison, Charles Kingsford Smith, Eric Chaseling and Bill Taylor flew sortie after sortie out of Essendon in ANA's Avro Tens. Ulm's fleet of light aircraft continued to search the country surrounding Benalla and Wangaratta. Searching mountainous terrain in single-engine machines was hazardous work. An engine failure could mean disaster, so for security they operated in pairs. At its peak, it is estimated that 30 military and civilian aircraft were involved in the search.

Finally, after 18 days of continuous effort, the coordinators reluctantly reached the conclusion that the passengers and crew of *Southern Cloud* could no longer be alive. Colonel Brinsmead officially suspended the search and requested that ANA withdraw its aircraft. He could see that to restore public confidence, it was important that scheduled services be resumed as soon as possible. It was sound advice, and Ulm and Kingsford Smith complied, but ANA Avros still searched sporadically whenever an aircraft was available.

The people who lost their lives on that fateful Saturday were Travis Shortridge, the pilot; Charles Dunnell, co-pilot; and passengers Elsie Glasgow, Claire Stokes, Hubert Farrell, Julian Margules, Charles Hood and William O'Reilly. Three more people had booked seats, but for various reasons did not board the flight.

The Minister for Defence quickly wrote a memorandum to the Air Accidents Investigation Committee requesting an inquiry into the disappearance of the *Southern Cloud*. It was to be conducted 'with particular reference to the weather at the time, and to what warning the pilots had been given of the cyclonic conditions into which the machine was heading'.[7]

The inquiry met in Sydney and Melbourne during April 1931, chaired by Lieutenant Colonel H.B. Gibbs. The committee members were Wing Commander E. Harrison, and Deputy Controller of Civil Aviation Edgar Johnston, assisted by Leo Little KC.

Witnesses included Charles Ulm; ANA pilots Allan, Mollison, Chaseling and Stephens; Chief Engineer F.W. Hewitt; and Meteorologist H.E. Camm. Kingsford Smith was also called, but asked to be excused on the grounds of exhaustion.

The inquiry found that from the evidence available, it could not definitely assign any cause for the loss of the *Southern Cloud*, its passengers and crew. Members were of the opinion, however, that extreme weather conditions had contributed to the disaster.

It was convinced that all possible efforts had been made to locate the missing aircraft, which in its opinion was airworthy in all respects. Furthermore, the pilot in command, Travis Shortridge, was highly qualified, licensed and medically fit, and Charles Dunnell, the co-pilot, was also medically fit and capable of performing his duties.

The committee was of the opinion that the weather conditions between Sydney and Melbourne on the day in question had been particularly severe and abnormal. Although the pilot probably foresaw moderately bad weather along the route, he had had no warning of the extreme conditions that actually existed. Importantly, the committee noted that under the arrangements that applied at the time, those extreme conditions could not have been foreseen prior to the departure of the aircraft.

The recommendations made by the inquiry were significant and far-reaching. Perhaps most importantly, the committee recommended that 'as soon as possible the carrying of two-way wireless and a qualified operator be made compulsory in aircraft engaged in regular passenger services'. This was to happen immediately on aircraft on the Sydney–Melbourne–Launceston runs. The Committee also recommended that 'the closest co-ordination, both in a professional and administrative sense, should be maintained between the aviation authorities and the Commonwealth Meteorological Bureau'. Observations were to be made of actual weather conditions along the air routes at 7 a.m. daily and forwarded to the weather bureau to allow updates to be made to the forecasts, which would then be immediately issued to all civil aerodromes and RAAF stations.

The Committee also decreed that 'a Departmental scheme for a ground wireless D.F. [direction finding] organisation be proceeded with as an urgent measure'. Research was to be conducted to ensure that the system adopted was of world standard.[8]

For Charles Ulm, the outcome of the Inquiry would no doubt have been bittersweet. He was about to get the infrastructure that he had been asking for, but, for Shorty Shortridge and his passengers, it had come too late. *The Southern Cloud* and her occupants would lie, undiscovered, in the Snowy Mountains for 27 years.[9]

CHAPTER 17

The Royal Air Mail

Ten days after the disappearance of the *Southern Cloud*, it was announced in England that Imperial Airways was about to conduct two experimental airmail flights between the United Kingdom and Australia as an extension of its regular service between London and Delhi. It was intended that Imperial would carry the mail to Darwin, where it would be transferred to a Qantas aircraft and flown to Brisbane. Australian National Airways would then take it on to Sydney and Melbourne.

It was just a trial, but Charles Ulm saw it as a significant development. ANA was struggling to stay afloat. Passenger numbers had declined after the loss of the *Southern Cloud*, not simply because of a decline in public confidence, but also because of the depressed economic conditions. People were simply not travelling, by rail, by sea or by air. But they were still writing letters and postcards and sending invoices and cheques. The Royal Mail was the lifeblood of both nation and empire. Ulm could see that, with a reasonable government subsidy, conveying it by air could be a lucrative business.

The first Australia-bound airmail left Croydon on 4 April on a regular scheduled Imperial Airways flight. At Karachi, it was transferred to a DH.66, the *City of Cairo*, which was to take it on to Darwin. On the last leg of its journey the aircraft ran short of fuel and was forced to land in a rock-strewn field near Koepang (Kupang) in Timor, sustaining damage to its wings, engines and undercarriage. Nobody was injured, and the mail-bags were not affected, but with the limited facilities available at Koepang it was not possible to make repairs.

This was a setback for both Imperial Airways and Qantas, but for ANA it was an opportunity. With only single-engine aircraft, Qantas could not venture across the Timor Sea, so Smithy and Scotty Allan came to the rescue in the *Southern Cross*. Picking up the mail in Koepang, they delivered it to Darwin where it connected with Qantas DH.61 *Apollo*, flown by Captain Russell Tapp, that had brought mail up from Brisbane. After the bags had been exchanged, the *Southern Cross* flew to Akyab (Sittwe, Myanmar) to connect once again with Imperial Airways, while the *Apollo* flew back to Brisbane with the mail from England. ANA then carried it on to the southern capitals.

Because of the crash of the DH.66 at Koepang, the first experimental mail flight from London to Brisbane took 24 days. On the second trip, Imperial Airways once again called on the *Southern*

Cross to bring the mail from Akyab to Darwin and then took it on to Brisbane in a DH.66 they had purchased from West Australian Airways, cutting Qantas out of the loop. The trip, which was incident free, took 18 days. At that time the sea mail took a month. It was a great leap forward.

Australian National Airways, with its three-engine aircraft and over-water experience, was largely responsible for the success of the experimental mail flights. The fact that Kingsford Smith had been involved, flying a world-famous aeroplane, had added lustre to the enterprise. The Dutch, who had recently carried out their own experimental mail flight from Amsterdam to Batavia, were impressed. There were meetings between ANA and KLM to discuss the possibility of joint operations to Europe, but Charles Ulm made it clear that he preferred an all-British link between Australia and England.

His patriotism was not rewarded. His subsequent appeal to the Australian government to operate a permanent, government-subsidised airmail service from Brisbane to Darwin and on to India was rejected. He was told that, while the government was aware that an airmail service linking Australia to Europe would be an imperative in the near future, for now it was adopting a 'wait-and-see' approach.

ANA continued to struggle financially and, in May, Ulm reduced the service to Melbourne from daily to once a week. In an effort to keep the company operating, he approached the Atlantic Union Oil Company for a loan of £20,000. Atlantic, which was one of ANA's major suppliers, refused. Company chairman Frederic Stewart then stepped in, offering to guarantee the company's bank overdraft to a limit of £18,000.[150]

It had been a matter of pride for both Ulm and Kingsford Smith that Australian National Airways had so far operated profitably and entirely without government subsidy. But circumstances had changed. The nation was in the grip of the Depression. The two other major operators, Qantas and West Australian Airways, both heavily subsidised, were still flying. Reluctantly, Ulm decided that it was time to level the playing field.

He approached the Commonwealth government asking for a subsidy of 1s 6d (15 cents) per mile, substantially less than the subsidies enjoyed by Qantas and West Australian Airlines.[151] This amount, he claimed, would be sufficient to keep the company afloat. Without it, ANA would be forced to suspend operations. There would no longer be a regular airline service between the capital cities on the east coast of Australia. The Avro Tens, the largest and most capable transport aircraft in Australia, would be sold, and ANA's team of highly skilled pilots and engineers would be dispersed. It would be a great loss to the nation.

Prime Minister Scullin was unmoved. Ulm was informed that, given the Depression, the government could not grant any further subsidies to airline operators.[152]

On 18 June 1931, ANA received a telling blow in the form of a writ from Atlantic Union for £4,705.[153] A week later the airline suspended all flying operations and it was Charles Ulm's duty to inform his team of pilots and engineers that they were out of a job. He did so with a heavy heart, for he knew that he was breaking up a team that he had personally assembled with great hope. The aircraft were put into storage and a small administrative and maintenance staff was retained on reduced wages. The directors voted to forgo their fees.

Writing in *Aircraft*, Edward Hart expressed his concern at the loss to Australian aviation and also applauded Ulm and Kingsford Smith for their attempt to operate without government subsidy:

> In effect, they said to the public, 'We will not worry about burdening you by asking for subsidies, which will have to be paid out of your own pockets. We will run an efficient airway, linking the eastern capitals, and all we ask as your contribution to a definitely progressive move is that you will patronise our airlines. The more you patronise us the cheaper it will be for you to travel, more time you will save in your business, and for your pleasure, and the more profit will go into your pockets eventually.'
>
> It was a courageous thing to do. Publicity and popularity have given Australian National Airways a prominence in the minds of the public which few others enjoy. The suspension of the services, therefore, must do much to shake the confidence of the public in the need for aerial services—a need we have been stressing so vigorously in the past.[154]

His wings may have been clipped, but Charles Ulm was far from grounded. He immediately presented the ANA board with a proposal containing detailed cost and revenue estimates for a weekly airmail service to link up with Imperial Airways in India, and sent a cable to Imperial seeking to open negotiations. The pompous George Woods Humphrey, the English airline's general manager, chose not to reply directly, preferring instead to communicate through Imperial's Australian representative, the Sydney travel agent Albert Rudder. Imperial Airways was not interested in a joint venture, Ulm was informed; they wanted sole control of the entire route. Furthermore, they intended to employ flying boats for the Australian section.

Although he corresponded with his masters with a civility that bordered on obsequiousness, Albert Rudder was no mere messenger. In the months to come, he would conduct a campaign of commercial espionage on behalf of Imperial Airways, sending a constant stream of intelligence about ANA and, to a lesser extent Qantas, which he favoured as a potential Imperial partner. He meticulously gathered news clippings, particularly those that were unfavourable to Ulm and Kingsford Smith, and forwarded them to London. This helped inform Imperial's opinion, which would be crucial when the time came for the Australian government to decide who would operate the nation's first overseas airline. Rudder also directly lobbied the prime minister. There is little doubt that his activities contributed to ANA's eventual demise.

Towards the end of August 1931, Charles Ulm obtained permission from his board to investigate the costs and potential profitability of an independent airmail flight to England. The figures looked promising, so Ulm approached the

Postmaster-General's Department, who promised their full cooperation. Several oil companies, and A.V. Roe, the manufacturers of the Avro Ten, offered financial assistance.

The 1930s were golden years for the postal system. The primary means of communication, both personal and for business, was still by post. The cheque and the postal order were the principal avenues for the transfer of funds. Philately was a popular hobby. Special stamps and envelopes, known as first-day covers, were often printed to mark momentous events. Charles Ulm knew instinctively that the first-ever airmail flight from Australia to the Mother Country, if properly promoted, would be a winner.

He was right. The public response was enormous. ANA had special envelopes printed and collectors fell over themselves to buy them. The airmail fee was 1 shilling (about 10 cents) per 14 grams in addition to the ordinary postage cost.[155]

The *Southern Sun* left Hobart on 19 November, under the command of Scotty Allan, with Bob Boulton in the right-hand seat and W.G. Callaghan working the radio. By the time the big Avro left Darwin, it was carrying a staggering 52,780 postal articles weighing 2700 kilograms. There was also one passenger: Colonel Horace Brinsmead, the Director of Civil Aviation, who was going to London for official talks with the British government.[156]

The early stages of the flight, through Darwin, Koepang (Kupang) and Singapore, were uneventful. But at Alor Setar the surface of the aerodrome was waterlogged after recent heavy rain. The *Southern Sun*, struggling into the air after a prolonged take-off run, struck an embankment bordering the field, stalled and crashed into a rice paddy. While nobody was injured, the aircraft was too badly damaged to be repaired there. The reason for the *Southern Sun*'s failure to become properly airborne was never ascertained. There were suggestions that the centre engine may have failed at a crucial moment, but the aircraft could also have been simply overloaded.

In Sydney, Ulm and Kingsford Smith were dismayed when they heard the news. The flight had departed in a blaze of publicity, now ANA's reputation was on the line. They had to get the mail to England, somehow. Kingsford Smith would come to the rescue.

With the aid of a skeleton staff, the *Southern Star* was wheeled from the hangar and prepared for the long flight. With all the staff pilots gone, the company's chief engineer, F.W. Hewitt, would accompany Smithy as co-pilot. ANA had insufficient funds to finance the flight, so Ulm was forced to ask H.P. Brown, the Director of Posts and Telegraphs, for an advance on the airmail revenue. To his relief, Brown readily agreed.

The *Southern Star* left Mascot on 30 November, and arrived at Alor Setar without incident. Upon landing, Smithy found that Colonel Brinsmead had elected not to wait and had boarded a Dutch airliner to complete his journey to England. It was a fateful decision: the KLM aircraft, also heavily loaded, crashed on take-off from a sodden Don Mueang Airport near Bangkok, killing the three crew members and two of their passengers. Brinsmead survived, but sustained serious injuries that would claim his life three years later.

As well as being a stalwart supporter of civil aviation, Horace Brinsmead was a personal friend and in the years to come Charles Ulm and Jo would do all they could to ease his suffering. He was partially paralysed, and lost the ability to write or speak, so, when he stayed at their home in Dover Heights, Ulm gave him a small portable typewriter so that they could converse.

At Alor Setar, Scotty Allan joined the crew and the *Southern Star* eventually arrived in London on 16 December. They were 13 days late, but the first all-Australian airmail had been delivered to England. ANA's reputation was intact.

Back in Sydney, Charles Ulm no doubt breathed a sigh of relief.

Southern Star was flown to the Avro works at Manchester to be overhauled, but, upon returning to Croydon, Allan encountered thick fog, forcing him to land in an orchard. The aircraft was extensively damaged and taken by road to Hamble for repairs, which cost £1500. The insurance company paid £900, and the ever-generous Frederick Stewart advanced a loan of £400 to partially cover the balance of £600, which Ulm cabled to Kingsford Smith in London. ANA was sailing perilously close to the wind.

The mishap to the *Southern Star* delayed the return flight by a fortnight and Scotty Allan eventually departed Hamble on 7 January 1932.

Twelve and a half days later the aircraft arrived in Darwin, and the mail was flown on to Brisbane, Sydney, Melbourne and Hobart.

Mission accomplished.

Australian National Airways had completed the longest commercial flights ever undertaken, anywhere, and despite the fact that there had been two crashes in the process, Ulm felt that the company had proven that it was capable of operating regular airmail services in conjunction with Imperial Airways. Whether Imperial would see it that way was another matter entirely.

But when the feeling of triumph subsided, the question of day-to-day survival remained. Ulm wrote to newly elected Prime Minister Lyons in a last-ditch attempt to save ANA from liquidation by way of a government subsidy: 'Although the following proposals each contain requests for financial assistance by way of subsidy they also contain an offer to the government to assume, without liability, a one-half interest in the capital of the company; this offer being made possible by the company shareholders agreeing to transfer to the government one-half of their holdings.'[157]

It was the offer of a desperate man.

Two detailed proposals followed. The first was that the Australian Government guarantee ANA's bank overdraft of £30,000 to provide some initial capital, and then subsidise the company to operate daily air services between Sydney and Brisbane, or between Melbourne and Tasmania, for a period of five years. The rate of subsidy proposed was again much less than the government subsidies then being paid to Qantas and West Australian Airways and would reduce in stages over the five years. Alternatively, the government could subsidise a daily service between Melbourne and Tasmania on a similar basis.

The second proposal was that the government guarantee the overdraft up to £35,000 and subsidise an air service outside Australia to connect with the Imperial Airways service between India and England. Ulm suggested that ANA aircraft could operate weekly from either Wyndham or Darwin to Delhi, Rangoon (Yangon) or Singapore. Supporting figures indicated that when the weight of airmail carried reached 450 kilograms, the government would show a profit over and above the subsidy, and the service would be self-supporting in just a few years. Furthermore, as a shareholder, the Australian government would be entitled to dividends.[158]

As usual, Charles Ulm had done his homework.

On 21 February, he had a serious flying accident. After attending a reunion of the Australian Flying Corps Association at Laverton, near Melbourne, he and a friend were returning to Essendon when their Avro Avian collided with high voltage power lines and crashed to earth in a blinding flash. Fortunately, neither Ulm nor his friend was seriously hurt. In an explanatory letter to Edgar Johnston, the Acting Director of Civil Aviation, Ulm stated that he was not drunk and claimed that the engine had separated from the fuselage in flight, causing the aircraft to stall.[159] There were no repercussions.

Shortly after he submitted his proposals to the government, Ulm received a letter from Norman Brearley, the chairman of West Australian Airways, suggesting that WAA and ANA combine forces to put a joint proposal to the federal government to operate the Australian section of the England–Australia air route. Brearley believed that the unexpired portion of his current east–west subsidy could be applied towards the funding of the new service.

Ulm immediately forwarded the letter to the prime minister, who suggested that he and Brearley discuss their plans with Johnston. Ulm then invited Hudson Fysh, the managing director of Qantas, to join the discussion. The aim was for the three major airline companies to combine and submit a joint proposal to the government.

It was an uneasy alliance. Charles Ulm, with ANA's services suspended and no prospects for new ones, had everything to gain and nothing to lose. Brearley and Fysh were worried that they might lose their subsidies. In the weeks that followed they met and corresponded, ostensibly in a spirit of cooperation, but behind the scenes there was deep distrust.

Hudson Fysh felt particularly vulnerable. Since its founding in 1920, Qantas had grown a modest but vital route network linking remote communities in Queensland and the Northern Territory. Its success was not the result of a series of spectacular record-breaking flights, but of steady progress backed by sound financial management. But now change was in the air and Fysh was deeply concerned. With his current fleet of single-engine aircraft, he could not hope to offer an overseas service. Moreover, he feared that if Charles Ulm and Norman Brearley were to join forces in a new company, he could lose his influence and Qantas its entire domestic network. Therefore, in an effort to cultivate a stronger relationship between Qantas and

Imperial Airways, Fysh began a private correspondence with Albert Rudder, knowing that the contents of his letters would be dutifully passed on to London. In one letter, he wrote:

> Kingsford Smith is entirely 'a law unto himself' and as he would be difficult to work with and impossible to control, I don't at the moment see any possibility there. Reference Ulm and Brearley, they have not even acknowledged my letters to them written weeks ago. It would be of good value if you can discover what their movements are. Though silent at the moment you can depend on it they are up to something telling.[160]

Hudson Fysh's strategy paid off. In a letter to George Woods Humphrey on 2 December 1931, Rudder wrote:

> The correspondence from and to Mr Hudson Fysh (copies enclosed with your letter 21st October) is of much interest. The subject matters were discussed at some length when Mr Fysh was last in Sydney and as reported to you at that time I gave him every encouragement to present his ideas to you, so it seems inevitable that his company must be considered in any arrangements which may eventuate for a permanent service . . . they have been carrying out useful services over a wider area for many years and have really a greater right to support than the A.N.A. Besides this they are financially sound and their activities are in the right position geographically.[161]

In an earlier letter, Rudder frankly assessed Ulm and Kingsford Smith's value if ANA were to form an association with Imperial Airways.

> Without putting it unkindly, both Smith and Ulm may be looked upon as Aerial Adventurers, and in putting money into the concern FH Stewart was largely influenced by vanity. He wants to be the Transport King of Australia; a sort of Australian Sir Charles Wakefield. I feel reasonably certain that he would spend largely if it meant feeding his personal vanity. Ulm, from my point of view, does not fit into the picture as regards a combination of interest. He is very dominant, certain records show that he is unscrupulous, and generally is not looked upon with confidence. He is by no means lacking in ability of a kind, and has the reputation of being a good organiser. I think that you would be quite happy in association with both Stewart and Smith but have very great doubts about Ulm. This is an aspect of the position desirable to keep in mind.[162]

In March 1932, Imperial Airways sent one of its directors, Sir Walter Nicholson, to Australia to examine the situation in Australia first hand. He did not form a favourable impression of Charles Ulm.

> Mr Ulm creates a good enough impression on first acquaintance. It is generally agreed that he is an able man and, in a popular sense a good organiser, though

his talents do not run to sound finance. It is, however, also generally agreed that he is not straight, and he is undoubtedly a great bluffer and a past master in publicity of a somewhat reckless kind. He is the brains of A.N.A. and very probably does not trust either Stewart or Kingsford Smith to conduct any negotiations on the company's behalf. His story to me was that A.N.A. have made offers of friendship to Imperial airways which have been rebuffed; that the Australian interests are on the point of uniting (the implication was that it was at his inspiration) and that anyhow he was certain of assistance from the Commonwealth government to enable him to run an overseas service.[163]

Early in March, Albert Rudder wrote to Ulm, informing him that Imperial Airways was prepared to cooperate with a combination of the three airlines if they could work something out. He added that Imperial could probably operate an air service from Calcutta to Singapore to join up with an Australian service from Darwin. This was a significant change of attitude, as Imperial had previously been adamant that they wanted the entire London–Darwin route to themselves. Encouraged, Ulm immediately informed the prime minister.

After long and tortuous discussions with Norman Brearley and Hudson Fysh, he submitted a proposal to the Commonwealth government, suggesting an amalgamation of Australian National Airways, West Australian Airways and Qantas to provide a comprehensive aerial network within Australia, extending overseas to link up with Imperial Airways. In a wide ranging and highly detailed document, Ulm attempted to provide the committee with all the information that it needed to make informed decisions about the location, allocation and operation of air routes. He compared the suitability of various aircraft types, including the advantages of land planes over seaplanes on over-water routes, and projected loadings and cost and revenue estimates of the prospective Australian airmail services. It was a substantial piece of work and Prime Minister Lyons appointed an inter-departmental committee to consider it.

Unfortunately for Ulm, the clandestine relationship between Imperial Airways and Qantas was continuing to develop, as evidenced by a letter from the influential Qantas director Fergus McMaster to Albert Rudder:

> I have heard from Fysh that you expect the Imperial people to do something of a definite nature about the middle of January. Personally, I do not think anything will come out of the Qantas, A.N.A. or W.A.A. negotiations, but they have to be gone on with until a definite decision is reached. I think negotiations will break down, and if definitely broken down we should then be in a position to definitely place something before your people in either an organisation including Imperial Airways, or Qantas will have to stand alone. Personally I wish the Imperial Combination.

Well, old man, I will say goodbye and wish the Imperial Airways and Qantas will yet be closely associated in the development of aviation.[164]

In June, word came through that Kingsford Smith had been knighted for his services to aviation. The government also made him a gift of £3,000, tax free. There was no mention of similar *largesse* for Ulm.

With no air routes to operate, and no assistance from the government, ANA was in dire straits financially. Ulm put in a bid to carry out aerial meteorological work to stimulate some cash flow, but even this last-resort effort was unsuccessful.

Finally, on 24 February 1933, an extraordinary meeting of ANA shareholders voted to wind up the company and dispose of its assets. Ulm moved quickly to buy the Avro Ten VH-UMI *Southern Moon* at a knockdown price from the liquidator.

He had plans.

Australian National Airways would be reincarnated in 1936 and go on to become a major Australian airline.

But without Charles Ulm.

CHAPTER 18

Faith in Australia

As the inter-departmental committee deliberated over Ulm's proposal for the re-organisation of the nation's air services in June 1933, the Imperial Airways airliner *Astraea* arrived in Australia, ostensibly on a survey of the England–Australia air route. The four-engine Armstrong Whitworth A.W.15 was the largest aircraft ever seen in the country and it attracted large crowds wherever it went. Major H.G. Brackley of Imperial Airways told the press that the main purpose of the visit was to survey the air route from England to Australia. 'We have come to Australia,' he told reporters, 'as ambassadors of commercial aviation and not as poachers on existing services.'[1]

Charles Ulm thought otherwise. In his view, Imperial was wooing Qantas and he decided to do something before they announced their engagement, or worse, a wedding date. He decided that he would fly around the world, heading west, to demonstrate that Australia could operate its own overseas air services.

The route that he planned led north-west from Sydney across Australia, through the East Indies and Malaya, across India, through the Middle East and the Mediterranean to the United Kingdom, then across the Atlantic and the United States, and finally down the Pacific and back to Sydney. It would be a 'real' around-the world flight, crossing the equator, unlike most of the previous record-breaking endeavours, which had merely circled the globe at high latitudes. As a secondary objective, he would aim at setting a fast time to London.

It was an ambitious undertaking. After his struggles to keep ANA afloat, he had little money, so once again he prepared a proposal to attract the necessary funds. He was frank about the reasons for the flight: 'I believe the successful completion of same will be of far reaching publicity value for . . . Australian industries here and abroad, and . . . I need the international publicity I will gain from same, and the cash rewards I will earn therefrom, to fully develop my future plans in commercial aviation.'[2]

He also believed that it was equally important to demonstrate that Australians could build aircraft as well as fly them, adding that, 'After over eighteen months of preliminary investigation I have had designs completed for a wholly Australian-made aircraft, having a non-stop range of over 3,230 miles for this flight, and am now ready to have construction commenced immediately.'[3] This was typical Ulm. The aircraft in question was not 'wholly

Australian-made', but in fact the Dutch-conceived, British-built *Southern Moon* sitting in a hangar at Mascot.

Ulm's appeal for funds, while both plausible and persuasive, yielded little in the way of hard cash, but after mortgaging all his personal assets, he managed to scrabble together enough money to enable his friend and aeronautical engineer Lawrence Wackett to refurbish the aircraft at the Cockatoo Island Dockyard.

It was an extensive re-build. Wackett fabricated ten new aluminium tanks, strengthened the fuselage, extended the wing-span and installed three new 330-horsepower Wright Whirlwind engines and new propellers.[4] The aircraft emerged from the hangar bearing new registration letters, VH-UXX, and a new name, *Faith in Australia*. Ulm now had an aeroplane that could fly long distances; if all went according to plan, around the world. He also had an aeroplane that was almost 65 per cent heavier than its original design.

Take-offs, fully loaded, would be a challenge, to say the least.

Ulm gathered a crew from a select group of experienced ex-ANA people. As Kingsford Smith was engaged on other busi-ness, he engaged Scotty Allan as pilot and wireless operator, Bill Taylor as navigator and second pilot, and appointed himself relief pilot and commander.

Short of cash to pay secretarial staff, Ulm typed the contracts of employment himself. While there would be no pay for prelim-inary tests, the two men would be paid £10 per week during the flight, with a further lump sum payment of £500 upon its completion, together with reimbursement of all out-of-pocket expenses. They would be paid for six weeks following the flight, at £15 per week. Ulm was engaging them both 'on tick', but neither seemed to mind.[5] Perhaps they were happy simply to be flying.

Experience had taught him that prior to any long flight, attention to detail could mean the difference between success and disaster, on the ground as well as in the air. Clearances and permits had to be obtained for the countries where *Faith in Australia* would touch down, fuel supplies had to be organised and suitable airfields found. The small field at Albert Park in Suva had given them all a scare during the trans-Pacific flight in the *Southern Cross*, so Ulm despatched Bill Taylor on a quick trip to Fiji by steamer to find a more suitable place to land.

On 1 June 1933, *Faith in Australia* was wheeled from the hangar ready to begin the next stage of her life in the air. She looked very smart, with a newly sprayed silver fuselage, polished aluminium cowlings and engine mountings and undercarriage of battleship grey. The effect was spoiled somewhat by the top surface of the wing, which was bright orange; with Coffee Royal no doubt still in mind, it was the colour that Ulm believed gave her the best chance of being spotted from the air if by some mischance they were forced down.

To save weight, the engines had not been fitted with handle-operated inertia starters and it was hoped that they would fire with retarded ignition at the top of the compression stroke on the impulse from the magneto alone.

The engines would not start.

It was out of the question to push her back into the hangar and wait for inertia starters to be shipped from the United States. Improvisation was called for. Scotty Allan quickly devised and built a starting platform, consisting of a plywood floor supported by four tubular steel legs that raised it to the correct height. The whole thing could be easily dismantled and stowed aboard the aircraft. It was an ingenious device, but Bill Taylor didn't much care for the idea of standing on a rickety platform, heaving on a propeller, and then having 330 horsepower spring into life just centimetres from his face. After doing it a few times, he found that it was largely just a matter of confidence. But he still hated it.

> Somehow that platform typified our whole enterprise. A desperate effort to achieve something big with practically no resources. Extraordinary methods had to be devised to overcome difficulties, which would not have existed with a well-supported expedition. But therein lay the incentive that made this flight so worthwhile to those who took part in it and to those who built the machine. It actually *was* a desperate adventure, but something I would not give away for much that is regarded as wealth, for in such adventures there was a wealth of human association and endeavour in circumstance in which 'none was for the party and all were for the state'.[6]

Test flights at low weight revealed that VH-UXX was stable and easy to fly, except for a slight tendency for the nose to wander up and down. She had a top speed of 190 kilometres per hour, and cruised at a steady 160.

They carried out load tests at Richmond aerodrome. It was not possible to use ballast to simulate the fuel, because it would have been impossible to keep the aircraft accurately balanced, and to fill some of the tanks with water to make up the weight would have been courting disaster.

On the first flight, *Faith in Australia* ran for 550 metres before taking off with a gross weight of almost 5500 kilograms. The fuel load was increased, bringing her gross weight up to 6300 kilograms, and this time she ran for 820 metres before the big wing lifted her into the air. At this weight, she was too heavy for a safe landing. They could have cruised around for a few hours, burning off fuel, but that would have been a waste of time as well as petrol. It went against the grain, considering the precarious state of his finances, but Ulm opened the dump valve and released almost 1000 litres of the precious liquid into the air.[7]

Now they had to prove that *Faith in Australia* could lift the enormous weight of 7300 kilograms, the load that she would have to carry on the long trans-Atlantic leg of her flight around the world. The aerodrome at Richmond was too small for this purpose, so they took her to a big paddock at Forbes, in central western New South Wales. They had to remove a couple of fences and grade the surface in a few places, but finally they were satisfied that there was sufficient run for a protracted take-off.

They started the engines and Scotty Allan pushed the throttles forward. The engines responded with a shattering roar and the propellers drove the air shrieking across the tail to dissipate in a swirling dust cloud behind the aircraft.

Faith in Australia did not move. Her whole frame was quivering with the strain of a thousand horsepower, but it was not enough to break her away, to get her wheels turning, to overcome the friction of her tail-skid. Allan throttled back and the roar of the engines subsided to an easy rumble. The signs of stress in the airframe eased as she rested, regaining her breath.

Every available man rushed forward to add his muscle power to the exercise and Scotty opened the throttles again. Cracks erupted from the drought-hardened earth in front of the wheels, and *Faith in Australia* began to move.

Ulm had placed flags every hundred metres to check the distance they had run. At the first flag she was running slowly, heavy on her wheels, and still dragging the skid. The tyres bulged as they ran over slight undulations in the ground, absorbing the shock.

By 200 metres, she was running freely and the skid was clear, but this was a critical stage: she was still too slow for the wing to lift her weight, but fast enough to place great strain on the undercarriage. All on board anxiously waited for the tail to rise.

It came up. She lowered her head and began to go. The flags flicked by. At 1000 metres she had enough airspeed to fly, but Allan still held her down until there was no doubt, and then lifted her away. He held her low, in the cushion of air between wing and ground, waiting for the speed to build further, then eased her up to clear the trees beyond the runway.

They went up to 1500 feet, which took a while, then once again Ulm pulled the dump valve. *Faith in Australia* had passed the last of her preliminary tests. Now the main event could begin.

Early in the morning of 21 June they returned to Richmond, where the tanks were filled with enough fuel for 28 hours' flying, enough to take her 3200 kilometres across the continent to Derby, on the north-west coast. This was by no means a full fuel load, and they knew that they could take off quite comfortably from the length of run available.

Ulm placed a toy kangaroo mascot on the coaming in front of the pilots for luck and, after the usual starting ritual, and with all three motors running, they stowed the platform and climbed aboard. The take-off went smoothly and Scotty Allan took her around in a gentle circuit before straightening up on course. The direct course to Derby led across one of the highest parts of the Great Dividing Range, so they headed north for a while, parallel to the mountains, to spare the engines the task of climbing quickly with a heavy load of fuel. Forty minutes later, with the lower country of the Hunter River valley opening out before them, they turned away from the coast.

As the hours passed, they took turns at the controls. Charles Ulm gave himself the largest share of the flying, so that Allan and Taylor could attend to their other duties. The landscape rolled by below, changing from green, to brown, to red. From time to time they flew over a town, most often evidenced by a cluster of white roofs on the sun-baked earth, and they confirmed their position by checking it off on their chart. They flew on, into evening, and then the night.

Suddenly, all three engines backfired in rapid succession and stopped. Taylor, who was taking his turn in the left-hand seat, quickly eased *Faith in Australia* into a gentle glide. In an uncanny silence, she dropped her nose and began to sink into the black void. Ulm, who was in the right-hand seat, instantly went below to investigate the problem.

He knew that, when all three motors cut out at the same time, it could mean only one thing: fuel. The engines were fed from gravity tanks in the wing. These were obviously now empty and it was a simple matter to top them up by pumping fuel from the big tanks in the cabin. *Faith in Australia* was equipped with small, hand-operated rotary pumps for just that purpose and it wasn't long before one engine coughed and started, then another, then the third. Bill Taylor eased her out of the glide, re-trimmed her, and checked the heading on the compass.

After 20 minutes of pumping, Ulm re-appeared in the cockpit with worrying news: there was a leak in the line from the pumps and fuel was escaping and filling the cabin with fumes.

Suddenly, the engines stopped again. This time it was Scotty Allan who did the pumping. Once more Taylor re-trimmed and settled her back on course. In ten more minutes, they stopped yet again.

It now became obvious to all on board that while a leaking fuel line, with its attendant fire risk, was a serious problem, they now faced a much more insidious threat: their pumps could barely keep up with the engines. It would take a more or less continuous effort, working in noxious conditions, just to keep them in the air.

Bill Taylor took his turn on the pumps and, for the rest of the night, they worked in twenty-minute shifts in a continuous effort directed towards survival. One person had to fly the aeroplane at all times, for there was no automatic pilot; someone else had to be pumping fuel; while the third was at an open window, recovering from the fumes. Taylor had to find time to attend to the navigation, while Scotty maintained wireless communication.

Before they had left Richmond, Ulm had issued each member of the crew with a list of his duties at each stop along the way, together with overall procedures and responsibilities. For example, as well as planning the navigation for the next sector, Bill Taylor was to assist with refuelling, drain and replenish the oil tanks, check oil pipes and connections, grease the rocker arms (a messy job that he detested), check tyre pressures, obtain weather reports and assist during engine starts. Ulm required two people to be present in the cockpit during landings, take-offs and instrument flight. Upon arrival, all aerodromes were to be circled to ascertain the wind direction before landing. He even set out the hierarchy for decision-making and the order of accession should he become incapacitated. He also stated, 'The spirit of our flying must be that the one best suited to the job at the time it is to be done, just goes ahead and does it.'[8]

Somehow they kept the fuel flowing, kept *Faith in Australia* flying, and kept her on course. Shortly after daylight they sighted the coast and identified King Sound. Ulm eased her away to the south-west and in a few minutes they saw the white roofs of Derby. Scotty Allan took over and brought her in to land.

The arrival in Derby of *Faith in Australia* marked the end of the first non-stop transcontinental aerial crossing of Australia from the south-east to the north-west. Visitors were rare in this part of the world and Ulm and his crew caused quite a stir.

Over breakfast in the pub they discussed the implications of the problem with the fuel lines and the pumps. They had intended to stay in Derby for the rest of that day, for routine maintenance and rest, and to leave that evening for Singapore, flying through the night so as to arrive during daylight. But now they would have to delay their departure for at least another 24 hours.

They could repair the leaks in the lines, but the pumps were patently inadequate. They needed new pumps that could transfer fuel to the top tanks much faster than the engines could use it. In such an isolated part of the world the chance of locating such a thing seemed slim to say the least, but the word went out and before long somebody miraculously turned up with a huge semi-rotary device, which clearly belonged at the top of a well rather than in the cabin of an aircraft. It was heavy, but it could do the job, so Scotty Allan set to work to install and test it.

They left Derby at midnight the following evening. Flares had been laid to indicate the take-off run and Scotty arranged for a fire to be lit on a hill a few kilometres away to give him an aiming point during the first few critical minutes following the take-off.

The new pump worked perfectly and, as the night progressed, they were able to relax, secure in the knowledge that from now on there would always be fuel in the top tanks. There were no more leaks, and consequently no more fumes, so when he was off duty each man was able to stretch out on a board in the space between the tanks and enjoy an hour or so of restful sleep. They kept *Faith in Australia* over the sea, well clear of the mountains of Bali, until they reached Surabaya, where they turned north-west on a direct course for Singapore, where they landed.

After a good night's sleep they left Singapore at five o'clock the next morning and flew up the west coast of the Malay Peninsula in fine weather. But soon after Malacca cloud appeared ahead, and rapidly thickened, forcing them down to 1000 feet to keep underneath it. Then past the island of Penang the top cylinder head of the starboard engine began to vibrate badly. They fixed it at Alor Setar and resumed their journey early the next morning, flying almost immediately into heavy monsoon rain. The weather cleared and they reached Yangon (Rangoon) without further incident.

The flight to Calcutta, via the Burmese coast and across the Ganges delta, was uneventful and relatively short and *Faith in Australia* touched down at Dum Dum aerodrome at five o'clock in the afternoon, six hours and 50 minutes after leaving Yangon.

That evening they took stock of the situation. They stood virtually no chance of making really good time to England, so they decided to attempt three non-stop flights to reach London: to Karachi, then Cairo, and then on to Heston.

The take-off from Calcutta was a tense affair. *Faith in Australia* was heavily loaded for the long flight to Cairo and it was a near-run thing. They departed Dum Dum via a gap between two hangars, the motors at full bore, the big Fokker wing barely able to lift her above the fence bordering the aerodrome. Scotty Allan coaxed her upwards, flying straight ahead, unwilling to make even the slightest change in course lest he disturb her precarious hold on the air.

They never made it to Cairo. Over southern Iran they flew into a gigantic dust cloud, drifting in from the sun-bleached mountains far to the north. It rose to a great height, far above *Faith in Australia*'s ceiling, enveloping everything in a fine, gritty mist. They tried to climb above the dust to cooler air, but they still had a heavy fuel load and it was tough going. About 700 kilometres from Karachi the oil pressures began to fall. The engines were seriously overheating. They abandoned their attempts to climb and throttled back slightly to give the motors a break.

At once, *Faith in Australia* began to lose height.

They were now in an untenable position. The overheated engines needed more throttle to maintain height, but the more throttle they were given, the more they overheated. They could not stand the strain indefinitely.

Suddenly the port engine made terrific banging noises, so they shut it down. A few moments later the starboard engine coughed a few times, then picked up. They dumped fuel, but, even at reduced weight, there was now no question of maintaining height on two engines. *Faith in Australia* dropped her nose as if in defeat and began a slow descent towards the sun-baked earth.

It was 100 kilometres to the nearest landing ground, at Jask, in Persia (Iran) and they almost didn't make it. With 30 kilometres to go they were down to 1000 feet, so they started the port engine again to give them just enough extra power to maintain height. With the aerodrome in sight it gave up the ghost completely with a loud bang, leaving *Faith in Australia* to touch down trailing clouds of blue smoke.

By a bureaucratic oversight, they had not obtained a clearance to land in Persia and Charles Ulm had visions of spending time in gaol, but his fears were unfounded. They were greeted warmly and put up in a private house owned by a British couple.

They spent four days in Jask, during which Scotty Allan worked wonders with the engines. A piston in the port engine had disintegrated, leaving its remnants flailing about at the end of the connecting rod. It was a wonder that it had not lashed the cylinder to pieces. Working in the blistering sun, and assisted by Ulm and Taylor, Allan polished the cylinder, removing almost all traces of internal damage. He fitted a new piston, painstakingly lapping it to the correct clearances. They didn't have enough spares to completely overhaul all the others, but they had piston rings, so they checked the compression on every cylinder, and where necessary freed and replaced the piston rings that had been hard-baked into their grooves by the punishing heat. They worked in two shifts: from daylight until mid-morning, when the heat made any form of physical exertion impossible, and from late afternoon until dark, sometimes continuing into the night.

On their third day at Jask, the KLM flight arrived on its way to Batavia. Ulm regarded the gleaming Fokker, her smartly turned-out crew, and her sleek, relaxed, affluent passengers with a certain degree of awe; this could quite likely be his future competition.

When they were almost ready to leave, somebody discovered that Ulm and his crew had a shotgun sewn into a canvas bag stowed beneath the cockpit. This was regarded as a serious breach and approval to depart was withheld while officials consulted a higher authority.

The idea of spending more time in the dust and the heat did not appeal to Scotty Allan, so he sought permission to test the engines. Approval obtained, he filled the tanks, started up, taxied out, and took off.

They pressed on to Basra, Aleppo, through the Greek Islands to Athens, and then to Rome. There they were taken to a hotel, where they enjoyed baths, good food and a few hours of blissful sleep. The next day, over southern France, the starboard motor made more strange noises and lost power. There was an aerodrome beneath them, at Orange, so Ulm decided to land immediately. A few days earlier, they probably would have pressed on, but at this stage it wasn't just the engines that were nearing the end of their tether. After 13 days of almost continuous effort, both in the air and on the ground, Ulm, Allan and Taylor were exhausted. Although nobody cared to admit it, the further setback came as a great relief.

Even though they had arrived unannounced at a military airfield, the authorities at Orange were extremely hospitable. They were now within easy distance of London, so Ulm decided it was time to seek expert help with the engines. He sent a cable outlining the situation to Cecil 'Doc' Maidment, the Wright specialist, who had been one of the select few permitted to lay a spanner on the engines of the *Southern Cross* and who happened to be in England at the time. Doc arrived soon thereafter, bearing a comprehensive selection of spare parts, and set to work. It took him four days to get the engines into reasonable shape, and on 9 July they left Orange for Heston with the engines all running sweetly.

In a final symbolic gesture, they left the despised starting platform behind.

If the three fliers had forgotten the rest of the world during their epic struggle to get to England, the rest of the world had not forgotten them. Much to Bill's surprise, they arrived at Heston to a rousing reception. The plan now was to have the engines completely and thoroughly overhauled before flying her to Ireland, where they would begin their Atlantic crossing. For the remainder of their around-the-world journey, Ulm wanted Scotty Allan to be able to fully concentrate upon his piloting duties, so he engaged a young man named J.A. Edwards as wireless operator.

Finally, all was ready. No airport runway in Ireland offered enough length for them to take off with sufficient fuel for

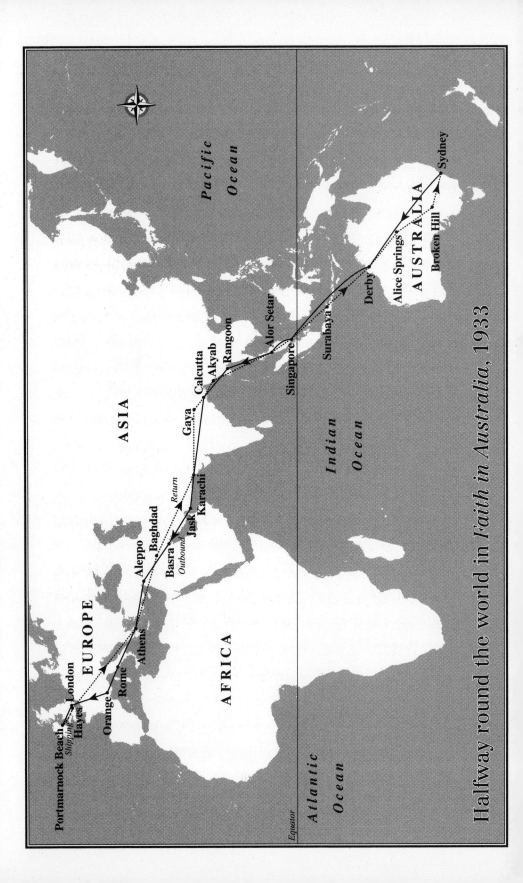

Halfway round the world in *Faith in Australia*, 1933

Newfoundland, so they planned to leave Heston late in the evening to arrive at Baldonnel aerodrome, in Dublin, early in the morning. From there, they would fly to nearby Portmarnock Beach, which offered a long expanse of sand, fuel up for the long haul across the Atlantic, and take off at noon.

The weather report was favourable, but, just before they were due to leave Heston, petrol began to drip from the wing: a tank was leaking. The plywood skin was peeled back, the leaking tank identified, and repairs made. When pressure tested, it failed again, but Ulm was not defeated: he scrapped the tank, had new connections made to bridge the gap of its housing in the wing, and the neighbouring tanks joined with a direct line. This meant that there would be 60 gallons less fuel in that wing, but to compensate twenty tins of fuel were taken on board so that the cabin tanks could be replenished in flight.

They flew to Baldonnel as planned and then to Portmarnock Beach, where police had been called in to control the large crowd that had gathered.

After the compasses had been swung, fuelling got under way. Drum after drum was rolled to the aircraft, hoses were attached, and pumps sent the petrol into the tanks. As the fuel flowed, *Faith in Australia* began to press down on her shock absorbers in response to the ever-increasing load that she was being called upon to bear.

Finally the fuelling was complete. Ulm and Allan left the aircraft and walked along the stretch of sand to check the take-off run, leaving Taylor in the cockpit.

Something broke.

With a sound of cracking and splitting wood, the machine sagged down onto its starboard side. Petrol began dripping from cracks in the plywood wing, trickling into the pilot's cabin. Bill Taylor lost no time in getting out.

Once on the beach, he could see that the damage was catastrophic. The starboard tie-rod of the undercarriage had failed and *Faith in Australia* had subsided drunkenly onto the sand. With one wingtip cracked and bent, and one wheel splayed uselessly beside her, she was no longer a creature of the air, nor of the earth. Soon, the sea would claim her.

She had to be moved, and quickly.

The first priority was to lighten the load. Hoses were hastily improvised and the fuel that had so recently been pumped aboard was piped back into the drums or allowed to run into the sand. The police, Irish Air Force personnel, and other willing helpers gathered in an attempt to manhandle the stricken aircraft clear of the rising tide, but she was still heavy, there were few handholds, and with only one wheel it was an impossible task. The best they could do was to swing her around to face the incoming waves, lift the tail skid onto a supporting drum to protect the fin and tail plane, and secure it with a rope. As the waters rose, she began to lift and drop, lift and drop, each advancing wave inflicting further damage. In the cabin, Ulm and his crew struggled to remove the wireless set and other delicate instruments, braving petrol fumes until someone slashed the fabric to allow the noxious gases to escape. The engines were wrapped in tarpaulins, to give them a degree of protection from the salt spray.

When they had done all they could, Ulm, Taylor and Allen retreated. A photograph taken that day shows Charles Ulm walking disconsolately up the beach, hands deep in his pockets, trousers rolled above his knees, his back to his aircraft as if he had abandoned her to the sea. He had invested all his personal resources in *Faith in Australia* and now it appeared that he was about to lose everything.

⚬➤⚬⚬➤ ⚬⚬ ➤⚬⚬➤ ➤⚬ ⚬➤ ➤⚬➤➤ ⚬ ⚬⚬⚬

The next day, at low tide, they assessed the damage. *Faith in Australia* was a sorry sight. The waves had stripped the fabric from most of the rear fuselage and tail surfaces, exposing the steel skeleton, which was broken in places and already partly covered by sand. The plywood skin of the wooden wing had split and there was almost certainly internal damage to the ribs and spar. The starboard undercarriage was a mess, but thanks to their covers, the engines appeared to be unaffected. The aircraft was not a total loss, but it was obvious that it would have to be substantially rebuilt. It would cost a lot of money. Charles Ulm's heart sank.

Later that day, he and his crew met to discuss the future of their enterprise. The situation looked bleak. The Atlantic crossing and the rest of the around-the-world flight were off the agenda, at least for the time being. No longer able to pay them, he released the men from their contracts. They were now free to find jobs in Britain or return to Australia.

275

Edwards, a local man, understandably decided to leave, but Scotty Allan and Bill Taylor elected to stay.

And then, as if on cue, came a bolt from the blue. A telegram came for Charles Ulm:

WOULD BE PLEASED TO BEAR THE COST OF REPAIRING
YOUR AIRCRAFT

SIGNED WAKEFIED OF HYTHE

Lord Wakefield, who had sent Ulm and Kingsford Smith a congratulatory telegram at the conclusion of the trans-Pacific flight, had been following their respective careers and had thrown Charles Ulm a lifeline.

With his hopes renewed, Ulm lost no time in having *Faith in Australia* shipped to the Avro works at Ringway, near Manchester. Work began to get her flying again. They still hoped to make the Atlantic crossing, but winter was approaching and westerly gales were already starting to blow along the route between Ireland and Newfoundland. Time dragged. At last, the resurrection of *Faith in Australia* was complete and they flew her to Brooklands, near London, to wait for a favourable weather forecast for the Atlantic crossing.

It didn't come.

By the middle of October, it became obvious that their window of opportunity had closed; conditions would not again be suitable until the northern spring. But Ulm could not wait. During his absence from Australia, the inter-departmental committee had considered his report on air communications and, largely ignoring his carefully considered recommendations, had re-organised the air routes and put them all up for grabs. Tenders closed on 31 January. Ulm had to return to complete his bid.

To go some way towards justifying the £1400 that Lord Wakefield had spent in rebuilding the machine, Ulm decided to fly back to Australia as quickly as possible. He hoped to break the record of seven days, four hours and 43 minutes, which had been established on 11 October by Kingsford Smith in a Percival Gull.

On 12 October, they took off from the Fairey Aviation Company airfield at Hayes, in Middlesex, and returned to Australia via Athens, Baghdad, Karachi, Gaya (where they made an unscheduled refuelling stop), Calcutta, Akyab, Alor Setar and Singapore. Once again, the engines gave them trouble, but they managed to arrive at Derby on 20 October: six days, 17 hours and 56 minutes after leaving England.[9] The fact that he had beaten Smith's recently established record no doubt gave Charles Ulm considerable satisfaction.

There was no time for a rest, even though it was warranted. Desperately short of money, Ulm decided to do some barn-storming in New Zealand, so *Faith in Australia* was thoroughly overhauled in preparation for the trip across the Tasman Sea. Scotty Allan signed on again as pilot, together with an engineer named Bob Boulton, who would also act as co-pilot. Ulm invited

Jo Ulm and Ellen Rogers to accompany them; they would be the first women passengers to fly from Australia to New Zealand.

Ulm still loathed barnstorming as much as ever. He attributed this to his mind being 'cast in a different mould'. It appears he was the only one:

> I well remember the official reception on the aerodrome at New Plymouth. Scotty Allan always amuses me on these occasions. He just stands there with a vertical smile and blinks at his surroundings with affable indifference. Bob Boulton was obviously nervous, knowing that any moment he would be called upon to speak into the microphone. My wife was patently and naturally excited, whilst the faithful 'Rog' looked as though she could not believe it had all happened.[10]

Leaving *Faith in Australia* in the care of Scotty Allan and Bob Boulton, Charles Ulm, Jo Ulm and Ellen Rogers returned to Australia aboard the SS *Makura*, arriving in Sydney on 13 January 1934. Ulm and Norman Brearley had just 18 days to lodge their tenders.

The federal government had decided to divide Australia's airmail network into a number of divisions. As well as the overseas division, from Darwin to Singapore, there was to be an eastern internal division (Darwin–Brisbane–Cootamundra), a southern division (Charleville–Cootamundra) and a western division (Perth–Katherine). It was possible to tender for shorter sectors within the divisions.

When he saw the way in which the Australian end of the Empire Airmail Service had been organised, Charles Ulm was appalled. Under the scheme worked out by the bureaucrats, it appeared that affluent, sophisticated passengers would board a stately Imperial Airways airliner in Croydon, England, and travel in considerable luxury halfway around the world only to end their magic carpet ride not in a major Australian city, but in the tiny New South Wales town of Cootamundra. Here, at three o'clock in the morning, they would be required to clamber aboard a train bound for Sydney or Melbourne. The reasoning behind this ridiculous state of affairs was quite simple: it was government policy that no subsidised air service be permitted to compete with a mainline railway. Apparently tenders were not called for ANA's defunct Brisbane–Sydney–Melbourne route for the same reasons. It may have made sense to the public servants and the politicians, but to airline executives like Charles Ulm it was downright anachronistic.

The choice of aircraft was limited. In 1934, everybody in civil aviation circles knew that the best airliners in the world were being manufactured in the United States, where Hudson Fysh had already flown coast to coast in the new, all-metal Douglas DC-2, and become an instant convert. However, in Australia it was deemed unpatriotic to buy anything but British. Ulm therefore specified de Havilland types in his tenders: the twin-engine Dragon for the inland sectors, and the new four-engine DH.86 Express for the overwater service to Singapore.[11] Brearley proposed to use the twin-engine Vickers Viastra in Western Australia.

The tender application form was an intimidating document running to many pages. As well as the expected detailed financial statistics, it sought an inordinate amount of supporting information. For example, as well as nominating the type of aircraft proposed to operate a particular sector, tenderers were required to supply its rate of climb at altitudes from 1000 feet to 5000 feet measured at 1000-foot intervals, the dimensions of the hangars in which it would be housed along the route, and whether it had a tail wheel.[12] Charles Ulm and Norman Brearley tendered for 21 sectors within eight divisions on behalf of their new company, ambitiously named Commonwealth Airways. It was exacting work and Ellen Rogers spent many hours at the typewriter keyboard.

Kingsford Smith's role at this important stage of the development of the Australian airline system was minimal. To exploit his celebrity status, Ulm and Brearley briefly considered asking him to join them, as did Fysh and Rudder. But both camps just as quickly dropped the idea, for similar reasons. They all knew that Smithy had no interest in airline administration. He was first and foremost a flyer, a free spirit and, in a corporate environment, uncontrollable. Kingsford Smith subsequently associated himself with a bid submitted by New England Airways, but his heart wasn't in it.

To ensure that their precious documents met the 31 January deadline, Ulm and Brearley decided to convey them to Melbourne in person by train. Some hours after leaving Brisbane, they discovered that a fellow passenger was Hudson Fysh, who introduced them to his companion, a Mr Dismore. As the train made its slow way south, they adjourned to Fysh's compartment for a yarn and a smoke. The conversation naturally turned to aviation, but Fysh took care not to reveal that Dismore was the company secretary of Imperial Airways in Australia on an important mission. Ulm did not know that the box on the floor of the compartment, on which he was resting his feet, contained tender applications from a new company, a joint venture of Imperial and Qantas.[13]

Its name was Qantas Empire Airways.

CHAPTER 19

Stella Australis

Early in February, as the government pondered the tenders, Ulm returned to New Zealand by sea to prepare for the first official airmail flight between New Zealand and Australia. He and Scotty Allan took *Faith in Australia* to Muriwai Beach, near Auckland, and filled the tanks with enough fuel to keep her in the air for 22 hours.

The flight captured the imagination of philatelists and there were brisk sales of first day covers. When Allan lifted her off the sand, *Faith in Australia* was carrying 300 kilograms of mail: 40,000 letters addressed to enthusiasts all over the world.

Ulm quickly followed this successful venture with the first official airmail flight from Australia to New Zealand, again carrying 40,000 letters. The journey was not without incident: severe turbulence popped rivets in a fuel tank, causing a serious leak. Ulm, who had been asleep, took control and flew the aircraft while Boulton plugged the holes with his fingers and Allan worked feverishly to transfer fuel from the leaking tank to the tanks in the wing.

Among those waiting to greet *Faith in Australia* as it landed in New Zealand was Sir Hubert Wilkins, from whom Ulm and Kingsford Smith had bought the Fokker that subsequently became the *Southern Cross*. There was also a letter of support from Perce Moodie from the Bathurst days, in the form of a first day cover. Ulm was delighted: 'On my return to my office today, I received your letter which was posted to me by the First Australia to New Zealand airmail. This is just a short note to say thanks very much, old man, for I appreciate your thoughtfulness.'[1] In the midst of his struggles, it must have been reassuring to know that he still had friends.

On 14 April, *Faith in Australia* was in the air again, carrying 20,000 letters on the return trip. Flights across the Tasman Sea were becoming almost a matter of routine. While Ulm was well aware that the volume of mail would drop off once the impetus of the first day covers had subsided, he hoped that the successful completion of so many overseas flights in such a short period of time would go a long way towards convincing the government that he was the man to carry the airmail to Singapore.

His hopes were soon dashed.

On 19 April 1934, the Australian government announced that the airmail contracts for the overseas division, from Singapore to Darwin, and the eastern division, from Darwin to Brisbane, had been awarded to Qantas Empire Airways (QEA).

Charles Ulm would not have been surprised. He had known for months that Qantas and Imperial Airways were contemplating a joint venture of some kind, but he had not anticipated that they would go so far as to form a conglomerate. It had been a clever move: the Imperial management, through its contacts with British cabinet ministers, would have been able to bring influence to bear on their Australian counterparts. The federal government wanted British loans. Wheels within wheels; it was the way the Empire worked.

He was confident that he had quoted lower than QEA and had supplied detailed cost and revenue estimates to support his bid. Moreover, he had runs on the board; between 1928 and 1933, he had operated a financially viable airline entirely without subsidy, carrying passengers, freight and mail between the east coast capital cities. He knew that the management of ANA had been sound and he knew that his airline could probably have traded its way through the Great Depression. But the loss of the *Southern Cloud* had been a fatal blow. And a faint odour of Coffee Royal still lingered.

Times were changing. The days of derring-do, with Kingsford Smith descending from the skies like a god in a Greek tragedy to rescue passengers and mail from sodden airfields, were over. People required a higher degree of certainty now. They wanted to be able to post an airmail letter, or to book a seat on an aeroplane, in the expectation that it, or they, would reach their destination speedily, safely and with a minimum of fuss. 'With a minimum of fuss' would in fact become the catchphrase of Imperial Airways' successor, BOAC.

In his heart, Charles Ulm knew that Qantas had been providing such a service for years.

He made contact with Hudson Fysh and congratulated him.[2]

Never one to sit and brood, Ulm immediately wrote to Prime Minister Joseph Lyons, suggesting that the *Faith in Australia* make a goodwill flight across the Tasman Sea carrying a message from Lyons to the prime minister of New Zealand, together with messages from the governor-general, the governors of each Australian state, the lord mayors of each capital city, the president of the RSL and other prominent citizens, to their counterparts across the ditch. Lyons responded positively to the idea, as did Lord Wakefield, who offered to pay all expenses.

On 11 May, *Faith in Australia* once more departed Richmond and set course on the now well-worn track across the Tasman Sea. After landing at New Plymouth, they flew on to Wellington, where Ulm personally delivered Lyons' message to the prime minister of New Zealand. From a public relations viewpoint the exercise was an outstanding success and, for Charles Ulm, the beginning of a much-improved relationship with the Australian government. At last, people in high places were beginning to take him seriously.

Within weeks this took tangible form when the Director of Posts and Telegraphs, H.P. Brown, worked with him to organise the first official airmail flight from Australia to New Guinea.

Faith in Australia, crewed by Charles Ulm, Scotty Allan and Bob Boulton, left Point Cook near Melbourne on 24 June, carrying 26,000 letters and two passengers. More mail was taken on board at Mascot and Brisbane and after an overnight stop they flew on via Rockhampton and Townsville to Port Douglas, where they landed on the broad expanse of the palm-fringed Four Mile Beach.

The next day they left early, in the dark, guided by a row of flares. After a rough trip through storms and heavy cloud, they arrived at Port Moresby at 9 a.m. Aviation was already playing a vital role in the development of New Guinea. It was a mountainous country and in some places a journey that had hitherto taken up to ten days on foot could now be accomplished in minutes by air. When gold was discovered at Wau in the highlands, Guinea Airways flew in everything needed to establish the mines—materials, manpower and machinery—saving the prohibitive cost of a road through the rugged terrain. Guinea Airways' German-built, all-metal Junkers aircraft could shift sixteen tons of material (including complete motor vehicles) in a day, making it the world's leading airfreight operator.[3] Charles Ulm was no doubt mightily impressed.

After spending a couple of days in New Guinea, they returned to Melbourne along the same route, carrying 40,000 letters. Although the revenue from the airmail flights had barely covered costs, the public relations value was beyond measure.

Due to the federal government's policy of not providing subsidy to any air service that competed with the railways, there was now a complete lack of scheduled services linking Sydney, Melbourne, Adelaide and Tasmania. Charles Ulm was confident that he could draw upon his experience with ANA to restore those services, entirely without subsidy, and make a profit.

It was his intention to form a new company, Interstate Speedlines, to connect with the New England Airways' service at Sydney, the QEA England–Australia service at Cootamundra, the Tasmanian service at Melbourne, and Norman Brearley's West Australian service at Adelaide. It would then be possible to travel by scheduled airline completely around Australia.

The name Interstate Speedlines was possibly inspired by the American airline Varney Speed Lanes, which at the time was operating single-engine, six-passenger Lockheed Orion airliners between Los Angeles and Mexico City. The first of its class to be fitted with a retractable undercarriage, and flaps to reduce the landing speed, the Orion was faster than many current military aircraft.[4] Ulm seriously considered it as the aircraft to operate his new service.

He sought the support of Ernest Fisk, a highly experienced company director, and the founder and owner of the large radio manufacturing and broadcasting company Amalgamated Wireless of Australasia (AWA). Ulm had first met Fisk when he commissioned AWA to design the wireless equipment for ANA's Avro Tens. When he realised the scope of Ulm's ambition, Fisk deemed the name Interstate Speedlines too restrictive. Charles quickly compiled a long list of alternatives:

Air Communications Limited

Airlines Limited

Air Transport Limited

Air Transportation Limited

Austral-International Air Transport Limited

Austral-International Airways Limited

Australian-International Airways Limited

Australian-overseas Airlines Limited

Australian and International Speed Airlines Limited

The C.T.P. Ulm Air Transport Company Limited

The C.T.P. Ulm International Airlines Company Limited

International Air Transport Limited

International Air Travel Limited

International Airlines Limited

International Overseas Airlines Limited[5]

Ultimately they rejected them all and decided to create an entirely new company. They called it Great Pacific Airways.

The Articles of Association of the new company reflected a major change in Ulm's thinking. Interstate Speedlines had been an operating company, but, acting upon Fisk's advice, Great Pacific Airways was incorporated as a holding company, enabling its board to create any number of subsidiaries. This gave the management great flexibility.

Great Pacific Airways was registered on 23 September 1934, with Ernest Fisk as chairman, Charles Ulm as managing director and Edward Ludowici, Ulm's trusted associate from the ANA days, as company secretary. The nominal capital was £500,000.

Five hundred thousand pounds was a lot of money in 1934 and for Charles Ulm it represented a whole new range of possibilities. He remembered the late nights, not so long ago, smoking and yarning with Smithy at Lavender Bay, when he had fantasised about owning airlines that not only linked Australia's capital cities, but also spanned the Pacific. Back then, it had been merely a pipe dream. Now, with Great Pacific's capital and some hard work, he knew he could turn it into reality.

His plan was to create a trans-Pacific air service from Sydney to Auckland and Suva, then to Honolulu via Fanning Atoll (Tabuaeran) or Kanton Island, where passengers could connect with steamer services to Vancouver, San Francisco or Los Angeles. It was ambitious, but with the modern airliners then becoming available, Ulm believed that it was eminently possible.

The aircraft that he wanted was the Douglas DC-2. Not British, but the best.

The new Douglas airliner sported novel features such as all-metal construction, a retractable undercarriage and variable pitch propellers. Powered by two 835-horsepower Wright R-1820 air-cooled radial engines, in its standard form it could convey 18 passengers almost 1700 kilometres at 320 kilometres per hour.[6] Ulm intended to re-configure it to carry eight passengers, 160 kilograms of mail and extra fuel for the long legs between the Pacific islands.[7] It seemed ideal.

As usual, he prepared preliminary cost and revenue figures to present to the Great Pacific board, together with a timetable and other operational details for a weekly service each way between Sydney and Honolulu, utilising three aircraft.

> This is a sound and perfectly safe schedule to operate.
>
> There is only <u>one</u> night landing called for (at Canton Island) and fogs do not occur at this point. Strong winds are seldom experienced here. There are no obstructions to approaches. There will be only 3½ hours (approximately) of night flying before reaching Canton Island. The crew will be in continuous wireless communication with Canton Island throughout night flying period. Navigation to Canton Island presents no difficulties if wireless beacon and emergency beacon light is used. Aircraft will carry its own landing lights. Flares on the ground as emergency. Visibility generally very good. The take off from Canton Island will be only just before dawn and presents no difficulties whatever.
>
> At two points only do passengers have to arise early:
>
> <u>At Canton Island</u> at before dawn, say 4:15 a.m. There is nothing to view here, and passengers will have slept at the company's hotel on the aerodrome.
>
> <u>At Auckland</u> at, say 6 a.m. to leave hotel at 6:30 a.m.
>
> Passengers sleep ashore and have reclining day-beds (adjustable) in the aircraft. Passengers leave Sydney at a comfortable hour (10 a.m.) and arrive at Honolulu similarly (5:30 p.m.).
>
> Time of journey including stops is 2 days 7½ hours.[8]

While it was evident that he had carefully considered the operational aspects of the new air route, his estimates reveal that he grossly underestimated the cost and logistics involved in the establishment of a base on an island in the middle of the Pacific. Ulm had allowed £11,250 for the preparation of the airstrip and £12,500 for the construction of the associated buildings.[9] According to his timetable, passengers would have an overnight stay on Canton Island, yet there is no allowance for the construction, staffing and supply of a hotel.

In the second half of 1934, Pan American Airways were carrying out a similar exercise, constructing luxury overnight accommodation for passengers on their new trans-Pacific Clipper service between the United States and China. To establish bases on the islands of Midway, Wake and Guam, Pan Am chartered the 15,000-ton SS *New Haven* out of San Francisco to transport 74 construction workers, 44 airline technicians, a doctor, 300,000 gallons of aviation fuel, power generators, weather and wireless stations, hotel supplies, water distillation units, refrigerators, tractors, tools and prefabricated housing. When the island soil proved unsuitable for growing fresh vegetables, garden soil and hydroponic equipment was brought in. The prodigious exercise was completed in just three months. The cost would have been enormous.[10]

It is not clear whether Charles Ulm was aware of Pan American's activities, but as he began to plan a demonstration flight to convince the Great Pacific board of the feasibility of his proposal, it is almost certain that he had not the slightest inkling of the logistics and cost of the task that lay head.

He planned to fly from Vancouver to Melbourne via San Francisco, Honolulu, Fanning Atoll (Tabuaeran), Suva, Auckland and Sydney. Although he eventually intended to use the American DC-2 commercially, for this flight he placed an order for the smaller, six-passenger Airspeed Envoy, which was lighter, less expensive and, being British-built, more politically expedient.

The landing ground at Suva's Albert Park had given them all a fright during the 1928 crossing in the *Southern Cross*, so through his Fijian contacts Ulm requested a more suitable place for them to put down and it is believed a site was chosen near the present Nadi International Airport. Although his proposal specified Canton Island as a refuelling point, Ulm changed his mind and arranged for an airstrip to be prepared at Fanning Atoll instead, probably for political reasons.

Curiously, it appears that the Great Pacific Board were reluctant to back their managing director financially, but the Australian government was at long last beginning to take him seriously and offered him a guarantee of £8000 towards expenses. While very welcome, this was insufficient, and Ulm was forced to fall back on his own resources. Once again, with Jo's full support, he mortgaged their personal assets, including their house, to fund the flight.

He had difficulty finding a crew. Scotty Allan, now flying for QEA, was unavailable, as was Bill Taylor, who was about to embark with Kingsford Smith on the first west-to-east crossing of the Pacific in the Lockheed Altair *Lady Southern Cross*.

Taylor and Allan both recommended George Littlejohn, the chief instructor of the New South Wales Aero Club. Ulm was reluctant as Littlejohn had virtually no experience in flying heavy multi-engined aircraft, nor in flying by instruments. But the demonstration flight was still underfunded and when Littlejohn offered to make up the shortfall with his own money, Ulm agreed to take him on.[11] He offered the position of wireless operator to Leon Skilling, whom he had met aboard the SS *Otranto* in 1929.[12] Already an experienced shipboard operator, Skilling agreed to undertake further studies to upgrade his airborne skills.

Early in September 1934, Charles Ulm sailed for England via the United States. During the long days at sea he took the opportunity to write, completing the autobiographical sketch 'Wings and The Man', and two short pieces entitled 'Flying and The Man on the Ground' and 'Barnstorming in New Zealand'. He also wrote an account of the forthcoming flight as if it were already a fait accompli, leaving blank spaces for statistics to be added when they came to hand. He wrote in longhand, posting the manuscripts back to Ellen Rogers in Sydney for transcription.

Before he took delivery of his new Airspeed Envoy, he intended to learn as much as he could about the Douglas DC-2, and talk to operators who were already flying it in airline service, so he visited the Douglas factory in California and the Transcontinental & Western Air Express at their headquarters terminal in Kansas City. He reported on the experience to Fisk:

At the Douglas works I was given the opportunity of very thoroughly examining the Douglas transport type aircraft in all stages of construction and of conferring with the designers; and at T.W.A. I was able to study the whole of this company's operations, and particularly with reference to the cost of operating Douglas transport aircraft.

I personally flew the transport across the USA Continent an average speed of 198 mph [318 kilometres per hour] at an average power output of 69 per cent of full power. As a result of my conferences with the designers of the transport, the Douglas company can now guarantee to supply a long-range version of the DC-2 certificated to a gross weight of 20,000 lbs [9071 kilograms] and which for the purposes of a regular trans-Pacific Air Service will carry eight passengers and their baggage and 300 lbs [136 kilograms] of airmail.

In the same letter, Ulm revealed that he was concerned about a friend. Kingsford Smith was proposing to fly the Lockheed Altair from Australia to America: 'This is a particularly foolhardy undertaking and is looked upon with great disfavor in aviation circles both in America and England. If he does start I do hope he gets through all right, although there is much more likelihood of his breaking his neck, and although those within the industry will realise that it is a foolish business, I'm afraid the public will be tremendously upset if Smithy comes to harm.'[13] Considering that Ulm was about to embark upon an equally hazardous journey in the opposite direction, it was a classic case of the pot calling the kettle black.

Ulm now turned to his attention to the new aeroplane for his own hazardous undertaking, the demonstration flight. The aircraft he had chosen, the Airspeed Envoy, was a low wing monoplane of wooden construction powered by two Armstrong Siddeley Cheetah engines, each of 277 horsepower. Fitted with a retractable undercarriage, in its standard form the Envoy could carry six passengers for 400 miles (640 kilometres) at a cruising speed of 150 miles per hour (240 kilometres per hour).[14]

Ulm's brusque, impatient manner did not endear him to the people at Airspeed's Portsmouth factory, particularly when he insisted on a complete re-configuration of his new aircraft. To increase the range he had the passenger seats and lavatory removed and replaced by a very large fuel tank immediately behind the cockpit, completely isolating the navigator–wireless operator, who was forced to occupy the rear half of the cabin.

Stella Australis carried the latest navigational aids, including a very accurate earth inductor compass, and sensitive wireless equipment capable of picking up directional beams, but the only way that the navigator could communicate with the pilots was via a primitive speaking tube. It was incongruous. Experience should have told Ulm that in a noisy cabin they would soon have to resort to a fishing rod and scribbled notes, but if his inner voice told him so, he failed to take heed.

After he and Littlejohn had test-flown and accepted the machine, Ulm christened her *Stella Australis* (Star of Australia) and she was shipped to Toronto. They then flew her in easy stages across Canada to Vancouver, where Skilling joined them on several local shakedown flights, after which they flew down the west coast to San Francisco to await suitable weather.

At 3.41 p.m. on Monday, 3 December 1934, the famous aviator Amelia Earhart was among the reporters and wellwishers who gathered at Oakland Airport to wish Ulm and his fellow travellers well on the long ocean crossing to Honolulu. They had planned a mid-afternoon take-off so as to arrive in the Hawaiian Islands early the following morning, giving them a whole day to search for a landfall should the need arise.

By early evening, the crew of *Stella Australis* had settled into a routine and radio messages received by shore stations indicated that the flight was proceeding normally. Possibly because Ulm had not contracted with a news outlet to provide copyrighted progress reports of the flight, most of Skilling's transmissions contained little other than the state of the weather and position reports.

Eight hundred kilometres out from San Francisco, Skilling established radio contact with the liner SS *Lurline*. At 11.25 p.m. the naval shore station at Wallupe, on Oahu, picked up messages between the aircraft and the SS *President Coolidge* and, from the position reports that were exchanged, the operator was able to estimate that *Stella Australis* was about 1600 kilometres from the island. The flight seemed to be proceeding smoothly.

The first indication that anything was wrong came at 5.40 a.m., when Skilling transmitted,

WE ARE UP AT 12000 FEET STOP WEATHER IS BAD STOP
CAN YOU PLEASE GET A WEATHER REPORT FOR US STOP

The US Coast Guard cutter *Itasca* and the radio station at Wheeler Field both responded, sending the latest report, but received no reply. At 6.40 a.m. came a further message, some of the words obscured by static.

PAN PAN PAN [the international code for extremely urgent]
WE ARE IN --- SHORT OF --- BEACON ON MAKAPUU PT
STOP WE ARE LOST

Half an hour later it became apparent that the situation was indeed desperate.

WE HAVE VERY LITTLE GASOLINE LEFT AND WE NEED THE
BEACON URGENTLY STOP WE DO NOT WANT TO GIVE THE
SOS [the international distress call] STOP PLEASE TELL
THEM TO SHAKE IT UP ON THE BEACON STOP

The beacon at Makapuu Point had in fact been operating since midnight and experienced wireless operators would later postulate that Skilling was not picking up the signal either because *Stella Australis* was too far off course, or he had not tuned his receiver properly. The truth will never be known.

At 7.24 a.m. Ulm sent another message, again distorted by static.

> ---LIKE HELP STOP WE DO NOT KNOW IF WE ARE SOUTH
> OF THE ISLANDS OR NORTH WILL YOU GET BEARINGS ON
> US I WILL SEND FOR FIVE MINUTES

The operator at Globe Wireless at Kaena Point on Oahu, who had been monitoring the situation, immediately contacted the *Itasca* and asked her to try to get a bearing on *Stella Australis* using her radio compass, but Skilling failed to make a continuous transmission so that the *Itasca* could get a fix. Globe Wireless then informed Ulm directly that the Makapuu beacon was on, and gave him the location of the Globe transmitter should he wish to use that instead of Makapuu.

Ulm responded:

> WILL YOU SEND VS [directional signal] WE HAVE ABOUT
> AN HOURS SUPPLY OF GASOLINE STOP

The Globe operator complied, sending a continuous signal so that Skilling could tune his receiver to the beacon.

At 8.25 a.m. Ulm was on the air again:

> URGENT STOP WE DO NOT HAVE ENOUGH GAS STOP KEEP
> RADIO BEACON GOING AND HAVE A LAUNCH READY
> BECAUSE THERE IS NOT ENOUGH GAS STOP

It was now apparent that Ulm and his crew were in dire distress. Aircraft were launched immediately to conduct a visual search and at the same time to attempt to get a wireless bearing using their on-board equipment.

They found no sign of *Stella Australis.*

At 8.40 a.m. Ulm's message was unambiguous:

> SOS SOS SOS WE ARE SOUTH OF HONOLULU BUT ARE
> HEADING BACK ON THE RIGHT COURSE

The signals then continued intermittently, weak and difficult to understand.

Finally, at 9.21 a.m.:

> WE ARE TURNING INTO THE WIND
> COME AND PICK US UP SOS SOS SOS . . . [15]

And then, nothing.

Immediately after it was learned that the *Stella Australis* had gone down, the US Navy began a determined search, which eventually involved 32 aircraft and 23 surface vessels. The searchers were handicapped by conflicting information in Ulm's radio transmissions: in one message, he stated that he had just passed the SS *President Coolidge* and was about 800 kilometres short of Hawaii, while another, sent not long afterwards, indicated that he believed that they had overflown the islands entirely and were turning back. With such a wide expanse of ocean between those limits the best that the navy could do was to send ships and aircraft 400 kilometres in all directions, and hope. Japanese fishing sampans, operating offshore, were also called upon to join the search.

As the days passed, reports of floating wreckage came in and were investigated, without result. There was much conjecture about the reasons for the disappearance of the *Stella Australis*, but as the search continued, an editorial writer for the *Honolulu Star Bulletin* probably came closer to the truth than most:

Captain Ulm's Mishap

Until Captain Ulm is able to make a detailed report of his experience in his flight from Oakland towards Oahu, all the details of his failure and forced descent upon the sea must remain subjects of speculation. But it is apparent now that a contributing element was in navigation and to some degree in his inability to pick up the Navy radio beacon, we had been on [the air] from midnight Monday, although Captain Ulm, before descending, had asked for it. At 6 o'clock yesterday morning, besides, he reported that visibility was 'practically nil' at an altitude of 12,000 feet; something of great importance to a man hoping to sight land soon.

In brief, the 'Star of Australia' lost her way, and some of the reasons are those outlined. She was out long enough to make Hawaii, had the course been true. A landing here might have been made in about 18 hours or less, granted excellent flying conditions. All told, she was in the air about 20 hours, and during that time her motors carried her until her fuel failed.

This mishap, therefore, is nothing to shake our confidence in present craft or engines. It does emphasise that the Pacific Ocean is very large, that in its wide wastes Hawaii is a succession of pinheads, and that navigation cannot be too good, especially when Captain Ulm's fuel supply allowed him very little time to spare. Apart from possible pilikia [trouble] with some part of the radio equipment, which might have prevented the 'Star of Australia' from keeping on the radio beam, the cause of the failure seems human not mechanical.[16]

In Australia, the loss of Charles Ulm and his crew received wide coverage. Kingsford Smith was shocked and deeply saddened. Despite their differences, his friendship with Ulm had remained intact. Assuming the gravitas of Sir Charles Kingsford Smith, he told the press:

> Charles Ulm was many things besides a great pilot and navigator. He was gifted, and possessed in his unusual character temperament many of the qualities of greatness. He had a great business capacity, punch and vigour, and had he lived would have fulfilled his dream of becoming the head of a great, worldwide aviation organisation, a position for which he was admirably suited. There is no saying to what goal his abilities would have taken him.

But later, as Smithy, Ulm's old mate, he wrote to a mutual friend,

> Poor old Charles came to a tragic end. It is impossible
> from the scarcity of information available to form any
> definite opinion of how it all happened, but it looks as
> though they were somewhat uncertain of their position
> throughout the flight, and were relying on picking up
> the wireless beam at Honolulu. Whether their uncer-
> tainty of position was due to bad weather conditions or
> laxity or inefficiency in navigation I do not know, but it
> seems almost inconceivable that with Charles in charge
> the latter could be the cause.[17]

Charles Ulm was indeed in charge. But when he installed
an extra fuel tank immediately behind the cockpit, probably to
keep the centre of gravity within acceptable limits, his navigator became isolated from the pilots. Consequently, when they
became lost, Ulm could not get to Leon Skilling to confer with
him and help him get *Stella Australis* back on track. Furthermore,
Littlejohn had never before been called upon to maintain an
accurate course for hour after hour, in the dark, across a wide,
featureless body of water, and Skilling usually worked at a tidy
navigation table on board a big ship, not a miniscule desk in a
cramped and noisy cabin. Their training for this mission had
been minimal. Ulm should perhaps not have selected such an
inexperienced crew. Unfortunately, it may well have been the
case that nobody of experience was prepared to go with him.

The Director of Civil Aviation wrote a personal letter to Jo Ulm:

My dear Mrs Ulm,

I have refrained from writing this letter as long as there was any prospect of Charles and his companions being safe. I am afraid, however, the time has now arrived when we must abandon all hope. Your great loss is shared by all Australian aviation, as Charles's interests were whole-heartedly in flying, and all of us have grown to regard him as a leader who would have done even greater things for aviation in the future. To me also he was a very dear friend and I shall miss his friendship as well as his valuable views, suggestions, and comments on aviation matters. It must be some small consolation to us all to know that he died as he lived—in endeavouring to advance the cause of commercial aviation. If there is anything at all I can do to help you please do not hesitate to let me know.

Yours very sincerely,

Edgar Johnston

In reply, Jo Ulm wrote:

Dear Capt. Johnston,

I deeply appreciate your nice remarks regarding Charles. We have continued to hope that he and his companions may yet be found on one of those islands but I'm afraid that my faith has now dwindled.

I simply cannot contemplate the future without him. Still the thought that his life was worthwhile may be a big consolation to me.

Many thanks for your generous offer of assistance.
If there should be any way in which you can help me I
shall communicate with you.

With all good wishes,

Yours sincerely,

Mrs Jo Ulm[18]

Charles Ulm had mortgaged all his assets, including his house and life insurance policy to finance the flight, and consequently Jo was now in financial difficulty. Realising her predicament, Prime Minister Lyons and his cabinet agreed to pay her the full value of the insurance policy, together with the value of the other assets that had been mortgaged. Jo Ulm had been her husband's staunch supporter through thick and thin, and it was her due.

Ever since the triumphant Pacific flight in 1928, there had been repeated calls from both press and public for Charles Ulm to be knighted. Many people believed that he should have received the award at the same time as Kingsford Smith. At last, in November 1934, Prime Minister Joseph Lyons agreed to recommend him for a knighthood at the completion of his Pacific flight.

Tragically, Ulm never knew.

Ellen Rogers had lost not just a respected employer, but a valued and much-loved friend. Alone in the office at Challis House, she completed the transcription of her boss's account of the never-to-be completed flight of the *Stella Australis*, blank spaces and all.

The significance of those spaces was not lost on Ellen.

She slipped one last page into her typewriter and tapped out her own farewell.

Exit, Charles Ulm.[19]

Epilogue

Charles Ulm was always an adventurer.

While still a boy he put his age up and ran away to war; was wounded and sent home; recovered, and enlisted again.

While overseas, he saw his first aeroplane and was captivated, but it took him a long time to learn to fly. His war wounds were partly responsible for this, but for Ulm the primary allure of aviation lay not in taking an aeroplane into the air and bringing it safely back again; he was more interested in taking an aeroplane and putting it to commercial use.

In post-war Australia, his ambitions to establish a charter business far exceeded the capabilities of the airframes and engines that he could afford, but he persisted, picked himself up after every setback, and carried on.

His relentless drive left little tolerance for those who did not share his vision and many found his manner brusque. He could be ruthless in his relationships with employees and even friends.

Much has been written about his relationship with Charles Kingsford Smith, but one thing is abundantly clear: in the early days of their partnership, each was highly dependent upon the other. Ulm needed a pilot of great skill who could help him realise his dream of flying the Pacific. Smithy, who shared that dream, needed a man with the entrepreneurial flair to find and fund a suitable aircraft.

In the euphoria that followed their momentous flight, it is perhaps understandable that its charismatic pilot should receive the lion's share of the glory, but without the courage, the tenacity, and the brilliant organisational skills of Charles Ulm, the *Southern Cross* would never have left the ground. This lack of recognition rankled and, when Kingsford Smith later released his autobiography, Ulm had no hesitation in taking legal action to make sure he received the credit that he deserved.

A born publicist and a master of spin, Ulm quite early realised the power of the mass media, particularly radio, and throughout the trans-Pacific flight he exploited it with great skill. But he was soon to learn that the media can quickly change its tune and his relationship with the press soured when the official enquiry into the Coffee Royal affair revealed that he sometimes operated in the shady margin between exaggeration and untruth. This taint on his reputation dogged him for the rest of his days.

The formation of Australian National Airways, a world standard airline, was arguably Charles Ulm's greatest achievement. Smithy and Ulm were co-directors, but Ulm was the driving force. ANA prospered without any form of government subsidy and, but for the loss of the *Southern Cloud*, would probably have survived the Great Depression.

Had Ulm not been lost, the adventure would have continued. He had plans to manufacture modern airliners under licence in Australia and establish a regular, scheduled airline service between Australia and America.

The powerful Pan American Airways, backed by the United States Government, had its eyes on the Pacific too.

Ulm would have had a fight on his hands.

Charles Ulm had never been one to walk away from a fight.

Acknowledgements

This book could not have been written without the assistance of Charles Ulm's son, John. Although he was only 13 years old when his father died, John Ulm still has personal recollections, which he has generously shared. Perhaps more importantly, John has been able to view his father's contribution to the Australian airline industry through the prism of his own long career as a Qantas executive and I found this unique perspective most helpful. I thank him and Valda for their hospitality.

I would also like to express my appreciation to John for his foresight in recognising the historical significance of his father's papers. With the assistance of Charles Ulm's secretary, the late Ellen Rogers, John spent many years gathering and collating thousands of documents, which are now kept in the National

Library in Canberra and Sydney's Mitchell Library. Both collections were a treasure trove for me.

I thank the staff at the National Library for their help during my week-long visit and I also wish to express my appreciation of Trove, their wonderful online research facility, which gave me immediate and easy access to the newspapers of the 1930s. I also wish to thank Andy Carr of the Mitchell Library, Judith Paterson of the National Archives of Australia, and Patricia Lai of the Hawaii State Archives.

I thank my overseas researchers. Simon Fowler, the History Man, delved into the files on my behalf at the British National Archives, and at the British Airways archive at Heathrow, where curator Jim Davies was able to point him in the right direction. In Honolulu, Sarah Tamashiro located all the Hawaiian newspapers published at the time of Charles Ulm's disappearance.

In Melbourne, I spent several enjoyable days combing through the files at the Airways Museum at Essendon Airport and I wish to thank Roger Meyer and Maurice Austin for their friendly assistance.

Through John Ulm, I met John Scott of the Australian Aviation Historical Society's New South Wales branch. Past issues of John's regular online feature 'Loops and Landings' were of great help when I was delving into Charles Ulm's early days in Bathurst.

I also wish to thank John Darcy Williams of Tasmania for once again casting a friendly yet critical eye over my manuscript and for access to his extensive Charles Ulm files.

I also acknowledge the continued support of Tim Curnow, who has been my friend and literary agent for more than 30 years.

I once again thank Tom Gilliatt, Publishing Director at Allen and Unwin, for his confidence in my initial concept, and Angela Handley, A&U's Editorial Manager, and copyeditor Aziza Kuypers for turning the manuscript into a book.

As always, I deeply appreciate the love and patient support of my wife, Bronwyn, who has travelled the Charles Ulm trail with me. Bronwyn also prepared one of the maps for the book.

Finally, I wish to thank my late brother-in-law Don Gough and his wife Lynn for their friendship and hospitality. We shared a lot of laughs during my research visits to Sydney. Don sadly passed away before the writing was completed and I have dedicated this book to his memory.

Notes

CHAPTER 1

1 Papers of Charles Ulm, 1931–1969 [manuscript], 4 December 1934, National Library of Australia (NLA), Canberra, MS 215 (account written by Ulm while at sea, en route for England just before his final flight).
2 NLA MS 215.
3 NLA MS 215.
4 National Archives of Australia (NAA), Canberra, Australian Imperial Force, Base Records Office, B2455, ULM Charles Thomas Phillippe (AKA JACKSON Charles).
5 NAA B2455 (letter).
6 Ellen Rogers, *Faith in Australia: Charles Ulm and Australian aviation*, Book Production Services, Crows Nest, NSW, 1987, p. 11; NAA B2455 (medical record).
7 NLA MS 215.
8 Charles Ulm, 'I get the urge to fly: My first steps towards the Air Mail', February 1935, *The Herald* (Sydney): one of a series of articles from Ulm's papers, published posthumously as 'The life story of Charles Ulm as told by himself'. From the archive of John Williams.

9   A.J. Jackson, *De Havilland Aircraft Since 1909*, Putnam Aeronautical Books, London, 1987, p. 154.
10 C.H. Barnes, *Handley Page Aircraft Since 1907*, Putnam Aeronautical Books, London, 1995, p. 147.
11 Terry Moyle, *Art Deco Airports: Dream designs of the 1920s and 1930s*, New Holland, London, 2015, pp. 78–9.
12 NAA B2455.
13 Author's interview with John Ulm (Charles Ulm's son), 12 July 2016.
14 John Scott, 'Loops and Landings', supplement to *Southern Skies, Journal of the Aviation Historical Society of Australia*, no. 361, April 2003.
15 Scott, 'Loops and Landings'.
16 NLA MS 215 (letter).
17 NLA MS 215.
18 John Scott, 'Loops and Landings', *Journal of the Aviation Historical Society of Australia*, no. 362, May 2003.

CHAPTER 2

1   Charles Ulm, 'I get the urge to fly: My first steps towards the Air Mail', *The Herald* (Sydney), February 1935. From the archive of John Williams.
2   *Wingham Chronicle and Manning River Observer*, 30 October 1925, p. 1.
3   Ian Mackersey, *Smithy: The life of Sir Charles Kingsford Smith*, Warner Books, 1998, p. 97.
4   Ulm, 'I get the urge to fly', *The Herald* (Sydney), February 1935.
5   'Faces towards east', *The Sun* (Sydney), 9 April 1924, p. 1. Retrieved 26 October 2016 from <http://nla.gov.au/nla.news-article223387518>.
6   '"The Sun" aloft', *The Sun* (Sydney), 9 April 1924, p. 1. Retrieved 26 October 2016 from <http://nla.gov.au/nla.news-article223387512>.
7   Charles Ulm, 'The life story of Charles Ulm as told by himself', Unpublished manuscript. From the archive of John Williams.
8   Ulm, 'The life story of Charles Ulm'.

CHAPTER 3

1   The aeroplane's name—NYP—was an abbreviation of New York–Paris.
2   In 1919, Raymond Orteig, a wealthy French-born New York hotelier, offered a prize of US$25,000 to the first aviator to fly between New York

and Paris in either direction. Although the principal aim was to enhance Franco-American friendship, the challenge was open to flyers from any allied country. Eight years later, Orteig awarded the prize to Charles Lindbergh at the Breevort Hotel in New York City on 16 June 1927.

3 Lindbergh had in fact already considered flying across the Pacific. See Charles A. Lindbergh, *The Spirit of St Louis*, Charles Scribner's Sons, New York, 1953, p. 107.

4 Ellen Rogers, *Faith in Australia: Charles Ulm and Australian aviation*, Book Production Services, Crows Nest, NSW, 1987, pp. 15–16.

5 It is quite possible that he also saw a man who stole his girl. Keith Anderson had recently announced his engagement to Bon Hilliard, with whom Smithy had been keeping company for some time. By all accounts, Smithy was not a vindictive man, but this may have coloured his decision. The Anderson–Kingsford Smith–Hilliard triangle is outside the scope of the Charles Ulm story; for more detail, see Ian Mackersey, *Smithy: The life of Sir Charles Kingsford Smith*, Warner Books, 1998, p. 93.

6 George Bond and Company later became well known for its Chesty Bond singlets.

7 Mackersey, *Smithy*, pp. 100–1.

8 *The Sun* (Sydney), 20 June 1927.

9 The tyre had been inflated in Sydney, under cold conditions, but in the heat of western Queensland the air expanded, causing it to burst.

10 A type of flying suit that derived its name from its Australian inventor, Sidney Cotton.

11 *The Sun* (Newcastle), 1 July 1927, p. 3.

12 John McCarthy, 'Ulm, Charles Thomas Philippe (1898–1934)', *Australian Dictionary of Biography*, National Centre of Biography, Australian National University, <http://adb.anu.edu.au/biography/ulm-charles-thomas-philippe-8896/text15627>, published first in hardcopy 1990, accessed online 6 March 2017.

CHAPTER 4

1 Ian Mackersey, *Smithy: The life of Sir Charles Kingsford Smith*, Warner Books, 1998, p. 103.

2 Interestingly, the big Fokker was identical in almost every respect to *Southern Cross*, the aircraft which would soon carry Ulm and Smithy all

the way to Sydney, but with three engines such a machine was expensive, and at the time way beyond their wildest dreams.

3 Mackersey, *Smithy*, p. 102, and <https://en.wikipedia.org/wiki/Dole-Air-Race>, accessed 14 March 2017.

4 Conversation recalled by Kingsford Smith, *Keith Vincent Anderson v Charles Edward Kingsford Smith and Charles Thomas Phillippe Ulm*, Supreme Court of NSW in equity: Case No. 5633 of 1928. Transcript in evidence in NSW State Archives, Sydney, ref K1800390, p. 42.

5 Mackersey, *Smithy*, p. 107.

6 Conversation recalled by Kingsford Smith, *Keith Vincent Anderson v Charles Edward Kingsford Smith and Charles Thomas Phillippe Ulm*, p. 44.

7 *Hitchcock v Kingsford Smith and Others*, p. 3.

8 <https://en.wikipedia.org/wiki/Dole-Air-Race>, accessed 14 March 2017.

9 Papers of Charles Ulm, 1931–1969 [manuscript], 4 December 1934, National Library of Australia, Canberra, MS 215 (letter from Wilkins to a Mr Byrne).

10 Mackersey, *Smithy*, p. 111.

CHAPTER 5

1 Ian Mackersey, *Smithy: The life of Sir Charles Kingsford Smith*, Warner Books, 1998, p. 111.

2 Mackersey, *Smithy*, p. 113.

3 Papers of Charles Ulm, 1931–1969 [manuscript], 4 December 1934, National Library of Australia (NLA), Canberra, MS 215 (letter from Locke Harper to Walter B. Phillips, Atlantic Union Oil Company, Australia).

4 Kingsford Smith, in Mackersey, *Smithy*, p. 115.

5 Charles Ulm, 'I get the urge to fly: My first steps towards the Air Mail', *The Herald* (Sydney), February 1935. From the archive of John Williams.

6 NLA MS 215 (letter from Harper to Phillips).

7 Mackersey, *Smithy*, p. 117.

8 Mackersey, *Smithy*, p. 118.

9 Ulm, 'I get the urge to fly'.

10 Ulm, 'I get the urge to fly'.

11 This cable and those following were annexures dated 19 July 1928, in *Keith Vincent Anderson v Charles Edward Kingsford Smith and Charles*

Thomas Phillippe Ulm, p. 42. 'CHILLACHAS' was a combination of one of Smithy's nicknames (Chilla) and Ulm's nickname (Chas).

12   NLA MS 215 (letter).

CHAPTER 6

1   Harry Lyon, in Lloyd S. Gates, 'Harry Lyon and the Southern Cross', *American Aviation Society Historical Journal*, vol. 24, no. 4, 1979, p. 282.
2   Ralph M. Heinz, 'How the Americans described the Southern Cross flight', *Popular Hobbies* (magazine), 1 August 1928.
3   Papers of Charles Ulm, 1931–1969 [manuscript], 4 December 1934, National Library of Australia, Canberra, MS 215 (letter from Harper to Phillips).
4   Charles Kingsford Smith and Charles Ulm, *Story of 'Southern Cross' Trans-Pacific Flight 1928*, Penlington and Somerville, Sydney, 1928, p. 153.
5   Cable in Ian Mackersey, *Smithy: The life of Sir Charles Kingsford Smith*, Warner Books, 1998, p. 134.

CHAPTER 7

1   Papers of Charles Ulm, 1931–1969 [manuscript], 4 December 1934, National Library of Australia (NLA), Canberra, MS 215.
2   *The Sun* (Sydney), 1 June 1928, p. 1.
3   QST is an international code indicating that a radio message is directed to amateur operators; S ARD denoted messages directed exclusively to the *Examiner*.
4   NLA MS 215.
5   NLA MS 215.
6   Ian Mackersey, *Smithy: The life of Sir Charles Kingsford Smith*, Warner Books, 1998, p. 137.
7   NLA MS 215.
8   Mackersey, *Smithy*, p. 143.
9   *The Sun* (Sydney), 3 June 1928, p. 1.
10 Note and two maps in ML MSS 3359: Charles T.P. Ulm collection of historical aviation records, Mitchell Library, State Library of New South Wales.
11 NLA MS 215.

12 I'd love to take credit for this wonderfully evocative expression, but I can't. It was coined by P.G. 'Bill' Taylor when writing about his exploratory flights in a Catalina flying boat through the far reaches of the South Pacific.

13 Mackersey, *Smithy*, p. 148.

14 Ulm's log, in Michael Molkentin, *Flying the Southern Cross: Aviators Charles Ulm and Charles Kingsford Smith*, National Library of Australia (NLA), Canberra, 2012, p. 99.

15 NLA MS 215.

16 NLA MS 215.

17 Mackersey, *Smithy*, p. 153.

CHAPTER 8

1 Papers of Charles Ulm, 1931–1969 [manuscript], 4 December 1934, National Library of Australia (NLA), Canberra, MS 215.

2 The sub-editors in Sydney turned it into something much more prosaic: 'The machine bounced, then touched thirty yards ahead, and taxied towards the corner at the foot of a short, steep rise, came around to the left between two trees, and pulled up. The plane had nothing whatever to spare. It was described as a perfect landing': *The Sun* (Sydney), 5 June 1928, p. 1.

3 NLA MS 215.

4 NLA MS 215.

5 Ian Mackersey, *Smithy: The life of Sir Charles Kingsford Smith*, Warner Books, 1998, p. 156.

6 Mackersey, *Smithy*, p. 157.

7 Mackersey, *Smithy*, p. 157.

CHAPTER 9

1 *The Sun* (Sydney), 8 June 1928, p. 1.

2 Ian Mackersey, *Smithy: The life of Sir Charles Kingsford Smith*, Warner Books, 1998, p. 160.

3 Papers of Charles Ulm, 1931–1969 [manuscript], 4 December 1934, National Library of Australia (NLA), Canberra, MS 215 (cable).

4 NLA MS 215 (cable).

5 NLA MS 215.

6 Mackersey, *Smithy*, p. 161.
7 Mackersey, *Smithy*, p. 162.
8 Mackersey, *Smithy*, p. 165.
9 Mackersey, *Smithy*, p. 165.
10 Mackersey, *Smithy*, p. 166.

CHAPTER 10

1 *The Sun* (Sydney), 11 June 1928, p. 9.
2 Ian Mackersey, *Smithy: The life of Sir Charles Kingsford Smith*, Warner Books, 1998, p. 174.
3 *The Sun* (Sydney), 14 June 1928; Papers of Charles Ulm, 1931–1969 [manuscript], 4 December 1934, National Library of Australia (NLA), Canberra, MS 215 (cable).
4 *The Sun* (Sydney), 14 June 1928; NLA MS 215 (cable).
5 *The Sun* (Sydney), 14 June 1928; NLA MS 215 (cable).
6 Ellen Rogers, *Faith in Australia: Charles Ulm and Australian aviation*, Book Production Services, Crows Nest, NSW, 1987, p. 62.
7 *Hitchcock v Kingsford Smith and Others*, Supreme Court of NSW in equity. Transcript in evidence in NSW State Archives, ref unknown, pp. 1–2.

CHAPTER 11

1 Sir Richard Williams, *These Are Facts: The autobiography of Air Marshal Sir Richard Williams, KBE, CB, DSO*, The Australian War Memorial and The Australian Government Publishing Service, Canberra, 1977, p. 202.
2 Sir Richard Williams, in Ian Mackersey, *Smithy: The life of Sir Charles Kingsford Smith*, Warner Books, 1998, p. 173.
3 Edward Hart, in Mackersey, *Smithy*, p. 173.
4 Mackersey, *Smithy*, p. 185.

CHAPTER 12

1 Papers of Charles Ulm, 1931–1969 [manuscript], 4 December 1934, National Library of Australia (NLA), Canberra, MS 215 (reminiscences of his father by John Ulm).

2 Ian Mackersey, *Smithy: The life of Sir Charles Kingsford Smith*, Warner Books, 1998, p. 429.
3 The Charles T.P. Ulm collection of historical aviation records, Part 1, 1919-1965, Mitchell Library, State Library of New South Wales (SLNSW), Sydney, MLMSS3359 (prospectus).
4 SLNSW MLMSS3359 (minute book).
5 NLA MS 215.
6 Charles Grey, *The Aeroplane*, 20 February 1929; *Aircraft* (London), 30 April 1929.

CHAPTER 13

1 Ian Mackersey, *Smithy: The life of Sir Charles Kingsford Smith*, Warner Books, 1998, p. 200.
2 Department of Air memorandum in Australian archives, in Mackersey, *Smithy*, p. 206.
3 Mackersey, *Smithy*, p. 207.
4 Although it is widely accepted that the name Coffee Royal originated from the concoction of brandy laced with coffee, Ulm told the journalist John Marshall that these beans tasted like coffee when roasted, implying that this was the origin of the name. The truth will never be known.
5 National Archives of Australia, Canberra, CP662/7/4.
6 *Aircraft*, 30 April 1929, p. 317.
7 *The Bulletin*, 10 April 1929.
8 Two obsolescent DH.9A biplanes that were hopelessly inadequate for the task.
9 In fact, the main spar had been fractured during the landing, but the damage was not outwardly visible. Major repairs were made in Sydney before they started again for England: Mackersey, *Smithy*, p. 216.
10 Mackersey, *Smithy*, p. 216.

CHAPTER 14

1 National Archives of Australia (NAA), Canberra, NAA CP662/5, 6/6/29 (Transcript of evidence regarding the loss of the *Southern Cross* and *Kookaburra*), 4 June 1929, folios 749–833; Ian Mackersey, *Smithy: The life of Sir Charles Kingsford Smith*, Warner Books, 1998, pp. 233–4.

2 Mackersey, *Smithy*, p. 229.

3 Mackersey, *Smithy*, p. 232.

4 NAA CP662/5, 6/6/29 (Transcript of evidence); Mackersey, *Smithy*, pp. 233–4.

5 NAA CP662/7 (Exhibits presented to the Air Enquiry Committee into the loss of the *Southern Cross* and *Kookaburra*).

6 NAA CP662/7/3 (Air Inquiry in connection with the Flights of Aeroplanes *Southern Cross* and *Kookaburra*).

CHAPTER 15

1 National Library of Australia (NLA), Canberra, NLA ORAL TRC 771.4 (audio recording).

2 Scotty Allan, in Ian Mackersey, *Smithy: The life of Sir Charles Kingsford Smith*, Warner Books, 1998, p. 246.

3 Ellen Rogers, *Faith in Australia: Charles Ulm and Australian aviation*, Book Production Services, Crows Nest, NSW, 1987, p. 56.

4 Papers of Charles Ulm, 1931–1969 [manuscript], 4 December 1934, National Library of Australia, Canberra, MS 215 (R.E. Ludowici, summary of ANA operations).

5 NLA MS 215 (brochure).

6 Rogers, *Faith in Australia*, p. 58.

7 NLA MS 215.

8 NLA ORAL TRC 771.1 (audio recording).

CHAPTER 16

1 National Library of Australia (NLA), Canberra, NLA ORAL TRC 771.1 (audio recording).

2 R.E.G. Davies, *Airlines of the United States Since 1914*, Putnam, London, 1972, p. 25.

3 Davies, *Airlines*, p. 83.

4 Edward Hart, 'Southern Cloud mystery', *Aircraft*, 6 April 1931.

5 Macarthur Job, *Air Crash: The story of how Australia's airways were made safe*, vol. 1, Aerospace Publications, Canberra, 1991, p. 36.

6 Sir Gordon Taylor, *The Sky Beyond*, Cassell Australia, Sydney, 1963, p. 30.

7 Job, *Air Crash*, pp. 33–5.

8   Air Accidents Investigating Committee Report on Loss of Aircraft VH-UMF 'Southern Cloud', The Property of Australian National Airways Limited, Which Occurred Between Sydney and Melbourne on Saturday 21st March, 1931', National Archives of Australia, MP115/1.

9   The story of the discovery on the wreckage of the *Southern Cloud* in the Snowy Mountains on 26 October 1958 is beyond the scope of this book. For further details, I recommend Carter, *Southern Cloud*, and Job, *Air Crash*.

CHAPTER 17

1   Ellen Rogers, *Faith in Australia: Charles Ulm and Australian aviation*, Book Production Services, Crows Nest, NSW, 1987, p. 72.

2   Rogers, *Faith in Australia*, p. 72.

3   Papers of Charles Ulm, 1931–1969 [manuscript], 4 December 1934, National Library of Australia (NLA), Canberra, MS 215 (letter).

4   Rogers, *Faith in Australia*, p. 72.

5   Edward Hart, 'Why the Government Must Help Our Aircraft Companies', *Aircraft*, vol. 9, no. 10, July 1931, p. 1.

6   Rogers, *Faith in Australia*, p. 74.

7   Rogers, *Faith in Australia*, p. 74.

8   Ulm sent a copy of his proposal to his friend Edgar Johnston, the Director of Civil Aviation. It is now held in the Edgar Johnston Collection, Civil Aviation Historical Society Airways Museum, Melbourne.

9   Rogers, *Faith in Australia*, p. 77.

10 Edgar Johnston Collection, Civil Aviation Historical Society Airways Museum, Melbourne.

11 Archives of British Airways, London, File no. 12706.

12 Archives of British Airways, London, File no. 12706.

13 Archives of British Airways, London, File no. 12771.

14 Archives of British Airways, London, File no. 12771.

15 Fergus McMaster, in John Gunn, *The Defeat of Distance: Qantas 1919–1939*, University of Queensland Press, Brisbane, 1985, p. 165.

CHAPTER 18

1   John Gunn, *The Defeat of Distance: Qantas 1919–1939*, University of Queensland Press, Brisbane, 1985, p. 173.

2 Papers of Charles Ulm, 1931–1969 [manuscript], 4 December 1934, National Library of Australia (NLA), Canberra, MS 215.

3 NLA MS 215.

4 A.J. Jackson, *Avro Aircraft Since 1908*, Putnam, London, 1965, p. 277.

5 Papers of Sir Patrick Gordon Taylor, 1922–1967 [manuscript], National Library of Australia, Canberra, MS 2594.

6 P.G. Taylor, *VH-UXX: The story of an aeroplane*, Angus & Robertson, Sydney, 1937, p. 16.

7 Taylor, *VH-UXX*, p. 17.

8 NLA MS 2594.

9 Ellen Rogers, *Faith in Australia: Charles Ulm and Australian aviation*, Book Production Services, Crows Nest, NSW, 1987, p. 123.

10 Charles T.P. Ulm collection of historical aviation records, part 1, 1919-1965, State Library of New South Wales (SLNSW), Sydney, ML MSS 3359.

11 SLNSW ML MSS 3359 (tender document).

12 SLNSW ML MSS 3359 (tender document).

13 Gunn, *The Defeat of Distance*, pp. 184–5.

CHAPTER 19

1 Charles T.P. Ulm collection of historical aviation records, part 1, 1919–1965, State Library of New South Wales (SLNSW), Sydney, ML MSS 3359 (letter).

2 Ellen Rogers, *Faith in Australia: Charles Ulm and Australian aviation*, Book Production Services, Crows Nest, NSW, 1987, p. 105.

3 Museum of Australian Commercial Aviation, <www.aviationcollection.org>, accessed 17 March 2018.

4 R.E.G. Davies, *Airlines of the United States Since 1914*, Putnam, London, 1972, p. 177.

5 SLNSW ML MSS 3359.

6 Bill Yenne, *McDonnell Douglas: A tale of two giants*, Bison Books, London, 1985, p. 93.

7 SLNSW ML MSS 3359.

8 SLNSW ML MSS 3359.

9 SLNSW ML MSS 3359.

10 James Trautman, *Pan Am Clippers: The golden age of flying boats*, Boston Mills Press, Ontario, Canada, 2007, p. 115.

11 Nancy Bird Walton, *'My God! It's a Woman!'*, HarperCollins, Sydney, 1990, fn p. 37.

12 Rogers, *Faith in Australia*, p. 113.

13 SLNSW ML MSS 3359.

14 A.J. Jackson, *British Civil Aircraft Since 1919*, vol. 1, Putnam, London, 1959, p. 24.

15 I was unable to locate the official transcript of the messages received from Ulm during his final flight, as I was informed that it probably is stored, uncatalogued, in the vast US Navy Archive in San Francisco. The radio messages reproduced here appeared in the *Honolulu Star Bulletin*, 6 December 1934.

16 *Honolulu Star Bulletin,* date uncertain, possibly 6 December 1934.

17 Rogers, *Faith in Australia*, pp. 117–18.

18 Papers of Charles Ulm, 1931–1969 [manuscript], 4 December 1934, National Library of Australia (NLA), Canberra, MS 215.

19 SL NSW ML MSS 3359.

Index